Sensory Marketing in Retail

Arto Lindblom

Sensory Marketing in Retail

An Introduction to the Multisensory Nature of Retail Stores

Arto Lindblom
School of Business
Aalto University
Helsinki, Finland

ISBN 978-3-031-47514-6   ISBN 978-3-031-47515-3 (eBook)
https://doi.org/10.1007/978-3-031-47515-3

Translation from the Finnish language edition: "Vaikuta Vihjein" by Arto Lindblom, © Arto Lindblom 2023. Published by Oppian. All Rights Reserved.

© The Editor(s) (if applicable) and The Author(s), under exclusive license to Springer Nature Switzerland AG 2023

This work is subject to copyright. All rights are solely and exclusively licensed by the Publisher, whether the whole or part of the material is concerned, specifically the rights of translation, reprinting, reuse of illustrations, recitation, broadcasting, reproduction on microfilms or in any other physical way, and transmission or information storage and retrieval, electronic adaptation, computer software, or by similar or dissimilar methodology now known or hereafter developed.
The use of general descriptive names, registered names, trademarks, service marks, etc. in this publication does not imply, even in the absence of a specific statement, that such names are exempt from the relevant protective laws and regulations and therefore free for general use.
The publisher, the authors, and the editors are safe to assume that the advice and information in this book are believed to be true and accurate at the date of publication. Neither the publisher nor the authors or the editors give a warranty, expressed or implied, with respect to the material contained herein or for any errors or omissions that may have been made. The publisher remains neutral with regard to jurisdictional claims in published maps and institutional affiliations.

Cover illustration: thananit suntiviriyanon/gettyimages

This Palgrave Macmillan imprint is published by the registered company Springer Nature Switzerland AG
The registered company address is: Gewerbestrasse 11, 6330 Cham, Switzerland

Paper in this product is recyclable.

Preface

This book focuses on sensory marketing and the multisensory nature of retail stores. To be more specific, the book introduces how sensory cues can be used as means of influencing our choices in a physical retail setting.

Cues are sensory stimuli that may be features in store design, lighting, music or even the body language of the staff—things that we as consumers may sense and experience in various ways during a visit to the store, and which may convey various meanings to us and influence our behaviour on a conscious or unconscious level. The book sheds light on the joint effects of cues in particular and emphasises that the retailer must possess the skill and vision to manage and coordinate cues from this standpoint as well. For example, the retailer should understand how the congruity of cues is reflected on how pleasant the store is to visit, or how the management of cues and tensions between them can be used to influence the arousal level of consumers.

After reading this book, the reader will be able to:

- Identify various cues in a retailing setting
- Categorise cues into different groups
- Explain how cues affect consumers when they make their daily choices
- Understand the multisensory nature of retail stores and the meaning of cue (in)congruence
- Describe how consumers are likely to respond differently to cue combinations than single cues
- Apply cues in practice and assess their outcomes.

One of the main messages of the book is that in our age of increasing hyper-competition and constant flood of stimuli, it is more important than ever to create environments that engage a consumer's every sense, enabling pleasant experiences that provide positive memories. This is particularly important for retail companies which still rely on brick-and-mortar locations in many ways while competing against digital platforms and algorithms.

This book delves into sensory marketing through analysis of an extensive range of academic research, explaining key research findings in clear, plain language. This is to say that the book provides a curated selection of top research, not just personal observations of the author. The book also steers away from normative guidelines, intentionally leaving it up to the reader to evaluate whether the sensory cues presented are viable in practice, and if so, how they might best be implemented. When using cues and other means of influencing behaviour, it is crucial for them to always be evaluated and managed from the company's own perspective and with an understanding of what ultimately resonates with its customers.

Helsinki, Finland
December 2023

Arto Lindblom

Contents

1	**Why Do We Choose How We Choose?**	1
	1.1 The Difficulty of Explaining Choice	1
	1.2 Freedom of Choice	4
	1.3 Choice as an Object of Influence	5
	References	6
2	**Consumer Psychology and Psychological Factors Affecting Our Choices**	9
	2.1 Senses and Sensory Information	9
	2.2 Motives	12
	2.3 Attitudes	12
	2.4 Mental Images	14
	2.5 Expectations	15
	2.6 Emotions	16
	2.7 Unconscious Mind	18
	2.8 Summary	21
	References	22
3	**The Goal and Scope of This Book**	27
	3.1 Focus on Sensory Marketing in Retail	27
	3.2 The Elements of the Retail Marketing Mix	30
	3.3 The Retail Store as a Context of Our Choices	31
	3.4 The Retail Store as a Bundle of Cues	33

	3.5	Ethical Considerations in Influencing Consumer Choices	36
	3.6	Summary	38
	References		39
4	**Identifying Cues and Their Effects in a Retail Store**		**43**
	4.1	Ambient Cues	43
		Background Music	43
		Scents	50
		Lighting	55
		Temperature and Airflow	58
	4.2	Design Cues	60
		Store Design	61
		Colours	69
		Names, Signs and Symbols	76
		Store Layout	79
	4.3	Social Cues	83
		Retail Store Employees	83
		Employee Clothing	86
		Social Presence of Others and Interpersonal Touch	88
		Spontaneous Mimicry	89
		Queues and Crowding	90
		Red Carpet Treatment	92
	4.4	Haptic Cues and the Need for Touch	93
	4.5	Merchandise-Related Cues	97
		You Are What You Sell	98
		You Get What You Pay For	99
		The Number of Alternatives and the Compromise Effect	101
		Product Display and Shelf Position	104
		The Scarcity Principle	107
		Product Packages	109
	4.6	Pricing-Related Cues	111
		Odd-Ending Pricing Versus Even Pricing	111
		Absolute Versus Relative Price Discounts	113
		Premiums Versus Price Cuts	114
		Within- Versus Between-Store Price Promotion Cues	116
		Red Versus Black Prices	116
		Price Presentation Order	118

		Multiple-Unit Price Promotions	119
		Setting Purchasing Goals and the Goal-Gradient Effect	120
	4.7	Summary	122
	References		124

5 The Multisensory Nature of a Retail Store and Joint Effects of Cues — 137

- 5.1 From Unisensory to Multisensory Approaches — 137
- 5.2 $1 + 1 + 1 = 4$ — 138
- 5.3 Sensory Overload and Degraded Responses — 141
- 5.4 Cross-modal Interaction — 143
- 5.5 Cue Congruence — 146
- 5.6 Cue Incongruence — 148
- 5.7 The Seesaw Effect in a Multisensory Retail Environment — 149
- 5.8 Summary — 151
- References — 153

6 Factors That Accelerate or Inhibit the Effects of Cues in a Retail Store — 157

- 6.1 Shopping Motives — 157
- 6.2 Mood — 159
- 6.3 Self-Control — 162
- 6.4 Rules of Thumb — 163
- 6.5 Routines and Habits — 164
- 6.6 Involvement — 166
- 6.7 The Presence of Others — 168
- 6.8 Time Pressure — 170
- 6.9 Familiarity of the Environment — 172
- 6.10 Summary — 173
- References — 174

7 Key Points of This Book — 179

- 7.1 Cue Diversity — 179
  - Explicit and Implicit Cues — 181
  - Tactical and Strategic Cues — 182
- 7.2 Cue Impact — 184
  - Emotional Response — 185
  - Cognitive Evaluations — 186
  - Spontaneous Impulse Purchases — 188
  - Conscious and Unconscious Impacts — 189
  - Response Moderators — 191

		Linking Cues to the Quality of the Shopping Experience	192
	7.3	Summary: The Overall View of the Impacts of Cues on Our Choices	193
	References		196
8	**Engaging in Sensory Marketing in Practice**		**199**
	8.1	Integrating Sensory Marketing into Retail Marketing	199
	8.2	The Connection of Cues to the Customer Promise	201
	8.3	Managing Cue Congruence	205
	8.4	Measuring Cue Effectiveness	206
	8.5	Responsibilities and Limitations Related to Sensory Marketing	209
	8.6	Cultural Specificity of Cues	210
	8.7	Summary	212
	References		214
9	**What to Explore Next?**		**217**
	9.1	Joint Effects and Sensory Overload	217
	9.2	Studying How Cues Are Related to Perceived Safety	218
	9.3	The Ethics of Influence in Consumer Marketing	218
	9.4	Sensory Marketing in an Omnichannel Environment	219
	9.5	Digital Sensory Marketing	220
	9.6	Neuroscience and Neuromarketing	221
	References		223
10	**Concluding Remarks**		**225**
	References		227
Glossary			**229**
Index			**235**

About the Author

Arto Lindblom Ph.D., is Professor of Retailing at the Aalto University School of Business in Finland. Professor Lindblom has been lecturing for more than 15 years on topics such as retail concepts and business models, retail strategies and retail marketing, and has published a wide range of articles on topics related to retailing and marketing in esteemed international journals. Lindblom has also run several large research projects in the field of retailing and collaborated with the largest retailing and manufacturing companies in Finland.

List of Figures

Fig. 2.1	Two dimensions of emotion and eight major emotional states (Donovan & Rossiter, 1982; original source: Russell & Pratt, 1980)	17
Fig. 3.1	Cues examined in this book	36
Fig. 4.1	Slow-tempo music vs. fast-tempo music (e.g., Milliman, 1982; Oakes, 2003; Sweeney & Wyber, 2002)	46
Fig. 4.2	Low-volume music vs. high-volume music (Biswas et al., 2019)	48
Fig. 4.3	Low-arousal scents vs. high-arousal scents (Zhou & Yamanaka, 2018)	51
Fig. 4.4	Cooler light (3000 K) vs. warmer light (5000 K) (Park & Farr, 2007)	56
Fig. 4.5	Frontal airflow vs. dorsal airflow (Izadi et al., 2019)	61
Fig. 4.6	Visual coherence vs. visual complexity	64
Fig. 4.7	The relationship between the attractiveness of environment and complexity	64
Fig. 4.8	Four visual features of environments (modified from Kaplan et al., 1989)	66
Fig. 4.9	The cathedral effect (Meyers-Levy & Zhu, 2007)	68
Fig. 4.10	Cool colours vs. warm colours (Bellizzi & Hite, 1992; Bellizzi et al., 1983)	72
Fig. 4.11	Semantic space of colours and examples of three-colour combinations (Solli & Lenz, 2010; see also Horiguchi & Iwamatsu, 2018)	75
Fig. 4.12	Three basic retail store layout options	81

Fig. 4.13	Effects of employee clothing formality (Yan et al., 2011)	87
Fig. 4.14	The influence of a mere social presence (Argo et al., 2005)	89
Fig. 4.15	The effects of red carpet treatment (Steinhoff & Palmatier, 2016)	94
Fig. 4.16	Shelf-space cues	106
Fig. 4.17	Scarcity cue vs. popularity cue (Das et al., 2018)	108
Fig. 4.18	Odd-ending pricing vs. even pricing	113
Fig. 4.19	Absolute vs. relative price discounts (Chen et al., 1998)	115
Fig. 4.20	Within- vs. between-store price promotion cues (Krishnan et al., 2006)	117
Fig. 4.21	Multiple-unit pricing (Wansink et al., 1998)	120
Fig. 5.1	Multisensory integration and multisensory enhancement (e.g., Spence et al., 2014; Stein & Stanford, 2008; Stanford et al., 2005)	140
Fig. 5.2	High-arousal cues and sensory overload	143
Fig. 5.3	A simplified example of cross-modal effects	144
Fig. 5.4	Seesaw effect in a multisensory retail environment	151
Fig. 7.1	Linking cues to the quality of the shopping experience	193
Fig. 7.2	Overall view of the impacts of cues on our behaviour	194
Fig. 8.1	Retail store as a bundle of cues	202
Fig. 8.2	Examples of the effects of cues in a retailing setting	203
Fig. 8.3	A customer promise directs the use of cues in practice	204
Fig. 8.4	Cross-channel conversion in the case of showrooming	208

List of Tables

Table 7.1   Explicit and implicit cues   182
Table 7.2   Tactical and strategic cues   183

1

Why Do We Choose How We Choose?

1.1 The Difficulty of Explaining Choice

As consumers, we frequently make choices, some of them consciously, others less so. The sheer number of choices we make just in the course of our weekly shopping can easily be seen from the receipt—and would probably come as a surprise to most of us. While looking through the receipt, we may wonder why we chose these specific products from all the ones available. We may also ask ourselves how we wound up buying things we had no intention of purchasing.

It is likely that we are not able to give a clear answer as to how we choose the things we do, and we may not even be interested in debating our choices with any particular depth; we simply choose what we choose. Meanwhile, researchers are fascinated by our choices—like the ones we make while grocery shopping—and can approach and explain them in a variety of ways.

An economist could say that our choices reveal our preferences, or the things we consider important. A sociologist might speculate that our choices could be explained by our habits, or that we make choices to communicate our taste or style. A psychologist could claim that most of our choices are made unconsciously, while a social psychologist might say that our choices are guided by reference groups that are important to us, like our family or friends, and our understanding of what they consider good or acceptable behaviour. A marketing researcher would claim that we make choices at the store based on the mental images created by marketing and the promises made by commercials. A representative of the field of cultural consumer research would emphasise cultural influences and the importance of viewing our consumer choices as part of cultural structures and the related established practices. Suffice to say there are many alternative approaches to analysing our choices.

It is clear that there is no single correct perspective, but rather all perspectives are needed to fully understand the choices we make. The factors influencing our choices take many different forms and can therefore be described and classified using many different methods. Our choices can be explained through psychological (e.g., motives, attitudes and emotions), personal (e.g., income level, lifestyle and life situation), social (e.g., family and friends) or cultural (e.g., shared values, norms and practices) factors.[1] This is to say that a host of potential explanations can be found behind our choices, and they present in different ways in connection with different choice settings. The key issue is to understand that the core cause of a given choice is difficult, if not impossible, to reduce to a single factor. Many different factors twist together every time we make a choice, and we may not even be aware of all of them ourselves. Additionally, some of these factors, such as attitudes and mental images, are shaped by many different forms of influence often long before the actual choice is made.

Various situational factors during our shopping also influence our choices, often at the very moment the choice is being made. Such situational factors may have to do with the shopping environment or the other people present.[2] Just the way products are displayed at the store may have a significant impact on what we choose to put in our shopping basket. Typically impulse purchases are the result of such situational factors.[3]

There is also a temporal dimension to our choice behaviour. This means that every choice becomes an experience, and these experiences and the expectations they generate are reflected on each new moment of choice we encounter. Many of our daily choices can even be memory-based choices, meaning that they are based on information retrieved from memory.[4] Over time, we may also develop a choice tendency or habit which can guide our choices in the future.[5] This all means that we never enter a moment of choice as a blank slate.[6]

---

[1] Hemsley-Brown and Oplatka (2016) and Armstrong and Kotler (2020).
[2] Belk (1975).
[3] Beatty and Ferrell (1998) and Barros et al. (2019).
[4] Lee (2002).
[5] Büttner et al. (2014).
[6] Panula (1997).

Our choices and the factors that influence them are both diverse and highly individual. While one person makes choices to bolster their identity, another chases pleasure, and a third seeks to identify with a specific reference group. For some, a spontaneous choice made in the moment may arise from the pure need to satisfy a basic physiological need, like hunger or thirst, while others may pick products out of sheer curiosity, without experiencing a need as such. Even when we make the exact same choice as another consumer, it is unlikely that the factors influencing our choices in the background are the same.

Further, our choices may be rational, less rational or even entirely irrational. Rationality in this context means the degree to which we employ reason to make our choices. We may sometimes go to great lengths to find the very best solution out of several alternatives, but quite often we make choices based on habit, emotions, various rules of thumb or perhaps our friends' expectations. We also make choices unconsciously. No matter which factor guides the choice ultimately being made, it may make sense to ourselves, even though it may appear irrational to an outside observer. In general, it is very difficult to assess a choice as rational or irrational from the outside.

In textbooks, consumer choice is typically presented as a multi-stage process featuring distinct phases from the recognition of the need for a product, to the gathering of information, to the evaluation of alternatives, to the choice and then the evaluation of the choice. However, the process of consumer choice varies greatly depending on the type of situation. In fact, when we discuss consumer choice, and specifically choices made in a retail environment, we must understand the moment of choice and its nature. Essentially, we could say that the moment of choice may be a routine shopping event, in which the choice is made in a habitual manner without major consideration (simple decision-making), or the situation may be complex or somehow important or unfamiliar for the consumer, in which case the consumer will want to spend more time assessing various factors, such as the quality and price of the product, before making the decision (complex decision-making).[7] The choice may also be made on a whim with no conscious premeditation. This means that it is difficult to understand a consumer's choices without understanding the situation in which the choices are being made.[8]

---

[7] Baumgartner (2002) and Niosi (2021).
[8] Dijksterhuis et al. (2005).

1.2 Freedom of Choice

Questions relating to consumer behaviour and consumer choice in particular are becoming increasingly important, as many of the restrictions previously associated with our consumer choices have for all intents and purposes been removed. The selection of products has increased dramatically, and we can now choose from a dizzying number of options. A normal hypermarket is a good illustration of the overabundance of the selection of products available. We can easily see shelves upon shelves dedicated to various product groups, with too many brands, flavour variants and package sizes for us to even count. Today's hypermarkets may have a selection of up to 50,000 products, and new ones are frequently being introduced. It has been estimated that more than 30,000 new products are brought to the market annually.[9] It is likely that nobody knows the number of smaller product innovations and packaging redesigns launched each year.

Meanwhile, digitalisation has introduced consumers to innumerable new shopping venues all around the world, while making shopping extremely easy on any day of the week and any hour of the day. Global marketplaces, such as Amazon, Alibaba and Rakuten, are examples of the modern version of the market square, where millions of seller companies around the world hawk their wares to consumers. It has been said that Amazon's marketplace alone is currently being used by nearly two million small or mid-size seller companies with a combined product selection counted in the tens, if not hundreds of millions.

Simultaneously, many of us also have an increasing amount of disposable income which we can use to make choices for our enjoyment. The amount of free time has grown, and few of us are prevented or restricted from consuming by a lack of time. This means that there are currently no specific outside restrictions or strict rules regarding what, when, where or who can consume. It remains to be seen whether this situation continues in the future. We are currently living in an age of abundance in many ways, and we are all faced with a vast number of alternative consumption options, various consumer environments and ways of shopping that just keep getting easier. The product selection of the entire world is just a few clicks away.

---

[9] Emmer (2018).

1.3 Choice as an Object of Influence

While our freedom of choice has increased, we continue to encounter an increasing amount of different types of commercial influencing. Marketers both small and large are tirelessly vying for our interest and consumer choices, and we are exposed to an increasing number of stimuli and messages which we may not even be aware of. One example of this type of influencing is social media platforms, such as Facebook, Instagram or TikTok, and the contents and commercial messages we encounter there. Influencer marketing has rapidly become more common on social media. Today, bloggers, Instagrammers and YouTubers play a significant role in the daily lives and choices of many consumers. It is also increasingly common for regular consumers to be harnessed into becoming informal brand ambassadors for various companies, and they may, for example, be encouraged to pass on commercial messages in the form of competitions.

It says something about the flood of stimuli and its rapid increase that while in 2016, there were three million active advertisers on Facebook, in 2020 they numbered 10 million.[10] We are exposed to advertisements hundreds, if not thousands, of times during a given day. According to some estimates, the average American consumer encounters 4,000–10,000 advertisements daily.[11] We can expect that the amount of commercial influencing will continue to increase. For example, Statista has calculated that global drive-to-store advertising spending will reach 80 billion US dollars in 2023 while just few years ago it was around 60 billion.[12] Statista also estimates that digital advertising spending worldwide will reach over 835 billion US dollars by 2026 while today the spending is around 600 billion.[13] While the amount of influencing is increasing, it is also becoming more intelligent, and marketing is likely to be more tightly connected with things such as AI and algorithms which can produce better targeted commercial and other content to evoke our interest and intent to purchase.

On the other hand, media literacy is also improving,[14] and more and more of us are viewing things that seem commercial in a critical or even negative light. There has long been talk of anti-consumerism, which means minimising consumption or even opposing it altogether.[15] We must assume

---

[10] Statista (2021).
[11] Simpson (2017).
[12] Statista (2023a).
[13] Statista (2023b).
[14] Kanerva and Oksanen-Särelä (2021).
[15] Jyrinki et al. (2012).

that these kinds of highly critical attitudes towards consuming will increase in the future, as people become more environmentally conscious. This will surely be reflected on the way commercial messages are received.

Thus, marketers' attempts to influence us, for example through advertisements, do not pass directly into our minds. We observe things selectively, and the internal factors of our psyche prevent and shape the effects in many different ways. Our state of alertness alone influences the degree to which we pay attention to various stimuli, such as commercial messages. In fact, in our daily lives, we might ignore most of the messages we face. On the other hand, we are also exposed to various forms of subliminal advertising, and we may not be able to recognise what kinds of effects different stimuli cause in us.

It is clear that our choices and the ways in which they can be influenced through commercial messages or changes in the shopping environment cannot be explained without understanding how we perceive things and how the mind works. Chapter 2 seeks to explain both how we experience the world around us and the factors in our minds that help us understand our choice behaviour. The analysis in Chapter 2 is based on consumer psychology. Consumer psychology investigates the choice behaviour of consumers and the ways it can be influenced, with a focus on various internal factors in the consumers' minds. As Bettman formulated already several decades ago: "The focus of consumer psychology is on understanding and explaining the psychological factors that influence these choice, purchase, and usage behaviour".[16] Consumer psychology is an interdisciplinary field of research that combines theories from psychology, marketing, economics, sociology and anthropology.[17]

References

Armstrong, G., & Kotler, P. (2020). *Marketing: An introduction* (14th ed.). Pearson.
Barros, L. B. L., Petroll, M. d. L. M., Damacena, C., & Knoppe, M. (2019). Store atmosphere and impulse: A cross-cultural study. *International Journal of Retail & Distribution Management, 47*, 817–835.
Baumgartner, H. (2002). Toward a personology of the consumer. *Journal of Consumer Research, 29*, 286–292.
Beatty, S., & Ferrell, E. (1998). Impulse buying: Modeling its precursors. *Journal of Retailing, 74*, 169–191.

---

[16] Bettman (1986, pp. 257–258).
[17] Jia et al. (2018).

Belk, R. (1975). Situational variables and consumer behaviour. *Journal of Consumer Research, 2*, 157–164.
Bettman, J. R. (1986). Consumer psychology. *Annual Review of Psychology, 37*, 257–289.
Büttner, O., Florack, A., & Göritz, A. (2014). Shopping orientation as a stable consumer disposition and its influence on consumers' evaluations of retailer communication. *European Journal of Marketing, 48*, 1026–1045.
Dijksterhuis, A., Smith, P., van Baaren, R., & Wigboldus, D. (2005). The unconscious consumer: Effects of environment on consumer behaviour. *Journal of Consumer Psychology, 15*, 193–202.
Emmer, M. (2018). *95 percent of new products fail. Here are 6 steps to make sure yours don't, Inc.* Accessed 9 September 2021: https://www.inc.com/marc-emmer/95-percent-of-new-products-fail-here-are-6-steps-to-make-sure-yours-dont.html
Hemsley-Brown, J., & Oplatka, I. (2016). Personal influences on consumer behaviour. In *Higher education consumer choice*. Palgrave Pivot.
Jia, H., Zhou, S., & Allaway, A. W. (2018). Understanding the evolution of consumer psychology research: A bibliometric and network analysis. *Journal of Consumer Behaviour, 17*, 491–502.
Jyrinki, H., Leipämaa-Leskinen, H., & Laaksonen, P. (2012). Välttämätön kuluttaminen nuorten aikuisten kokemana—Avain vastuullisuuden lisäämiseen? *Kulutustutkimus. Nyt, 1*(2012), 4–19.
Kanerva, A., & Oksanen-Särelä, K. (2021). *Aikuisten medialukutaidon edistämisen hyvät käytännöt ja kehittämistarpeet, Kansallisen audiovisuaalisen instituutin julkaisuja, 1/2021.* www.medialukutaitosuomessa.fi
Lee, A. Y. (2002). Effects of implicit memory on memory-based versus stimulus-based brand choice. *Journal of Marketing Research, 39*, 440–454.
Niosi, A. (2021). *Introduction to consumer behaviour.* BCcampus.
Panula, J. (1997). Vaikutussuhde, käyttösuhde, merkityssuhde: Näkökulmia todellisuuden, joukkoviestinnän ja yleisön väliseen suhteeseen, Atena Kustannus Oy.
Simpson, J. (2017). Finding brand success in the digital world. *Forbes.* Accessed 9 September 2021. https://www.forbes.com/sites/forbesagencycouncil/2017/08/25/finding-brand-success-in-the-digital-world/?sh=66468c50626e
Statista. (2021). *Number of active advertisers on Facebook from 1st quarter 2016 to 3rd quarter 2020.* Accessed 9 September 2021. https://www.statista.com/statistics/778191/active-facebook-advertisers/
Statista. (2023a). *Drive-to-store advertising spending worldwide 2018–2023.* Accessed 7 June 2023. https://www.statista.com/statistics/1053564/drive-to-store-advertising-spending-worldwide/
Statista. (2023b). *Digital advertising spending worldwide 2021–2026.* Accessed 7 June 2023. https://www.statista.com/statistics/237974/online-advertising-spending-worldwide/

2

Consumer Psychology and Psychological Factors Affecting Our Choices

2.1 Senses and Sensory Information

We begin our journey into the mind of the consumer by examining the senses. The five basic human senses are vision, hearing, smell, taste and touch. These senses give us information on factors outside our consciousness. In other words, through our five senses, we become aware of the outer world. For example, we are constantly receiving a great deal of visual information, even when we are not consciously thinking about it.[1] Incoming sensory information about the outside world can take many forms. The stimuli for smell and taste are both chemical substances (e.g., odorant molecules), while touch is physical stimuli that interact primarily with the skin. Sight is based on light stimuli received through the eyes, and hearing is the perception of sound waves, which is a physical stimulus similar to touch.[2] Almost always sight is ranked as our highest sense, and visual stimuli are seen as a dominant mode of sensory information.[3] However, non-visual stimuli (e.g., sounds and scents) and other senses than sight are equally important and also deserve our full attention when discussing how we receive incoming sensory information from the world around us.

Our senses can generate information from the briefest exposure to a sensory stimulus. For example, eye-tracking studies have found that if our

---

[1] Ansorge et al. (2014).
[2] Gordon Betts et al. (2013).
[3] Hutmacher (2019).

gaze pauses for even 100 milliseconds, we will consciously register the visual observation.[4] A millisecond is one-thousandth of a second. However, studies show that our attentiveness has a strong impact on how we actually observe our environment and what we perceive in it.[5] It is also known that we can be rather selective when scanning the environment and the information it provides to us.[6] In fact, we have a tendency to consciously or unconsciously seek out sensory information that we feel is somehow relevant and matching with our thoughts, while ignoring or even avoiding information that we feel is irrelevant or somehow against our thoughts. One could say that being selective helps us cope with a constant barrage of sensory information.

Incoming sensory information such as scents or sound must reach a certain minimum intensity level to be detected by our sensory organs.[7] However, humans have evolved to have exceptionally accurate senses and we can spot various stimuli even with relatively low intensity levels. We are also capable of recognising a wide range of stimuli. It has been claimed, for example, that our nose can distinguish tens of thousands of different scents.[8] The ability to sense also differs from one individual to the next. For example, women have been found to have a more acute sense of smell on average than men. The senses are also connected to each other, supporting or supplementing the information each one provides. For example, the sense of taste is closely linked to the sense of smell, and we frequently need our vision and sense of touch to complement our experiences of taste and smell. We often remain unaware of how our senses actually interact. As Spence states: "The senses talk to, and hence influence, one another all the time, though we often remain unaware of these cross-sensory interactions and influences".[9] As a whole, our senses form a completely unique, expertly honed machine which enables our connection to the world around us. We often only realise the significance of our senses when we lose access to one of them.

Sensory information received through our senses is transmitted to our central nervous system where the information is processed.[10] Odours are the only type of sensory information that has been found to have a direct route to our limbic system, the part of our brain that regulates emotions

---

[4] Kuisma (2007).
[5] Alho and Salmela (2017).
[6] Niosi (2021).
[7] Ibid.
[8] Lyly et al. (2022).
[9] Spence (2020, p. 14).
[10] Molnar and Gair (2021).

and memory.[11] The way we receive and process sensory information is often labelled as perception or perceptual process. The information processing as a part of perception includes, for example, organising and storing the information. An important step in sensory information processing is interpretation. By interpreting the sensory information, the information acquires meaning and we can take action based on it. Interpretation is often seen as a deliberate and conscious part of information processing.[12] This means that we are aware of the interpretations we make. As a result of the interpretation, the perceived sensory information may become an opinion or understanding of something, for example. One could say that interpretation is a mental process that helps us to make sense of the information that we perceive in our daily lives. Our interpretations, like all information processing, are influenced by a number of factors, including our expectations, previous experiences and knowledge stored in our memory.

However, because our information processing capabilities are limited, we only process a small amount of the incoming sensory information in a systematic manner.[13] Actually, very often we ignore a large part of the sensory stimuli that we are exposed to, and the information that reaches our minds is processed with less elaboration. Particularly, in the case of low levels of involvement and motivation, it is likely that we only engage in very simple and quick information processing.[14] This is often called heuristic processing.[15] It is said that heuristic processing is a relatively automatic mode of processing information and hence a more efficient and less time-consuming way to make "good enough" judgements. On the other hand, heuristic processing might sometimes lead to errors in our judgement and thus cause poor decisions. It should be noted that sensory information can also bypass our conscious information processing completely. This means that sensory information such as subtle cues can affect us unconsciously, outside of our awareness.[16] This is to say that the information provided by our senses can influence us and our choice behaviour in very different ways.

---

[11] Lyly et al. (2022).
[12] Niosi (2021).
[13] Hansen (2005).
[14] Petty and Briñol (2012).
[15] Chaiken and Ledgerwood (2012).
[16] Dijksterhuis et al. (2005) and Messner and Wänke (2011).

2.2 Motives

How we ultimately operate in moments of choice is largely dependent on internal factors within our minds. Of these internal factors, motives are central to our choice behaviour. Motives are the reasons behind our actions, they are our goals or purposes—factors that precede our actions and set us in motion. Motives can be said to guide us or pull us in a specific direction. The motives of our actions also influence how we observe our environment. We often look to motives to answer the question of why we behave the way we behave.[17] Just a visit to the store can come with a considerable range of motives: we may have a basic need we wish to satisfy, and we may want to see what products are on offer, sniff out the latest trends, or just pass the time.[18] In the context of consumption, we also talk about motives that have to do with taking care of our well-being, self-expression or the pursuit of social approval.[19] Our motives stem from our needs, and the needs that underlie our motives may be either conscious or unconscious. Consequently, it may be difficult to access the actual motives behind our behaviour. We may not even be able to explain the reasons behind our behaviour to ourselves. Even though motives are undoubtedly important for explaining our behaviour, they are not solely responsible for the choices we make. Particularly in today's environment of abundant choice where we have an untold number of options through which to satisfy our needs, the reasons behind our choices cannot be uncovered by merely examining our motives.

2.3 Attitudes

Our attitudes are central for our choice behaviour. Attitudes express our evaluations or opinions of something or someone.[20] Our attitudes may be positive (favourable) or negative (unfavourable) assessments. They arise gradually and describe our personal beliefs.[21] Furthermore, attitudes are made up of both cognitive (thoughts, knowledge) and affective (feelings) components.[22] Attitudes are usually thought to be generated and shaped through the information transmitted by our senses and our conscious processing of

---

[17] Collins and Montgomery (1969).
[18] Dawson et al. (1990).
[19] Belk (1988).
[20] Stangor et al. (2014) and Niosi (2021).
[21] Fishbein (1966) and Ajzen (1989).
[22] Stangor et al. (2014) and Niosi (2021).

it (the information processing approach to attitude formation), even though attitudes may also arise through other routes.[23] This means that we may not have an exact understanding of where our attitudes ultimately come from, or how they influence us.[24] Attitudes of which we are not aware, or are only partially aware, are called implicit attitudes, whereas attitudes of which we are aware and which we can elaborate and verbally explain to others are called explicit attitudes. Attitudes are relatively stable, but also susceptible to change, unlike values which are more permanent in nature.

Attitudes in particular have been thought to explain or predict our behaviour, or at least our intention to behave in a certain way.[25] It is said that our attitudes tend to guide our behaviour very quickly and effortlessly.[26] This behavioural response is often called the third component of attitude. As a simplified example, the more positive attitude a consumer holds towards environmental issues, the more likely they are to make environmentally friendly choices in their daily life. Or we can assume that the more positive a person's attitude towards Coca-Cola as a brand, the more likely they are to choose Coca-Cola when shopping for something to drink. Emphasising conscious attitudes as factors that explain or guide our behaviour suggests that our behaviour is more or less thoughtful and proceeds logically from attitude formation to actual choice. While the consumer may follow their attitudes and beliefs strictly in moments of choice that hold particular significance, it is extremely rare for a consumer to behave in such a straightforward manner. In fact, studies have shown that our attitudes may not necessarily be reflected in our actual behaviour.[27] For example, positive environmental attitudes do not automatically mean that the consumer always chooses environmentally friendly products.[28] Or even if we like Coca-Cola as a brand, we do not buy Coca-Cola every single time we feel thirsty.

---

[23] Fishbein and Middlestadt (1995).
[24] Gawronski et al. (2006).
[25] Ajzen (1991) and Stangor et al. (2014).
[26] Niosi (2021).
[27] The degree to which our attitudes guide our behaviour is at least partially related to the strength of the attitude. It has been said that the stronger the attitude, the more likely it is to guide our behaviour. The strength of the attitude is measured through how important and reliable we believe it to be, and how easily it comes to our mind (Stangor et al., 2014).
[28] Uusitalo (1997).

2.4 Mental Images

The concept of the mental image is often connected to discussions of attitudes. It has even been suggested they mean the same thing, even though mental images and attitudes do have their differences. Whereas an attitude is a relatively permanent opinion of a specific object based on (conscious) assessment and elaboration, a mental image is an impression or a belief of the object, such as a product or store, that is more holistic, but often also more superficial and based on less mental processing.[29] In accordance with Poiesz, one could say that mental images are comprehensive perceptions that locate at the lower end of the elaboration continuum.[30] Thus, we tend to form our mental images fast, and in our judgements, we can rely on some very simple information sources such as colours.[31] Poiesz also emphasises that our mental images often tell how the object, such as a brand, is positioned in our mind in relation to other similar alternatives.[32]

We all have our individual mental images or subjective impressions of various things, and these impressions can shift. For example, what may today be considered a trendy place to shop can be hopelessly out of fashion tomorrow. Or a product that may seem high quality to one person may seem entirely ordinary in someone else's eyes. We know that our mental images guide which things we observe around us and which ones we ignore. For example, if we have a very negative image of a particular object, we may make very limited observations on it. Mental images may also serve as heuristic choice rules,[33] and hence, images can guide our choices (particularly if the moment of choice is not particularly important) or at least make them easier, but mental images are rarely the sole reason for why we choose the way we choose. However, neither can we ignore the impact of mental images on our choices.

It has been said that our mental images, no matter how superficial, are based on the information we receive through our senses. It is as if the mental images are like organisms which feed on information.[34] The marketing carried out by companies naturally has an impact on our mental images. For marketers, mental images are a very important target for influence, as they are a key way for companies to differentiate themselves. It is well known that

---

[29] Poiesz (1989) and Kotler (2001).
[30] Poiesz (1989).
[31] Singh (2006).
[32] Poiesz (1989).
[33] Ibid.
[34] Karvonen (1997).

there is little actual difference between many companies or the products they offer, but the differences may arise in the realm of abstract mental images. For this reason, marketing is often seen as an effort aiming to generate or shape mental images.

2.5 Expectations

Mental images, as discussed in the previous section, are closely linked to our expectations. Mental images generate expectations, for example relating to the quality or usability of a product, or to the kind of service we expect to receive in a store. Our expectations can also be influenced by a variety of cues which we perceive either consciously or unconsciously when we enter a store or examine a product. Explicit and implicit promises by the firm also affect our expectations. One source of information that has been found to have a particular impact on our mental images and expectations is word-of-mouth, i.e., what we hear from our friends about a product or store.[35]

Expectations are centrally important because they are what we compare our experiences to and then experience either satisfaction or dissatisfaction based on the results.[36] Our expectations create a kind of standard against which we rate our experiences. If our actual experience does not meet our expectations, we feel dissatisfied, whereas our satisfaction increases in situations where our expectations are met or even exceeded. The degree to which we experience satisfaction or dissatisfaction will then in turn have an impact on our intention to revisit a store, or our willingness to recommend it to our friends.

This means that it is crucially important to understand and meet consumer expectations—a feat easier said than done, since there are so many different kinds of expectations and they may be difficult to identify. Ojasalo, among others, has described various types of expectations.[37] According to Ojasalo, some of our expectations may be "fuzzy", meaning we cannot fully express or describe them in detail. Sometimes our expectations may be abstract wishes or even daydreams. Meanwhile, other expectations may be very concrete and specific, and therefore easily explained. Studies also discuss implicit expectations, meaning expectations that the customer takes for granted and does not even think of consciously. Failure to meet such implicit expectations will result in extremely irritated customers. It is similarly problematic if, for one

---

[35] Clow et al. (1997).
[36] This is a central point in the "Expectancy-Disconfirmation" model (Oliver, 1980).
[37] Ojasalo (2001).

reason or another, customers have developed unrealistically high expectations. Meeting such expectations may be extremely difficult or even impossible. This also increases the risk of dissatisfaction. Consequently, there has been much talk of expectation management, or even of restraining customer expectations to ensure satisfaction.[38]

2.6 Emotions

In addition to attitudes, mental images and expectations, much has been said about consumer emotions, even though attitudes themselves also include an affective component.[39] All in all, an emotion is such a complex concept with so many meanings that it is very difficult to define exhaustively. Suffice to say that an emotion can refer equally to a physiological affective response (e.g., blushing), or the internal, subjective experiences and feelings inside our minds.[40] In this context, we are primarily interested in the internal sensations and emotional experiences of which we are aware and which can be thought to be based on some form of sensory information and its interpretation.[41] However, emotions may also be evoked automatically, outside our conscious minds.[42]

Feelings such as joy, hate, fear and sadness are known as our basic emotions. They are universal feelings which we express with very similar expressions and gestures, regardless of culture. Studies also discuss complex emotions, such as shame or envy. This book does not debate basic or complex emotions; instead, it discusses the emotional states in our minds, often intensive but relatively short-term mental states or emotional experiences, which arise as reactions to something. This means that our emotional states do not appear out of nothing, but are generated by a triggering factor. For example, environmental psychologists have found that cues in the environment influence us specifically through our emotional states.[43]

Our emotional states generally vary from unpleasant to pleasant and from non-aroused and inactive to active and aroused. In other words, our emotional experiences basically at any given moment can be defined in terms of how pleasant and aroused we feel. To be more specific, our emotional

---

[38] Ibid.
[39] Stangor et al. (2014).
[40] Nummenmaa (2017a).
[41] Lazarus (1991).
[42] Nummenmaa (2016, 2017b).
[43] Mehrabian and Russell (1974) and Baker et al. (1992).

responses to everyday settings can be described with the help of two bipolar dimensions:

- Pleasure–displeasure: refers to the degree to which a person feels joyful, happy or satisfied in the situation.
- Arousal–nonarousal: refers to degree to which a person feels excited, active or alert in the situation.[44]

These two bipolar, independent dimensions together form a "circumplex" that helps to identify and describe our current emotional states in more detail.[45] Figure 2.1 describes the model of eight major emotional states based on the combination of the dimensions of pleasure–displeasure (i.e., pleasant-unpleasant) and arousal–nonarousal (i.e., arousing-sleepy).[46] Each of these eight emotional states can be seen as a specific reaction to the environment that surround us. Over time, other competing circumplexes with different dimensions have emerged, but the original model is still very valid.

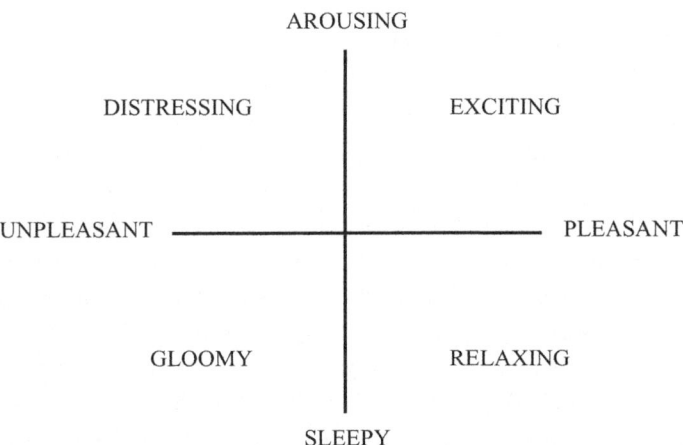

Fig. 2.1 Two dimensions of emotion and eight major emotional states (Donovan & Rossiter, 1982; original source: Russell & Pratt, 1980)

---

[44] Mehrabian and Russell (1974), Russell (1980), and Donovan and Rossiter (1982).

[45] It is also argued that the relationship between pleasure and arousal does not necessarily has to be independent (Kuppens, 2008). As Kuppens (2008, p. 1054) points out: "[…] it is possible that for some arousal and pleasantness are positively related, for some they are independent, whereas for others they are negatively related". This highlights the fact that the relationship between pleasure and arousal is rather complex.

[46] Donovan and Rossiter (1982).

Several studies have shown that such emotional states are very significant for our behaviour. These emotional states, as long as they exist in sufficient intensity, may result in behavioural reactions, for example, whether we approach something or remove ourselves from the situation.[47] For example, if the situation evokes unpleasant feelings among us, we engage very easily in avoidance behaviour, regardless of the degree to which the situation increases our arousal.[48] Our emotional states may also determine whether we want to communicate with the sales personnel. Additionally, emotional states may influence how much time we want to spend at the store, and how much money to spend on our shopping.[49] This is to say that our emotional states influence us in many ways. It should be borne in mind that describing such emotional states may be difficult, and as they are fleeting, we may not even remember them with any accuracy after the fact.[50]

Overall, emotions have become an important part of consumer research,[51] and they are also a typical target for marketers. This is understandable since emotions have such a great potential to influence our behaviour.

2.7 Unconscious Mind

In the preceding sections, we have briefly covered some key psychological factors that explain our choice behaviour. Many, but not all, of these factors are very often seen to form on a conscious level. This means that we consciously process the information that our senses provide us and based on this conscious information processing we can, for example, form an opinion or a mental image of something or someone. Conscious processing refers simply to something that we are aware of and that is under our personal control. It can involve either high or relatively low levels of elaboration and reasoning. An important feature of conscious processing is that it is verbally reportable, meaning that we can articulate why we behave as we do.[52]

Even though our conscious information processing and outcomes of it such as explicit attitudes may have a significant impact on why we choose the way we choose, research has also established that our choices are often

---

[47] Mehrabian and Russell (1974) and Donovan and Rossiter (1982).
[48] Ibid.
[49] Donovan and Rossiter (1982).
[50] Ibid.
[51] Havlena and Holbrook (1986) and Westbrook and Oliver (1991).
[52] Bargh and Morsella (2008).

far from conscious.[53,54] As Bargh and Morsella state: "Several theorists have postulated that the conscious mind is not the source or origin of our behaviour; instead, they theorize that impulses to act are unconsciously activated [...]".[55] It has even been claimed that up to 95% of our everyday choices are made unconsciously.[56] Whether the percentage is quite that high or not, it is clear that every day we make an immense number of choices which we do not consciously deliberate, and which we could not articulate or justify to others.[57] Like Martin and Morich emphasise: "[...] the majority, if not all, of human behaviour either begins as an unconscious process or occurs completely outside of conscious awareness".[58] A key feature of the unconscious behaviour is that it arises in the absence of conscious awareness and control. We just choose what we choose without being aware what actually drives our decisions. Explaining the choices that we make unconsciously in our daily lives is no easy task. It is said that in order to exhaustively explain unconscious choices, we would have to delve into the deeper parts of our minds. This would mean that we as researchers would not settle for the explanations consumers claim as reasons for their choices (because these reasons are likely to be more or less made-up reasons), but would instead investigate the unconscious motives or goals, hidden memories or implicit attitudes operating in the background or other factors that influence outside of conscious awareness.[59] Investigating these hidden factors is challenging because consumers themselves are rarely, if ever, able to report them directly. Zaltman proposes that we can try to reveal unconscious thoughts by inviting consumers to use metaphors as they think about a product or service.[60]

This book is interested in our unconsciously made choices in a store environment, but the goal is not to seek their causes from the hidden parts of our minds. Instead, the scope of the book is limited to cues, sensory stimuli that exist outside our minds and that can trigger unconscious choices. Impulse purchases are a good example of this, even though they should not be seen

---

[53] In accordance with Daniel Kahneman's (2011) famous book about the dual system of our brain (System 1 and System 2), one could say that our choices are either fast, automatic, unconscious (based on System 1, intuitive thoughts and quick thinking with minimum effort) or they are slow, conscious, controlled (based on System 2, conscious reasoning and reflective thinking).
[54] Dijksterhuis and Nordgren (2006).
[55] Bargh and Morsella (2008, p. 7).
[56] Mahoney (2003) and Zaltman (2003).
[57] Ozkara and Bagozzi (2021).
[58] Martin and Morich (2011, p. 483).
[59] Bargh and Morsella (2008).
[60] Zaltman (2003).

as an action taking place entirely outside our awareness.[61] For example, Messner and Wänke state that such decisions always involve some information processing.[62] However, impulse purchases are by definition choices which are made quickly, spontaneously, with no conscious premeditation, and which are typically triggered by some form of stimulus or cue. Cues that trigger such spontaneous purchases may be advertising slogans that communicate limited availability (e.g., "Only available today!") or similar verbal cues. The same impact may also be generated through very subtle cues, which the consumer may not even consciously notice.[63,64] In a retail environment, such cues may have to do with the background music, lighting or scents. This book focuses specifically on these types of cues which stimulate our senses in almost imperceptible ways, and on their ability to guide us beyond our full awareness.

It is important to note that large number of our daily unconscious choices are likely to be choices that are guided by our habits. It is well known that habits make us behave in a nearly automatic manner. In fact, it could even be said that our habits enable us to function as if on autopilot, without particularly thinking about the choices we are making during our shopping trip or in some other contexts.[65] Habitual choice behaviour is particularly common when the involvement or motivation is low in our purchasing decisions. Furthermore, it should also be mentioned that researchers have made an interesting observation relating to unconscious choices, namely that when we are making choices, we may be mimicking the behaviour of others, for example other consumers, without being aware of doing so. This is called spontaneous mimicry.[66] Unconscious choices are a very interesting phenomenon but also something that is difficult to grasp.

The goal of this section has been to explain and illustrate what a complex issue choice is. A simple task like grocery shopping is an eventful series of

---

[61] Rook and Hoch (1985).

[62] Messner and Wänke (2011).

[63] In academic literature, this type of influencing consumer choice is often called priming. Priming means that consumer choice is influenced through some form of hidden cue (a prime). Such a cue, of which the consumer would be unaware, could be a simple image or word that the consumer is exposed to before making the choice. Such subliminal exposure to a hidden cue is demonstrated to influence the customer at later moments of actual choice. Minton et al. (2017) specify that priming is based on the idea of manipulating or increasing knowledge activation in the consumer's mind to produce specific outcomes. Minton et al. continue that the priming outcome can be affective, behavioural or cognitive. Furthermore, primes can lead to responses that are either consistent or reactant to the prime (Minton et al., 2017). See more about priming, e.g., Mandel and Johnson (2002), Bargh et al. (2001), and Karremans et al. (2006).

[64] Dijksterhuis et al. (2005).

[65] Martin and Morich (2011).

[66] Martin and Morich (2011), Kavanagh and Winkielman (2016), and Johnston (2002).

interconnected conscious and unconscious influences and choices, and understanding these processes is challenging even for professional researchers. Few consumers can think about all the things that are happening in our minds and outside it while we shop.

2.8 Summary

As consumers, we make choices consciously or unconsciously in every situation we face. Whether it is a choice to purchase a particular product over another or a choice to approach the store or avoid it, or to move along a certain route, these all are choices we make. It is fascinating to study why we choose how we choose. Although the question seems simple, it is more than difficult to solve.

Relying on consumer psychology is seen as a promising avenue to shed a light on consumers' choices and psychological factors such as motives, beliefs and emotions behind these choices. Psychological factors that largely drive our choices are formed in our minds mainly through processing of the sensory information registered and conveyed by our senses such as sight, hearing and touch. Processing the information can be very systematic and may require a high degree of mental effort and intensive reasoning, or it can be relatively automatic and less demanding in terms of mental work.[67] The way we receive and process information is known as perception. The key part of information processing is interpretation. Through interpretation, we make sense of the sensory information that our minds receive and most of the psychological factors are formed or moulded based on our interpretations. However, some aspects of information processing, like our choices, may also take place on the unconscious level, outside our awareness. In fact, it is said that a large part of our daily life is experienced without conscious information processing or alternatively, the processing is based on minimum elaboration. Furthermore, it should be noted that psychological factors such as motives or mental images also affect where we focus our attention and how we process the incoming sensory information.[68] All in all, our senses and internal psychological factors form a complex and interrelated whole.

This book utilises consumer psychology as a general theoretical base and starting point when delving into the world of sensory marketing. The American Psychological Association defines consumer psychology as "the branch of psychology that studies the behaviour of individuals as consumers and the

---

[67] Chaiken and Ledgerwood (2012).
[68] Bettman (1986).

marketing and communication techniques used to influence consumer decisions".[69] One could say that consumer psychology is about unlocking the mysteries of the consumers' mind. One part of this unlocking is to understand how our unconscious mind works or how some of our actions take place without our awareness. It is largely acknowledged that most of our choices are done unconsciously and in the guidance of subtle cues that surround us.[70]

This book explores how the various sensory cues that we face in a retail environment affect us on a conscious or unconscious level. The cues are an essential part of sensory marketing and largely determine why we behave as we do.

References

Ajzen, I. (1989). Attitude structure and behaviour. In A. R. Pratkanis, S. J. Breckler, & A. G. Greenwald (Eds.), *Attitude structure and function* (pp. 241–274). Lawrence Erlbaum Associates Inc.

Ajzen, I. (1991). The theory of planned behaviour. *Organizational Behaviour and Human Decision Processes, 50*, 179–211.

Alho, K., & Salmela, V. (2017). Tarkkaavaisuus ja havaitseminen aivokuvantamisen näkökulmasta. *Niin & Näin: Filosofinen Aikakakauslehti, 24*, 99–104.

Ansorge, U., Kunde, W., & Kiefer, M. (2014). Unconscious vision and executive control: How unconscious processing and conscious action control interact. *Consciousness and Cognition, 27*, 268–287.

Baker, J., Levy, M., & Grewal, D. (1992). An experimental approach to making retail store environmental decisions. *Journal of Retailing, 68*, 445–460.

Bargh, J., & Morsella, E. (2008). The unconscious mind. *Perspectives on Psychological Science, 3*, 73–79.

Bargh, J., Gollwitzer, P. M., Lee-Chai, A., Barndollar, K., & Trötschel, R. (2001). The automated will: Nonconscious activation and pursuit of behavioural goals. *Journal of Personality and Social Psychology, 81*, 1014–1027.

Belk, R. (1988). Possessions and extended self. *Journal of Consumer Research, 15*, 139–168.

Bettman, J. R. (1986). Consumer psychology. *Annual Review of Psychology, 37*, 257–289.

Chaiken, S., & Ledgerwood, A. (2012). A theory of heuristic and systematic information processing. In P. A. M. Van Lange, A. W. Kruglanski, & E. T. Higgins (Eds.), *Handbook of theories of social psychology* (pp. 246–266). Sage.

---

[69] https://dictionary.apa.org/consumer-psychology.
[70] Dijksterhuis et al. (2005).

Clow, K. E., Kurtz, D. L., Ozment, J., & Soo Ong, B. (1997). The antecedents of consumer expectations of services: An empirical study across four industries. *The Journal of Services Marketing, 11*, 230–248.

Collins, L., & Montgomery, C. (1969). The origins of motivational research. *European Journal of Marketing, 3*, 103–113.

Dawson, S., Bloch, P., & Ridgway, N. (1990). Shopping motives, emotional states, and retail outcomes. *Journal of Retailing, 58*, 34–57.

Dijksterhuis, A., & Nordgren, L. (2006). A theory of unconscious thought. *Perspectives on Psychological Science, 1*, 95–109.

Dijksterhuis, A., Smith, P., van Baaren, R., & Wigboldus, D. (2005). The unconscious consumer: Effects of environment on consumer behaviour. *Journal of Consumer Psychology, 15*, 193–202.

Donovan, R., & Rossiter, J. (1982). Store atmosphere: An environmental psychology approach. *Journal of Retailing, 58*, 34–57.

Fishbein, M. (1966). The relationships between beliefs, attitudes and behaviour. In S. Feldman (Ed.), *Cognitive consistency*. Academic Press.

Fishbein, M., & Middlestadt, S. (1995). Noncognitive effects on attitude formation and change: Fact or artifact? *Journal of Consumer Psychology, 4*, 181–202.

Gawronski, B., Hofmann, W., & Wilbur, C. (2006). Are "implicit" attitudes unconscious? *Consciousness and Cognition, 15*, 485–499.

Gordon Betts, J., DeSaix, P., & Johnson, E. (2013). Anatomy and physiology. *OpenStax*. https://openstax.org/details/books/anatomy-and-physiology

Hansen, T. (2005). Perspectives on consumer decision making: An integrated approach. *Journal of Consumer Behaviour, 4*, 420–437.

Havlena, W., & Holbrook, M. (1986). The varieties of consumption experience: Comparing two typologies of emotion in consumer behaviour. *Journal of Consumer Research, 13*, 394–404.

Hutmacher, F. (2019). Why is there so much more research on vision than on any other sensory modality? *Frontiers in Psychology, 10*, 2246.

Johnston, L. (2002). Behavioural mimicry and stigmatization. *Social Cognition, 20*, 18–35.

Kahneman, D. (2011). *Thinking, fast and slow*. Farrar, Straus and Giroux.

Karremans, J. C., Stroebe, W., & Claus, J. (2006). Beyond Vicary's fantasies: The impact of subliminal priming and brand choice. *Journal of Experimental Social Psychology, 42*, 792–798.

Karvonen, E. (1997). *Imagologia. Imagon teorioiden esittelyä, analyysiä, kritiikkiä*. Tampere University Press.

Kavanagh, L., & Winkielman, P. (2016). The functionality of spontaneous mimicry and its influences on affiliation: An implicit socialization account. *Frontiers in Psychology, 7*, 458.

Kotler, P. (2001). *A framework for marketing management*. Prentice Hall.

Kuisma, J. (2007). Silmänliikemenetelmä painetun ja verkkomainonnan tutkimuksessa. *Kulutustutkimus. Nyt., 1*(2007), 41–52.

Kuppens, P. (2008). Individual differences in the relationship between pleasure and arousal. *Journal of Research in Personality, 42,* 1053–1059.

Lazarus, R. (1991). Progress on a cognitive-motivational-relational theory of emotion. *American Psychologist, 46,* 819–834.

Lyly, A., Wikstén, J., & Lundberg, M. (2022). Hajuaistin arvoitukset. *Duodecim, 138,* 1780–1786.

Mahoney, M. (2003, January 13). *The subconscious mind of the consumer (and how to reach it).* Harvard Business School, Research & Ideas.

Mandel, N., & Johnson, E. J. (2002). When web pages influence choice: Effects of visual primes on experts and novices. *Journal of Consumer Research, 29,* 235–245.

Martin, N., & Morich, K. (2011). Unconscious mental processes in consumer choice: Toward a new model of consumer behaviour. *Journal of Brand Management, 18,* 483–505.

Mehrabian, A., & Russell, J. (1974). *An approach to environmental psychology.* The Massachusetts Institute of Technology.

Messner, C., & Wänke, M. (2011). Unconscious information processing reduces information overload and increases product satisfaction. *Journal of Consumer Psychology, 21,* 9–13.

Minton, E. A., Cornwell, T. B., & Kahle, L. R. (2017). A theoretical review of consumer priming: Prospective theory, retrospective theory, and the affective–behavioural–cognitive model. *Journal of Consumer Behaviour, 16,* 309–321.

Molnar, C., & Gair, J. (2021). Concepts of biology (1st Canadian ed.) [ebook]. OpenStax College.

Niosi, A. (2021). *Introduction to consumer behaviour.* BCcampus.

Nummenmaa, L. (2016). Tunteiden neurobiologia. *Suomen Lääkärilehti, 10*(2016), 725–731.

Nummenmaa, L. (2017a). Mistä puhumme kun puhumme tunteista? *Tieteessä Tapahtuu, 35*(2).

Nummenmaa, L. (2017b). Tuntematon tunne. Aurora. 1/2017.

Ojasalo, J. (2001). Managing customer expectations in professional services. *Managing Service Quality, 11,* 200–212.

Oliver, R. (1980). A cognitive model of the antecedents and consequences of satisfaction decisions. *Journal of Marketing Research, 17,* 46–49.

Ozkara, B., & Bagozzi, R. (2021). The use of event related potentials brain methods in the study of conscious and unconscious consumer decision making processes. *Journal of Retailing and Consumer Services, 58.*

Petty, R. E., & Briñol, P. (2012). The elaboration likelihood model. In P. A. M. Van Lange, A. W. Kruglanski, & E. T. Higgins (Eds.), *Handbook of theories of social psychology* (pp. 224–245). Sage.

Poiesz, T. (1989). The image concept: Its place in consumer psychology. *Journal of Economic Psychology, 10,* 457–472.

Rook, D., & Hoch, S. (1985). Consuming impulses. In E. C. Hirschman & M. B. Holbrook (Eds.), *NA—Advances in consumer research* (Vol. 12; pp. 23–27). Association for Consumer Research.

Russell, J. (1980). A circumplex model of affect. *Journal of Personality and Social Psychology, 39*, 1161–1178.

Russell, J., & Pratt, G. (1980). A description of the affective quality attributed to environments. *Journal of Personality and Social Psychology, 38*, 311–322.

Singh, S. (2006). Impact of color on marketing. *Management Decision, 44*, 783–789.

Spence, C. (2020). Senses of place: Architectural design for the multisensory mind. *Cognitive Research: Principles and Implications, 5*, 1–26.

Stangor, C., Hammond, T., & Jhangiani, R. (2014). *Principles of social psychology.* BCcampus Open Publishing. http://opentextbc.ca/socialpsychology/

Uusitalo, L. (1997). Kuluttajien ympäristöä koskevat valinnat. *Liiketaloudellinen Aikakauskirja, 1*, 15–31.

Westbrook, R., & Oliver, R. (1991). The dimensionality of consumption emotion patterns and consumer satisfaction. *Journal of Consumer Research, 18*, 84–91.

Zaltman, G. (2003). *How customers think: Essential insights into the mind of the market.* Harvard Business School Press.

3

The Goal and Scope of This Book

3.1 Focus on Sensory Marketing in Retail

This book focuses on sensory marketing, defined in the literature as "marketing that engages the consumers' senses and affects their perception, judgment and behaviour".[1] In other words, sensory marketing is a marketing activity that aims to appeal to one or more of our five senses in order to trigger some specific responses in our mind or actual behaviour. As Hultén et al. summarise that sensory marketing puts human senses and sensory experiences at the centre of marketing.[2] Sensory marketing can be used in different fields and situations. In this book, sensory marketing is explored in the context of retailing, with a focus on cues as the main means of consumer influence in sensory marketing.

In a retail setting, cues may be factors relating to lighting, background music or even the body language of the staff—things which we may encounter and sense in various ways during a visit to the store, and which may then guide our choices either on the conscious or unconscious level.,[3,4]

---

[1] Krishna (2012, p. 333) and see also Krishna (2010).
[2] Hultén et al. (2009).
[3] Biswas (2019) and Puccinelli et al. (2009).
[4] It should be noted that in this book the term "choice" is interpreted rather broadly—it can refer to actual purchase decisions (including impulse purchases) but also conscious and unconscious decisions to approach or avoid the retail environment, or a willingness to investigate and browse the product

© The Author(s), under exclusive license to Springer Nature Switzerland AG 2023
A. Lindblom, *Sensory Marketing in Retail*, https://doi.org/10.1007/978-3-031-47515-3_3

For example, cues that we face in a retail store can guide us to make impulse buys, even though such spontaneous purchases are rarely the result of cues alone.[5] Similarly, cues may influence the amount of time we spend in the store, or how we move within it. Cues may also be a critical factor in shaping the way we think of the level of service, quality or price of the store. All in all, cues have a potential to elevate our shopping experience by engaging our senses while we are at the store. Sensory experiences that we can gain in a store are found to act as one of the main sources of shopping enjoyment.[6] However, managing cues is far from easy and requires, for example, that the retailer is able to control the meanings of the cues. Furthermore, cues should be managed in a way that the multisensory nature of the store is taken into account. This highlights the fact that cues should not be considered independently, but rather as a whole. As the retail store is multisensory in nature, it is important to understand how cues work together, and what kinds of joint effects the cues we encounter may have.

As this book will explain, cues often trigger transient emotional states in us, but the impacts of the cues may also manifest in our attitudes or mental images.[7] These impacts in our consciousness may then result in various behavioural reactions. Such a chain of influence is usually described in the literature with the letters S–O–R where "S" stands for Stimulus, "O" for Organism and "R" for Response.,[8,9] The S–O-R model emphasises that our mind (internal evaluations) acts as organism (O) that mediates the effects of cues (S) on our actual behaviour (R). The way our mind works can be explored, for example, with the help of information processing theory. The S–O-R model has become a very popular way to describe and explain the impacts of cues in a retail environment. Also, this book relies largely on the S–O-R model and its idea of consciousness acting as a mediating variable between sensory cues and behavioural responses. Although cues affect us through our consciousness, one should remember that they often have an

---

offering, among other things. Thus, choices can be seen as those behavioural responses that take place in a store environment during the shopping journey. This view comes close to the response taxonomy presented by Mehrabian and Russell (1974) (see Donovan & Rossiter, 1982).

[5] Beatty and Ferrell (1998).
[6] Cox et al. (2005).
[7] Spence et al. (2014) and Roggeveen et al. (2020).
[8] Donovan and Rossiter (1982).
[9] The S-O-R model was originally developed by researchers Albert Mehrabian and James Russell (1974) in the field of environmental psychology.

impact beyond our awareness and conscious control.[10] For example, scents are often thought of as cues which typically function subliminally.[11]

No matter how or where in the mind the impacts of the cues manifest, a cue should not be thought of as a "magic bullet" that automatically triggers a specific reaction. The impacts are always specific to the individual and situation. Just the financial situation of the consumer will influence the kinds of choices they can make at a given moment of choice. The consumer's mood or shopping motive will also influence how they operate and observe their environment. Similarly, our personalities and various social norms are always reflected in our behaviour, no matter what kinds of cues prevail around us while we are making our choices. These and similar factors do not mean that cues in the shopping environment cannot be a significant component in shaping our choice behaviour.

It is also important to understand that cues in the shopping environment, no matter what they may be like in style or nature, will radiate their influence towards the consumer in any case, regardless of whether the store is making conscious efforts to control them. The consumer is always exposed to a variety of environmental stimuli and their potential impacts. For example, a brick-and-mortar store will always look, sound and smell like something, no matter how minimalist its design. Consequently, it is important for the store to be aware of what these cues inherent to the retail environment and its various aspects are, and how creating and managing cues can be used to influence consumers. It is particularly important to understand how different cues fit together, and what kinds of combined effects they may have. This is crucial for sensory marketing to be effective and have the intended results.

This book delves into the use of cues by investigating an extensive range of academic research on the topic and by explaining the results in plain language. A broad range of research sources has been consulted, with a particular focus on the most esteemed academic journals in the fields of consumer research, marketing and retailing. The use of cues is also illustrated through brief case examples of existing companies. However, the book steers away from an excessively normative approach, intentionally leaving it up to the reader to evaluate whether the cues depicted in the book could be viable in practice, and if so, how they might best be implemented. It is important when using cues, or any other means of influence for that matter, that they are evaluated and managed from the company's own perspective, for example, guided

---

[10] Dijksterhuis et al. (2005).
[11] Holland et al. (2005).

by the customer promise and the chosen target groups. What may work for one company may not work for another, due to different target groups or similar reasons.

This book is intended for everyone interested in the myriad meanings of cues as well as consumer choice and the ways that choice can be influenced in a retail environment. It is particularly aimed at students, teachers and researchers interested in sensory marketing and consumer behaviour, but can also provide interesting information for consumers on the ways they are being influenced, showing them what sorts of influencing methods they are likely to encounter while shopping. Additionally, the book provides valuable insights for companies and entrepreneurs operating in a range of retail environments, particularly if they are looking to redesign their own retail environment, or possibly to develop a completely new retail concept. The book can help identify critical factors for generating a positive shopping experience as well as factors that influence consumer choice during store visits.

3.2 The Elements of the Retail Marketing Mix

The retail sector offers many different ways of influencing consumer choice. The practical implementation of influencing consumer choice has traditionally—and largely to this very day—been conceived of as being conducted through the management of the retail marketing mix. The retail marketing mix includes a selection of marketing tools or tactics. These tactics are the concrete means that can be employed to entice consumers to make purchases or to guide them to a specific retail location. However, the tactics are not just means for drawing attention or guiding consumers. Instead, they are a central part of generating customer value and building customer relationships. It is also important for the tactics to support the strategic positioning efforts and overall brand building of the store. It is clear that the use of marketing tactics must always be based on a strong understanding of consumers and the factors that influence their behaviour. Furthermore, how various tactics are ultimately emphasised in the retail marketing mix is always dependent on the company and its target groups and competitive situation.

Key marketing mix tactics in retail include, for example, assortment planning, space management and pricing. For a brick-and-mortar store, physical location is naturally another important marketing tactic. Customer service is also part of the retail marketing mix, as are customer loyalty programmes. Furthermore, marketing communication in all its forms (e.g., TV, radio, newspapers, Internet and social media) is also a crucial part of influencing consumers in the field of retailing. In particular, influencer marketing through various social media channels has become an increasingly prominent form of commercial influencing. For example, influencer-generated reviews have become a very popular way to promote products and services in the retail industry. Typically, such influencing primarily reaches younger age groups. In today's commercial landscape, marketing communication has also become more personalised and targeted as retailers are able to collect and handle extremely detailed information on their customers.

The central message of this book is that a physical store with all its many sensory cues is an important marketing tactic in itself. What the store looks like, smells like or sounds like is at the very core of influencing consumer choice, and, more broadly, determining what kind of value is being generated for customers and what kind of a relationship customers ultimately form with the store. The store could be called an extremely efficient means of communicating with customers. One could say that at its best the physical store is a place of storytelling that signals to the customers what the retailer stands for.[12] All in all, brick-and-mortar has a strong impact on how the retailer is positioned in the minds of the customers, and how the retailer can differentiate itself from the competition. It has been said that the competitive edge of a retailer is based specifically on the multisensory experiences that the store can create for its customers during shopping. For example, Cox et al. found that for many customers the sensory experiences that physical stores can provide are one of the key sources of shopping pleasure.[13] Sensory experiences might even be the reason why consumers choose to visit brick-and-mortar stores instead of making their purchases online. However, the importance of the physical store and its sensory experiences for the formation of the competitive edge is something that is easily overlooked in our intensely digitalising world.

3.3 The Retail Store as a Context of Our Choices

The physical retail environment is a unique shopping context where the consumer may make dozens of different choices in a short amount of time, consciously or unconsciously. Furthermore, in many stores there is an overwhelming number of alternatives that a consumer has to choose from. Also,

---

[12] Alexander and Cano (2020).
[13] Cox et al. (2005).

while walking in the store, the consumer is exposed to a large number of different stimuli from sounds to smells, which may significantly shape their behaviour. The retail environment is a genuinely multisensory setting which fully envelops the consumer during shopping and can create a strong base for shopping enjoyment and pleasure. This is the core advantage of a brick-and-mortar store when compared with digital environments. And it should be remembered that the physical stores themselves are also becoming digitised as retailers invest more and more in digital technologies such as digital shelf displays, self-checkout terminals and smart shopping carts to enhance and expand their in-store experiences. In many cases, retail stores are becoming platforms that combine a physical and digital experience together.

Its multisensory nature also makes the retail environment a fascinating research topic, particularly from the perspective of sensory marketing. Thus, it is not surprising that researchers have long been interested in how the shopping environment with all its multisensory stimuli influences consumers and their shopping behaviour. It goes without saying that consumer behaviour, and more specifically, the things consumers do or do not choose while shopping, is absolutely critical for the success of both retail and manufacturing companies. Consequently, it is no wonder that many different methods of influencing consumers are employed specifically at the moment of purchase.

The impact of the influencing methods used in retail environments—including sensory marketing—is reflected in the fact that the number of impulse purchases is typically very high in a retail setting. At a retail store, the majority of purchases may be goods that the consumer had not originally intended to buy, but decided to purchase them while shopping. This is a good illustration of how susceptible consumers are to different forms of influencing while visiting a store.

The above describes how significant an impact the physical store environment may have on us as consumers. The role of physical environments may of course vary in the daily lives of consumers. Sometimes a consumer may first find or test the products at a brick-and-mortar store, but ultimately make the purchase on an online platform. This is known as the "showrooming effect". Conversely, we may explore the product selection online before making our purchases at a physical location, a process known as "webrooming". A webrooming consumer studies the available products at online stores and then visits a brick-and-mortar store to make the purchase. These examples prove that physical environments are an important part of our daily lives and shopping behaviour in one way or another.

3.4 The Retail Store as a Bundle of Cues

This book focuses on cues as means of influencing consumer choice in a physical retail setting. At its simplest, a single cue may be defined as a sensory stimulus which generates information, which is then either consciously processed or influences us unconsciously.[14] More accurately, cues are incoming sensory information that our sensory organs receive and transmit further to our central nervous system, where the information is processed. Processing information refers to mental processes such as organising and interpreting the information. Information processing might involve deep thinking, or it can be quick and less systematic. After processing the information, we can act. However, in many cases, sensory information, particularly in the form of subtle cues, may steer our behaviour beyond our full awareness.[15]

A cue may address any of the five senses of the consumer. In other words, cues essentially influence consumers through their senses, such as sight, hearing and touch.[16] At their best, cues stimulate senses which are beyond the scope of other influencing methods. By stimulating senses with cues retailers can, for example, draw consumers' attention, elicit approach behaviours or guide their choices in a store.[17] Cues can also convey certain meanings about the features or benefits of the store to consumers. For example, consumers tend to associate some cues like bright lighting and Top 40 music with some specific features of the store, like affordable prices. In this book, coordinated use of sensory cues for influencing purposes is called sensory marketing.

During shopping, consumers may encounter several intentionally placed cues. However, it is likely that consumers themselves are able to name only few surrounding cues when they enter a store. In fact, a typical feature of sensory cues is that they are more or less "invisible" and thus, difficult to spot. This is why cues in the retail environment are often understood as "atmospheric variables"—the word "atmosphere" literally meaning "the air surrounding a sphere".[18] Although cues can be rather abstract stimuli, researchers have been able to describe and classify them in many meaningful ways. For example, Turley and Milliman divide retail store variables into several elements: the exterior of the store, the general interior variables, layout and design variables, point-of-purchase and decoration variables and

---

[14] Biswas (2019) and Helmefalk (2017).
[15] Dijksterhuis et al. (2005).
[16] Krishna (2012) and Roggeveen et al. (2020).
[17] Ballantine et al. (2010).
[18] Kotler (1973).

human variables.[19] Also, Brengman made a comprehensive classification of store environmental cues by classifying cues into the macro-environment, the store exterior, store ambient factors, interior aesthetic design factors, interior functional design factors or store layout, point-of-purchase displays and store social factors, including store personnel and customers.[20]

One established and well-known way to classify the cues or atmospheric elements in a store environment is to divide them into three categories:

- Ambient cues; e.g., background music, scents and lighting
- Design cues; e.g., store design, colour palette and layout
- Social cues; e.g., number of staff, their body language and dress code.[21]

Following Belk's thoughts, ambient, design and social cues can be defined as situational variables that concretise the surroundings of the store.[22] According to Belk, situational variables are factors that are particular to a time and place of observation, i.e., not related to stable individual features (such as personality) or to product or service object.[23] Furthermore, each cue category has potential effects on our senses (e.g., music and colours stimulate auditory and visual senses).[24] It is important to note that even the most abstract cues can be linked to conscious or unconscious sensory experiences. Many studies have used above classification as their basis, and this book also employs it to group cues. The general understanding is that the retailer can guide its clientele and influence their shopping behaviour by controlling these cues in the environment.[25]

However, even ambient, design and social cues can be seen as situational variables which drive our current behaviour, they often influence our shopping indirectly and in the background, and may thus be unable to influence us at the specific moment of choice. One could say that ambient, design and social cues are sort of peripheral elements of the store environment.[26] For this reason, this book examines the following types of cues separately:

---

[19] Turley and Milliman (2000).
[20] Brengman (2002).
[21] Baker (1986), Baker et al. (2002), and Kumar and Kim (2014).
[22] Belk (1975).
[23] Ibid.
[24] Roggeveen et al. (2020).
[25] Puccinelli et al. (2009).
[26] Hultén et al. (2009).

- Haptic cues, which stimulate our sense of touch
- Merchandise-related cues
- Pricing-related cues.

These are very concrete cues and can be expected to relate to the moment of choice, which makes them worthy of closer examination. It is unfortunately rare to find studies that examine these cues together with the abovementioned atmospheric cues. One exception is Roggeveen et al.'s DAST framework that also takes into account trialability and highlights its importance from the viewpoint of shopping experience.[27] Some of these concrete cues, such as cues related to pricing, are not even necessarily understood as a part of sensory marketing, but this book views all these cues as forming the greater whole of sensory marketing.[28]

Figure 3.1 describes the cues that are discussed in this book. The cues, their specific components and various meanings are discussed in more detail in Chapter 4. Here, it is crucial to understand that cues are not just visual stimuli, as they can also engage other senses, such as our hearing or sense of smell.

As a whole, this book seeks to provide a comprehensive understanding of cues relating to the physical retail environment, along with their meanings and impacts on our shopping behaviour.[29] As the book will endeavour to show, cues convey all sorts of information, and their impacts are diverse, resulting in reactions in our conscious and unconscious minds as well as actual behavioural reactions, such as impulse purchases or changes in how quickly we move inside the store.

It is also important to remember that when a customer enters a store, they experience the cues in the environment holistically.[30] This means that multiple cues influence customers simultaneously and different cues are entwined together in customers' minds and evoke joint effects. There is an increasing amount of research on the joint effects of cues (e.g., music x scent)

---

[27] Roggeveen et al. (2020).
[28] For example, Turley and Milliman (2000) state that studies around "shelf space" are not commonly recognized as a part of atmospheric studies (i.e., sensory marketing). However, as they argue, these shelf space studies explore variables such as shelf signs, price displays and merchandise arrangement, which can be considered as atmospheric variables in the atmospheric classification.
[29] The one sense excluded from this book is the sense of taste. Even though it is possible to engage the sense of taste to influence consumer behaviour in a retail setting (e.g., with samples or product presentations), this sense as well as the cues and factors that stimulate it fall beyond the scope of this book.
[30] Bitner (1992).

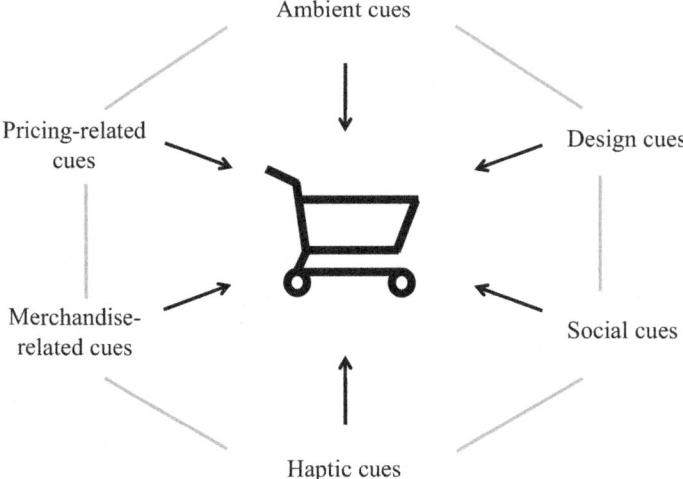

Fig. 3.1 Cues examined in this book

and how cues should be managed as a whole while considering such interactions.[31] Sensory marketing also involves some risks, such as sensory overload. These issues are described in Chapter 5 in more detail.

3.5 Ethical Considerations in Influencing Consumer Choices

When we discuss influencing consumers we will inevitably encounter certain ethical questions. For example, where is the line between acceptable and unacceptable influencing? Marketing is typically deemed to be inappropriate if it is in clear conflict with generally accepted social values.[32]

In selecting and using influencing tactics, it is important to understand to what degree the consumer can be expected to be aware of them.[33] If the consumer is unaware of a company using influencing methods to change their attitudes or behaviour, the marketer is engaging in manipulation instead of influencing.[34] Consumers may find manipulation to be extremely unpleasant, even though in practical terms, the difference between influencing and manipulation may be very subtle. These types of situations

---

[31] Mari and Poggesi (2013).
[32] Bargh (2002).
[33] Spence (2020a).
[34] Panula (1997).

where we are not aware of being influenced may occur in many ways in the course of our daily lives. For example, many of us may find it very difficult to discern between commercially aligned reality TV or influencer marketing, and pure entertainment with no commercial agenda. Product placement in cinema is a common example of influencing that we may not be aware of, even if it is mentioned at the beginning of the film. On the other hand, public discourse often underestimates the media literacy of consumers and assumes that consumers are fully at the whim of marketing techniques deployed by companies. This is certainly not the case. Most consumers are very aware and able to interpret the marketing messages they receive, and know to make their own independent decisions. This does not mean, however, that consumers are never influenced by marketing that uses misleading information, or subliminal manipulation, which becomes particularly problematic if the targets are underage children.

Spence states that a worrying trend is "neuromania" where the use of neuroscience might go too far and influencing becomes so effective that consumers ultimately lose their free will and ability to resist.[35] In the most extreme case, neuroscientists are afraid they might find our brain's "buy button", which marketers would inevitably seize upon and start to manipulate us beyond our awareness. Neuroscience-inspired influencing is very much a grey area where boundaries of good practices should be defined carefully.

It is also clear that the rapid development of digitalisation has introduced a host of new influencing methods, potentially based on very personal information or targeted content, and at their worst, on extremely ruthless manipulation. The Cambridge Analytica data scandal, in which the voting behaviour of Facebook users was influenced entirely without their knowledge leading up to the American presidential election of 2016, is a good example of unethical, and even illegal, influencing. This case is partially the reason why authorities have begun to monitor consumer influencing more closely, and some concrete steps have already been taken. For example, the EU's recently adopted General Data Protection Regulation (GDPR) means that every EU citizen has a right to access the personal data an organisation holds on them, to know how and for what purpose their personal data is being processed, and to object to the processing or request the erasure of the data. Besides formal measures, active discussion of ethical issues is one way to make sure that influencing is moving forward in a healthy and ethically sound direction.

The retail environment is fundamentally a commercial environment, and any consumer entering a store can be expected to be aware that they are being

---

[35] Spence (2020b).

targeted by commercial influencing, even if they are unable to identify the specific influencing tactics such as scents, lighting or music. This does not mean, however, that any kind of influencing is permissible inside a store. All marketing must comply with good practices. Retail companies should be particularly careful with how and for what purpose they use their ever-accumulating, and increasingly rich, consumer data. If marketing slips into the realm of the unethical, let alone illegal, the consequences can be extremely severe.

3.6 Summary

Sensory marketing has gained a great deal of interest among practitioners in various fields and is seen as a way to differentiate businesses from their competition while influencing customers and their behaviour. At its best, sensory marketing guides or helps customers to make certain choices in a way that they are unaware of what actually influenced their choices. Although sensory marketing sounds like an attractive way to "nudge" customers, it is a highly demanding practice that also involves risks and ethical concerns.

This book delves into the world of sensory marketing in a physical retail setting and aims to offer a comprehensive and coherent view of various sensory cues and their capacity to drive our behaviour through stimulating our senses and creating sensory experiences. Cues are sensory stimuli (sensory information) that can vary along a wide array of features. Some cues can be very concrete and easy to observe, while others may be more abstract and more difficult to spot and comprehend by customers. Typically cues are seen as some sort of background conditions of the store environment although certain cues can be linked directly to the moment of choice. The book particularly highlights the meaning of the multisensory nature of retail stores and emphasises how cues tend to affect us in combination rather than separately as single cues. Thus, after reading this book, the reader will be able to:

- Identify various cues in a retailing setting.
- Categorise cues into different groups.
- Explain how cues affect consumers when they make their daily choices.
- Understand the multisensory nature of retail stores and the meaning of cue (in)congruence.
- Describe how consumers are likely to respond differently to cue combinations than single cues.
- Apply cues in practice and assess their outcomes.

Furthermore, with the help of self-reflective questions, the book also challenges readers to think how they behave as consumers and how they react or response to various sensory cues when visiting a retail store. The book also includes decision-based questions that place readers into the position of store manager and in charge of setting cues in a store environment.

More theoretically speaking, as stated earlier in Chapter 2, this book is largely based on the premises of consumer psychology and its core thoughts of why we behave as we do. However, when explaining how sensory cues are perceived and how they affect us, different, more specific theoretical models and frameworks will be cited such as the Stimulus-Organism-Response (S–O-R) model, information processing model, fluency theory and social impact theory. All in all, the book has a pluralistic nature, and it purposefully utilises theories and constructs from various fields to create as comprehensive picture of sensory cues and their effects as possible.

References

Alexander, B., & Cano, M. B. (2020). Store of the future: Towards a (re)invention and (re)imagination of physical store space in an omnichannel context. *Journal of Retailing and Consumer Services, 55*, 101913.

Baker, J. (1986). The role of the environment in marketing sciences: The consumer perspective. In J. A. Cepeil et al. (Eds.), *The services challenge: Integrating for competitive advantage* (pp. 79–84). AMA.

Baker, J., Parasuraman, A., Grewal, D., & Voss, G. (2002). The influence of multiple store environmental cues on perceived merchandise value and patronage intentions. *Journal of Marketing, 66*, 120–141.

Ballantine, P. W., Jack, R., & Parsons, A. G. (2010). Atmospheric cues and their effect on the hedonic retail experience. *International Journal of Retail & Distribution Management, 38*, 641–653.

Bargh, J. (2002). Losing consciousness: Automatic influences on consumer judgment, behavior, and motivation. *Journal of Consumer Research, 29*, 280–285.

Beatty, S., & Ferrell, E. (1998). Impulse buying: Modeling its precursors. *Journal of Retailing, 74*, 169–191.

Belk, R. (1975). Situational variables and consumer behavior. *Journal of Consumer Research, 2*, 157–164.

Biswas, D. (2019). Sensory aspects of retailing: Theoretical and practical implications. *Journal of Retailing, 95*, 111–115.

Bitner, M. J. (1992). Servicescapes: The impact of physical surroundings on customers and employees. *Journal of Marketing, 56*, 57–71.

Brengman, M. (2002). *The impact of colour in the store environment: An environmental psychology approach*. Ghent University.

Cox, A., Cox, D., & Anderson, R. (2005). Reassessing the pleasures of store shopping. *Journal of Business Research, Elsevier, 58*, 250–259.

Dijksterhuis, A., Smith, P., van Baaren, R., & Wigboldus, D. (2005). The unconscious consumer: Effects of environment on consumer behavior. *Journal of Consumer Psychology, 15*, 193–202.

Donovan, R., & Rossiter, J. (1982). Store atmosphere: An environmental psychology approach. *Journal of Retailing, 58*, 34–57.

Helmefalk, M. (2017). *Multi-sensory cues in interplay and congruency in a retail store context: Consumer emotions and purchase behaviors*. Linnaeus University Dissertations No 297/2017.

Holland, R. W., Hendriks, M., & Aarts, H. (2005). Smells like clean spirit: Nonconscious effects of scent on cognition and behavior. *Psychological Science, 16*, 689–693.

Hultén, B., Broweus, N., & van Dijk, M. (2009). *Sensory marketing*. Palgrave Macmillan.

Kotler, P. (1973). Atmospherics as a marketing tool. *Journal of Retailing, 49*, 48–64.

Krishna, A. (2010). *Sensory marketing. Research on the sensuality of products*. Routledge.

Krishna, A. (2012). An integrative review of sensory marketing: Engaging the senses to affect perception, judgment and behaviour. *Journal of Consumer Psychology, 22*, 332–351.

Kumar, A., & Kim, Y.-K. (2014). The store-as-a-brand strategy: The effect of store environment on customer responses. *Journal of Retailing and Consumer Services, 21*, 685–695.

Mari, M., & Poggesi, S. (2013). Servicescape cues and customer behavior: A systematic literature review and research agenda. *The Service Industries Journal, 33*, 171–199.

Mehrabian, A., & Russell, J. (1974). *An approach to environmental psychology*. The Massachusetts Institute of Technology.

Panula, J. (1997). Vaikutussuhde, käyttösuhde, merkityssuhde: Näkökulmia todellisuuden, joukkoviestinnän ja yleisön väliseen suhteeseen, Atena Kustannus Oy.

Puccinelli, N. M., Goodstein, R. C., Grewal, D., Price, R., Raghubir, P., & Stewart, D. W. (2009). Customer experience management in retailing: Understanding the buying process. *Journal of Retailing, 85*, 15–30.

Roggeveen, A. L., Grewal, D., & Schweiger, E. B. (2020). The DAST framework for retail atmospherics: The impact of in- and out-of-store retail journey touchpoints on the customer experience. *Journal of Retailing, 96*, 128–137.

Spence, C. (2020a). Senses of place: Architectural design for the multisensory mind. *Cognitive Research: Principles and Implications, 5*, 46.

Spence, C. (2020b). On the ethics of neuromarketing and sensory marketing. In J. Martineau & E. Racine (Eds.), *Organizational neuroethics. Advances in neuroethics*. Springer.

Spence, C., Puccinelli, N. M., Grewal, D., & Roggeveen, A. L. (2014). Store atmospherics: A multisensory perspective. *Psychology & Marketing, 31*, 472–488.

Turley, L. W., & Milliman, R. E. (2000). Atmospheric effects on shopping behavior: A review of the experimental evidence. *Journal of Business Research, 49*, 193–211.

4

Identifying Cues and Their Effects in a Retail Store

4.1 Ambient Cues

Ambient cues are non-visual atmospheric factors in the background of the store environment. We tend to be less aware of these factors when moving around the store. We often only realise that ambient cues exist if their intensity exceeds some sensory or emotional tolerance limit, for example, if the lighting becomes too bright or the background music too loud. Even when ambient cues do not reach our immediate awareness, they may have significant impacts on our behaviour.[1]

Background Music

> **DID YOU KNOW?**
> - Customers often find silence more disturbing than background music.
> - The tempo of the background music can influence the speed at which customers in the store conduct their shopping.
> - Background music that is familiar to the customers may increase their arousal.
> - The genre of the background music may influence the price or quality impression of the store.

---

[1] Baker et al. (1992) and Roggeveen et al. (2020).

Background music, literally the music playing in the background while we shop, may be one of the most researched ambient cues. Background music is often used to increase the appeal of the store and the enjoyment of the shopping experience.[2] Music in general is known to have a capacity to affect both our feelings of pleasure and arousal.[3] As Hunter et al. stated that we tend to respond emotionally to music.[4] Music is also something that can bring memories to our mind rather spontaneously.[5] Besides creating an inviting and enjoyable shopping atmosphere, a store can also use background music to differentiate itself from competing stores, or to enhance the image the retailer wishes to create.[6] Further, background music can be used to mask any distracting noises, or, in some cases, to cover silence. In fact, studies have found that we are more disturbed by silence than by background music.[7] For example, it has been found that when we have to stand a short while in a queue, silence bothers us more than background music.[8] This is to say that background music serves many different purposes, and also that it should be selected carefully.

Background music varies along several characteristics such as volume, tempo, genre and familiarity. Researchers have been particularly interested in the impact of the tempo on consumers' shopping behaviour. Tempo is the speed at which the background music is played. The tempo is indicated as beats per minute (BPM). In a research context, background music with 60–70 BPM is typically considered slow-tempo, and music around 100–120 BPM fast-tempo. The impacts of tempo on shopping behaviour seem to be quite straightforward. Research has found that:

- Slow-tempo background music slows down our speed of shopping;
- Fast-tempo background music makes us shop faster.[9]

It is said that similar effects can be seen in many restaurants regarding how fast we eat.[10] It has also been established that we tend to buy more in the presence of slow-tempo than fast-tempo music. This may be ascribed to the fact

---

[2] Yi and Kang (2019).
[3] Kemp et al. (2019).
[4] Hunter et al. (2010).
[5] Jakubowski and Francini (2023).
[6] Sweeney and Wyber (2002).
[7] Spence et al. (2014).
[8] Oakes (2003).
[9] MillIman (1982).
[10] Milliman (1986) and Caldwell and Hibbert (1999).

that slow-tempo background music tends to prolong the time we spend shopping.[11] This sort of effect is likely to be related to the fact that slow-tempo music often makes us relaxed and evokes feelings of pleasure.[12,13] These kinds of feelings easily slow down us whatever we are doing. Fast-tempo music in turn tends to increase our arousal levels, and thus it can speed up our shopping behaviour. It is rather well documented in previous studies that music that is more arousing leads consumers spending less time on their activities.[14]

Although tempo in general is an important factor that tends to affect us as described above, it should be noted that the effects of tempo are likely to be dependent on music genre. Depending on whether the background music is pop, jazz, rock or classical, tempo (slow vs. fast) might generate responses that are somehow surprising. For example, Sweeney and Wyber found in their study that slow pop music (compared to slow classical music) evokes higher levels of pleasure although pop music in general is perceived to be more arousing.[15] Interestingly, in the same study it was also demonstrated that fast classical music is associated with the pleasure. All in all, the study conducted by Sweeney and Wyber shows that the interaction effects of two musical characteristics, tempo and genre, can lead to some specific emotional responses among us.

Taken together, if the store aims to promote relaxation and reduce our stress while we are shopping, slow-tempo music should work well (but bearing in mind that in some cases slow music might cause negative emotions). However, if the goal of the store is to increase the excitement and arousal of its clientele or even guide them to do shopping more quickly, fast-tempo music is more likely to serve this purpose than slow-tempo.[16] Figure 4.1 illustrates differences between slow music and fast music.

> The Australian youth clothing chain **Cotton On** plays chart-topping hits in its stores to appeal to its target audience. Cotton On has also experimented with a system based on RFID technology, in which the music played in the fitting rooms changes according to the clothes the customer tries on. For example, when trying on a specific type of jeans, the customer would hear either rock, indie or pop music.

---

[11] Garlin and Owen (2006).
[12] Oakes (2003).
[13] In some cases, slow-tempo music can also evoke negative emotions such as sadness or even depression (see e.g., Balkwill et al., 2004; Hunter et al., 2010).
[14] Caldwell and Hibbert (1999).
[15] Sweeney and Wyber (2002).
[16] Ibid.

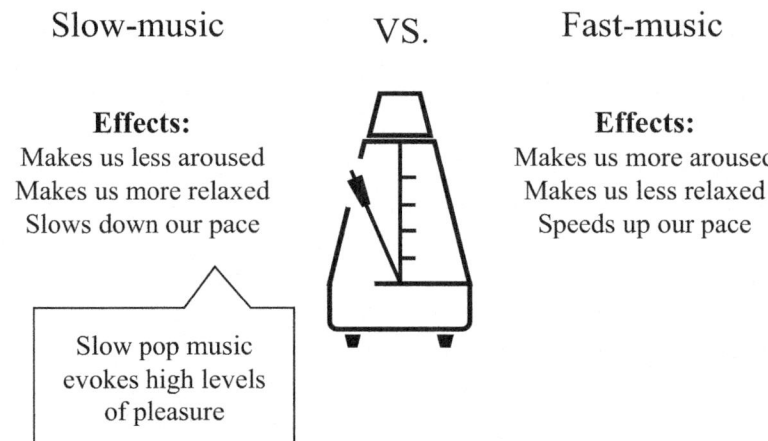

Fig. 4.1 Slow-tempo music vs. fast-tempo music (e.g., Milliman, 1982; Oakes, 2003; Sweeney & Wyber, 2002)

Studies have also found that our shopping experience is more enjoyable if there is a moderate discrepancy between the tempo of the background music and how crowded the store is. This means that we seem to enjoy our shopping more if the store plays slower-tempo music when there is a rush (high density), and higher-tempo music when the store is quieter (low density).[17] To simplify, we could say that we are more likely to be annoyed if we are exposed to fast-tempo music while being in a congested environment, but conversely may feel bored or even melancholy in a deserted store with very calm music in the background. It has also been found that people tend to become more irritated with slow-tempo music if they have to wait in queue for a long time. However, if the waiting time is short, slow-tempo music evokes positive feelings.[18] Above examples highlight the importance of "fit" when the background music is used as an ambient cue.[19]

In addition to tempo, many studies have examined the volume of the background music and its impacts on consumers. Volume is expressed as decibels (dB). The human hearing threshold is 0 dB and the pain threshold approximately 125 dB. The volume of human speech is typically just over 50 dB. It is said that music with high volume increases our excitement levels (and also our heart rate and blood pressure), whereas lower volume music tends to make us relaxed and calm.[20] In other words, as it was in the case

---

[17] Eroglu et al. (2005).
[18] Oakes (2003).
[19] Milliman (1982).
[20] Biswas et al. (2019).

of fast-tempo music, the louder the volume of the background music, the more aroused we are.[21] And the more aroused we are, the faster we tend to behave and the less time we are likely to spend in the space.[22] Quieter and thus more relaxing background music in turn entices us to spend more time in the store. As Garlin and Owen stated in their review article: "[…] most research has reported that consumers stay longer when […] the music is low rather than high in volume".[23] Particularly female customers seem to prefer the music played at a lower volume.[24] Yalch and Spangenberg remind that soothing background music should be selected if the aim is to facilitate discussion between customers and staff, whereas in self-service stores a different kind of music might be more appropriate.[25] This underlines the fact that the knowing what sort of behaviours are desired in a retail setting affects the choice of music and how loud it can be played.

Biswas et al. made an interesting finding that consumers tend to make healthier choices when ambient music volume is low than when ambient music volume is loud.[26] Biswas et al. argue that the effects of music volume on consumers' healthier food choices seem to be driven by relaxation evoked by music that is played with low volume. Biswas et al. specify that: "[…] in a relaxed state, consumers have greater self-efficacy in resisting tempting, unhealthy foods, leading to preference for healthier options".[27] If the music is played loud, it tends to cause higher levels of excitement and arousal (and potentially also stress) that in turn seem to enhance our preference for unhealthier choices. The study conducted by Biswas et al. is a good example of that just the loudness level of music can have specific consequences on our choice behaviour (Fig. 4.2).

Researchers have also been interested in how the familiarity of the background music influences customer behaviour in stores. There are conflicting results. Some studies have shown that familiar background music makes us spend a little longer in a store than unfamiliar background music.[28] On the other hand, one study established that when familiar music consisting mostly of Top 40 hits was playing, customers conducted their shopping faster than when less familiar, older instrumental music was played.[29] This study

---

[21] Ibid.
[22] Smith and Curnow (1966).
[23] Garlin and Owen (2006, p. 759).
[24] Kellaris and Rice (1993).
[25] Yalch and Spangenberg (1990).
[26] Biswas et al. (2019).
[27] Ibid. (p. 43).
[28] Garlin and Owen (2006).
[29] Yalch and Spangenberg (2000).

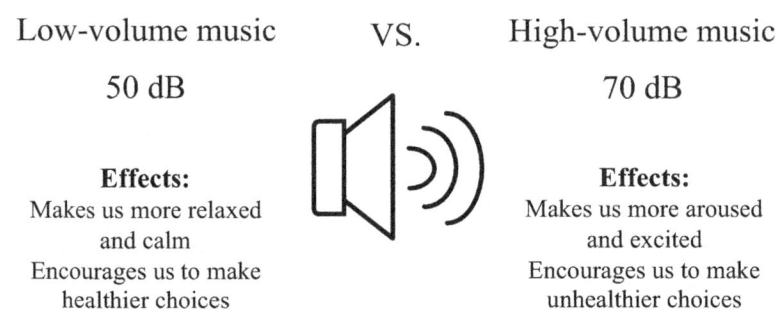

Fig. 4.2 Low-volume music vs. high-volume music (Biswas et al., 2019)

seems to indicate that familiar music makes us shop faster, while unfamiliar music makes us slow down. Researchers attribute these results to the fact that familiar music increases customer arousal, which leads to faster shopping. Unfamiliar music, in turn, makes individuals less aroused, and thus they also tend to shop longer. Researchers also found that individuals who are exposed to familiar music think that they use more time for shopping than they actually do. One potential explanation for this might be that individuals tend to remember familiar music better than unfamiliar music and this is likely to affect the perception of time.[30]

Even though the familiarity of background music seems to influence the shopping behaviour of consumers, studies show that it is ultimately more important that the customers like the background music than that it is familiar to them. As Sweeney and Wyber emphasised based on their findings: "[…] we recommend that priority is given to music that consumers like rather than music that they are familiar with".[31] Their study showed that consumers' liking of music plays a significant role in explaining consumers' emotional states and cognitive processes.[32]

> The Japanese lifestyle chain **Muji** is an example of a retail company that uses distinct but carefully curated background music to enhance the unique atmosphere of its stores. The background music played at Muji locations is traditional music from around the world, from Celtic folk songs to Parisian street musicians.[33]

---

[30] Ibid.
[31] Sweeney and Wyber (2002, p. 64).
[32] Ibid.
[33] Imada (2021).

As stated, studies have also established that the genre of the background music may be used to influence consumers, even though the most common choice for background music is neutral easy listening. For example, according to one widely cited study, when a grocery store played French music, it sold more French wine, and when it changed to German music, consumers began to prefer German wines.[34] According to another study, classical music played in the background made consumers spend more money on their shopping than if Top 40 music was played,[35] while another indicated that Top 20 music generates an impression of affordable prices, while classical background music communicates high quality and prestige.[36] This means that the genre of the background music can be used as a cue to convey or communicate certain meanings, for example, relating to the price or quality image of the store. However, such effects depend at least to some extent on whether the customers are familiar with the store or not. It is said that shoppers are more prone to make inferences based on the music in unfamiliar settings than familiar settings.[37] Furthermore, these kinds of effects are also likely to be dependent on matters such as whether the shoppers are younger or older people. Nevertheless, this all means that it is far from irrelevant what kind of background music (e.g., pop, classical or rock) a store plays.

It is clear that the chosen background music (e.g., genre, tempo and volume) must support or be aligned with the brand image of the store, and correspond to the preferences of the customer target groups. Incorrect choice of background music will probably only serve to confuse, or even annoy, the clientele, and may at worst lead to customers leaving the store or at least generating unwanted impressions of the store. In an ideal situation, a store will discover or develop its own background music which becomes a part of its brand and evokes the desired emotional responses and cognitive associations as well as behavioural reactions in the customers. One could sum up this section by saying that "audio branding" is a significant opportunity for retailers.[38]

---

[34] North et al. (1997).
[35] Areni and Kim (1993).
[36] Baker et al. (1994).
[37] Areni and Kim (1993).
[38] Spence et al. (2014).

Scents

> **DID YOU KNOW?**
> – Scents often generate immediate emotional reactions.
> – The effect of scents on our shopping behaviour tends to occur outside of our conscious awareness.
> – Scents typically function together with cues that stimulate our other senses.
> – Scents that are considered pleasant will attract more customers and make them spend more time in the store.
> – Women are more sensitive to scents than men.
> – Scents may trigger distant memories.

One important ambient cue of the retail environment is scent. Scents have been found to have a significant impact on our shopping behaviour. For example, Lindström has highlighted that scents affect us substantially more than we are aware of.[39] This is not surprising because our sense of smell is always on, very sensitive, and in direct contact with our limbic system, the part of our brain which governs our emotions and memories. Thus, it is no wonder that scents or olfactory stimuli can easily generate many different kinds of immediate emotional reactions in us. These spontaneous emotional reactions might not require any cognitive effort.[40] Just stepping inside a bakery where we can smell just-baked bread or croissants is likely to immediately evoke pleasure and positive feelings. Also, visiting the local café where we can sniff a wonderful aroma of roasted coffee beans and fresh-baked cinnamon buns will instantly put a smile on our face. Generally speaking, pleasant scents should cause pleasant emotional reactions in us while unpleasant scents should result in unpleasant emotional responses.[41]

More specific emotional reactions caused by various scents are well described in the literature. For example, the following observations have been made:

- Vanilla and peach are the most pleasing scents regardless of cultural background;
- Rose Maroc is perceived as moderately pleasant;
- Peppermint and cinnamon enhance motivation and alertness;
- Rose geranium decreases anxiety;
- Lemon invigorates and energises;

---

[39] Lindström (2005).
[40] Roschk and Hosseinpour (2020).
[41] Spangenberg et al. (2006).

- Lavender increases relaxation;
- Jasmine promotes a sense of calm;
- Pine decreases stress.[42]

The effects of scents are also illustrated in Fig. 4.3 which describes the effects of low-arousal and high-arousal scents.[43] Although the scents can be explored in terms of their ability to stimulate or activate us, it has been argued that scents and their effects are often analysed by focusing on the pleasantness or unpleasantness of scents whereas the arousing nature of scents is less researched in marketing environments.[44] Spangenberg et al. also point out that intensity should be considered when exploring the scents.[45] An increase in intensity might reduce positive reactions to otherwise pleasant scents. It is also important to bear in mind that pleasant scents do more for a retailer than no scent at all.[46] Roschk and Hosseinpour, in turn, state that familiarity is an important feature of scents because it tends to lead to liking.[47]

> The Singaporean luxury shopping centre **ION Centre** has become famous for its own signature scent, consisting of more than twenty scent components, such

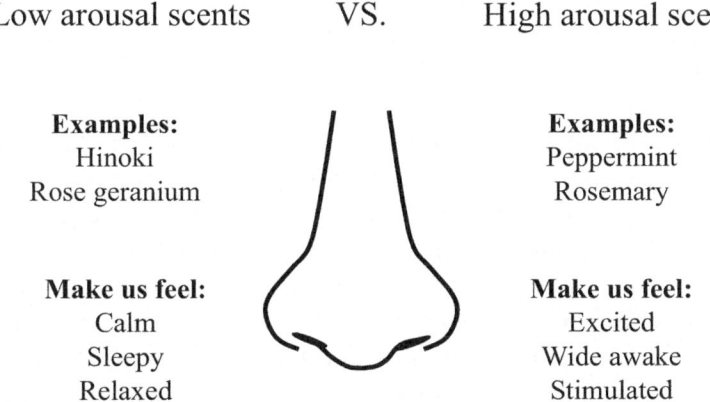

Low arousal scents VS. High arousal scents

Examples:
Hinoki
Rose geranium

Examples:
Peppermint
Rosemary

Make us feel:
Calm
Sleepy
Relaxed

Make us feel:
Excited
Wide awake
Stimulated

Fig. 4.3 Low-arousal scents vs. high-arousal scents (Zhou & Yamanaka, 2018)

---

[42] Zhou and Yamanaka (2018), Mattila and Wirtz (2001), Soars (2009), Spangenberg et al. (2006), and Arshamian et al. (2022).
[43] Zhou and Yamanaka (2018).
[44] Spangenberg et al. (1996).
[45] Ibid.
[46] Spangenberg et al. (2006).
[47] Roschk and Hosseinpour (2020).

> as fruits, white tea and peony. Diffusers spread the fragrance at all entrances as well as in the common areas of the shopping centre. In addition, all elevator lobbies are scented through a fragrance system installed in the ceiling. Using a signature scent is part of the multisensory marketing strategy of ION Centre, which has a goal of instilling an intense memory in the minds of all customers who visit the shopping centre.

Besides immediate emotional reactions, scents can also evoke images and generate more general mental impressions. As Holland et al. write: "[...] the processing of odors does not stop at the limbic system".[48] It is said that scents can influence cognitions and behaviour by activating semantic associations.[49] For example, it has been proposed that the scent of popcorn is associated with affordable prices.[50] Some specific scents like the smell of leather, sandalwood or rose are often associated with luxury. In some settings, the scent of citrus may be associated with high levels of hygiene and fresh cleanliness. An interesting side note is that we often find it rather difficult to describe such scents, even if they feel familiar.[51] As Roschk and Hosseinpour state: "While people distinguish well among many scents they have previously smelled, they have difficulty providing a verbal or semantic label for them and thus often experience a feeling of recognizing a scent, without being able to identify it".[52] Similarly, studies have shown that women are more sensitive to certain scents than men, and that women are also better able to recognise various scents.[53] It also seems that scent liking is learned and our smell preferences tend to change over time.[54]

Scents used to affect us through a cognitive route are typically very subtle cues. We do not necessarily even register the presence of faint scents, let alone the impacts they may have on us. Some researchers call this "odour priming".[55] This means that the effects of scents may manifest outside our conscious awareness.[56] Researchers have been able to demonstrate the nonconscious effects of scents empirically. For example, Holland et al. found through their research that in research settings, scents triggered various associations and behavioural reactions in the test subjects without the subjects

---

[48] Holland et al. (2005, p. 689).
[49] Ibid.
[50] Baker et al. (1994).
[51] Spence et al. (2014).
[52] Roschk and Hosseinpour (2020, p. 129).
[53] Spangenberg et al. (2006).
[54] Roschk and Hosseinpour (2020) and Lindström (2005).
[55] Schifferstein and Blok (2002).
[56] De Luca and Botelho (2019) and Spence et al. (2014).

being consciously aware of the effects.[57] In that study, when research subjects were exposed to the scent of lemon without their knowledge, their intentions to undertake cleaning tasks increased. Another research setting established that after being exposed to the scent of lemon, the subjects took more care of the cleanliness of their immediate surroundings than subjects that had not been exposed to the scent. Although the study was conducted in a laboratory setting, its insights of the unconscious influence of scents are also relevant from the viewpoint of retail stores and sensory marketing.

There has been considerable research into the impacts of scents in the retail environment. In general, studies have established that scents the customers find pleasant or appealing will increase approach behaviour and the time they spend examining the products and in the store in general.[58] For example, Spence et al. refer in their review to the study that showed that customers in a jewellery store spent more time at the store's counter when a fruity scent was introduced to the area.[59] This is to say that pleasant scents attract customers and entice them to stay longer in store. Unpleasant scents, in turn, tend to lead to avoidance behaviours.

It has also been proven that using scents in a retail setting may increase sales. For example, one study found that when a vanilla scent (feminine scent) was sprayed at the women's clothing department, and a sweet floral scent (masculine scent) in the men's department, the sales in these departments increased significantly after the adoption of the scents.[60] The findings of this field experiment indicate that gender-scent congruity is likely to boost the sales of a retail store. Roschk and Hosseinpour in turn estimated that the presence (vs. absence) of ambient scent is likely to cause a 3% increase in expenditures for an average setting and a 23% increase for a most favourable condition.[61] However, there are also studies that have been unable to prove any correlation between scent marketing and product sales.[62] It has been said that scents in a retail setting are likely to affect only those who have some interest to buy a product, whereas for all others scents alone are not sufficient stimuli.[63]

Studies have established that scents typically work in conjunction with other cues and stimuli that engage our other senses, particularly if the cues

---

[57] Holland et al. (2005).
[58] Morrin and Ratneshwar (2000, 2003), Spangenberg et al. (1996), and Soars (2009).
[59] Spence et al. (2014).
[60] Spangenberg et al. (2006).
[61] Roschk and Hosseinpour (2020).
[62] Schifferstein and Blok (2002).
[63] Ibid.

are compatible.[64] For example, the better the background music and scent fit together (e.g., relaxing music combined with a relaxing lavender scent), the more significant the impact on consumers as well as their emotional states and behaviour.[65] In a similar vein, Zhou and Yamanaka showed in their study that the arousal quality of scent modifies the perceived arousal level of music, and scent which is congruent with music on arousal increases the effects of the music.[66] The above means that scent marketing in a retail setting must be conducted in way that the retailer considers how scents are matched with other central cues.

> The coffee shop chain **Starbucks** is an example of a chain that heavily employs a variety of visual cues and scents to appeal to its customers. The sombre colour scheme of the cafés is carefully designed, and the lighting adjusted to be as pleasant as possible. The locations largely employ indirect lighting. The primary material for furniture is wood. Scents naturally play a key role, and the cafés in the chain grind their coffee from beans specifically selected to generate precisely the desired scent.

One specific feature of scents is that they can trigger memories (thanks to our limbic system). It has even been claimed that it is easier for us to remember smells than to remember things we have seen.[67] Thus, scents can be used to remind consumers of previous shopping experiences, or to trigger distant childhood memories, which may then result in the desire to purchase a specific product, for example.[68] Some scents may even evoke memories from decades ago. However, triggering memories through scents requires for the retailer to possess a profound understanding of the associations scents can evoke. It should also be borne in mind that there may be people among the clientele who are very sensitive to scents and in whom fragrances may trigger symptoms such as headaches and nausea. Thus, scent cues should be used with caution, and their effects carefully monitored.

Based on the above, one could argue that scented environments are likely to lead to more positive evaluations and behaviour than unscented environments.[69] Scents are a particularly powerful way to generate emotional reactions and memories among customers. However, one should remember that scents must support the retailer's positioning efforts and they should

---

[64] De Luca and Botelho (2019).
[65] Mattila and Wirtz (2001).
[66] Zhou and Yamanaka (2018).
[67] Krishna (2012).
[68] Ward et al. (2007).
[69] Spangenberg et al. (1996).

also be in line with other cues. Furthermore, as in the case of background music, creating a signature scent could offer retailers an opportunity to differentiate themselves from competitors and provide an engaging in-store experience. This is something that many airlines and hotels have already done. For example, Singapore Airlines has developed its own signature scent with floral notes to create a unique sensory experience for passengers during their journey.

> Youth wear chain **Abercrombie and Fitch** has become famous for its nightclub-like atmosphere. Club music is played at a loud volume in the dimly lit stores. The signature scent, which is easily recognisable and features elements of wood musk, is a key part of the atmosphere in the stores. The signature fragrance is also sold in the stores.

Lighting

> **DID YOU KNOW?**
> – Lighting plays a significant role in creating an ambiance.
> – Indirect and soft lighting make the store seem more pleasant.
> – Brighter lighting will increase the arousal of the customers but may generate a tense atmosphere.
> – Lighting can be used to influence the price and quality impression generated by the store.

Lighting and its effects on consumers are another extensively researched ambient cue, along with background music and scents. Studies indicate that lighting can be used to affect, for example, how pleasant the store environment is or to what extent shopping at the store is considered stimulating or relaxing. Hultén et al. state that: "[…] appropriate lighting can create an appropriate mood, which in itself attracts and captures the customer's interest".[70] In particular, combining lighting with certain colours makes it possible to draw consumers' attention.

The connection between lighting and our emotional states has been well documented in several studies. Some observations regarding the impact of lighting on our emotions that have arisen in research include:

---

[70] Hultén et al. (2009, p. 99).

- Bright lighting (5000 K) increases our level of arousal, whereas warm or soft lighting (3000 K) increases experiences of pleasure.[71]
- Cooler light is perceived as more approachable than warmer light, while warm-toned lighting is perceived as more attractive than cooler light.[72]
- Retail stores with indirect lighting are considered pleasant and relaxing.
- Contrasts in lighting makes the store environment feel more pleasant.
- A store can be made livelier by increasing sparkling or blinking lights, while the sense of privacy can be increased by using dimmer lighting[73] (Fig. 4.4).

In their study, Park and Farr demonstrated that consumers tend to prefer a bright light source when approaching a retail store, even though they find warm light more pleasing.[74] Lighting can also be used to evoke mental images and to convey meaning, just like background music or colours. For example, soft lighting is thought to communicate dignity and quality, while bright lighting suggests affordable prices.[75] Regarding the images that lighting can create, Hultén et al. state that hard discounters tend to use naked strip lights in a retail setting to communicate their low prices to customers.[76] All in all, lighting has been found to hold great significance for the ambiance of the

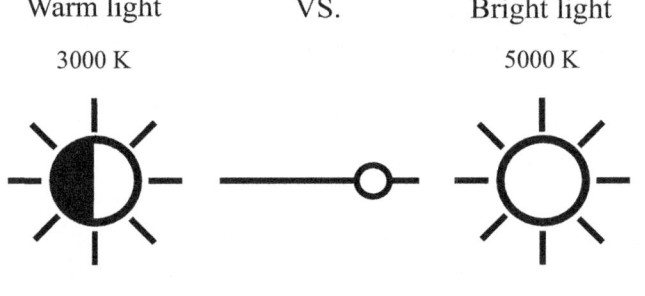

Fig. 4.4 Cooler light (3000 K) vs. warmer light (5000 K) (Park & Farr, 2007)

---

[71] Park and Farr (2007).
[72] Ibid.
[73] Custers et al. (2010).
[74] Park and Farr (2007).
[75] Baker et al. (1994).
[76] Hultén et al. (2009).

store and for the kinds of impressions the store environment generates among consumers.

> The stores of the Swedish candy shop chain **Lakritsroten**, which primarily specialises in salt liquorice, have a general appearance reminiscent of a traditional apothecary, with wooden shelves circling the walls and carefully designed product presentations. The colour palette of the stores leans on black and white, combined with grey concrete floors. Staff are dressed neatly and wear black aprons. The lighting in the stores is indirect and soft. The stores of the chain communicate a sense of exclusivity and high quality of the products.

Lighting can also be used to highlight specific products or sales areas as well as to guide shoppers within the store. One study found that bright lighting encouraged consumers to spend more time examining the products in comparison with environments that had softer lighting.[77] Another study showed that when bright spotlights were installed for a sales area, consumers would touch and collect more products into their shopping baskets than when the spotlight was turned off.[78] This indicates that the brightness of the lighting is connected to the extent to which consumers wish to examine the products on offer. This is understandable, as the brightness of the lighting can increase the level of arousal, and also make it significantly easier to see. On the other hand, as stated above, bright lighting may generate the wrong type of price impression of the store, reduce the coziness of the environment and make the store feel stressful or restless.[79] For example, bright fluorescent strip lighting, which is common in fashion stores, can make the store feel cold and sterile.[80] This is to say that bright lighting may not always be a desired feature.

All in all, lighting offers much potential in influencing customers, but it requires its own set of skills and must be in line with other cues and marketing tactics. It should also be possible to adjust the lighting for different needs and situations. Modern technology makes it rather easy to adjust the lighting to appeal to a particular clientele or even to correspond to a specific mood.

---

[77] Areni and Kim (1994).
[78] Summers and Hebert (2001).
[79] Custers et al. (2010).
[80] Kerfoot et al. (2003).

> **The fashion chain H&M** is an example of a chain with brightly list stores which also use bright LED spotlights to highlight products or product areas. The white colour scheme of the stores combined with reflective surfaces makes the spaces feel brighter still, while making the stores seem roomier than they are.

Temperature and Airflow

> **DID YOU KNOW?**
> - As the temperature rises, customers tend to make simpler choices.
> - As the temperature rises, customers tend to spend more money.
> - Higher outdoor temperatures tend to make customers more willing to purchase.
> - Frontal (vs. dorsal) airflow energises consumers in a retail environment.

The temperature in a retail environment can also be considered to be an ambient cue. Temperature as an ambient factor has mainly been studied in working environments, for example, from the perspectives of employee performance and stress, but its impacts on consumer choice behaviour has not been extensively researched at the time of writing. Some studies do exist. For example, Cheema and Patrick carried out five experimental studies on the impact of temperature on consumer choice.[81] The researchers found that shoppers exposed to a higher temperature (+25 °C) tended to avoid making difficult choices more than shoppers exposed to cooler temperatures (+19.5 °C). According to the study, consumers in a warmer temperature were more likely to choose a simple product over a more complex one, as the choice of the simpler product was thought to carry a lower cognitive load. It seems that higher-than-average temperatures lead to consumers making simpler choices. This could be attributed at least partly to the fact that warm temperatures deplete our resources, making us tire easily, which in turn makes us less alert and lowers our cognitive performance. Cheema and Patrick pose an interesting question in their conclusion: "But how does depletion work? Does it decrease the motivation to perform complex tasks or decrease the ability to perform these tasks?" For example, as Cheema and Patrick pointed out, depletion might just lower blood glucose level, and thus hamper our cognitive performance. However, there are also other potential explanations

---

[81] Cheema and Patrick (2012).

to why warm temperatures would be depleting. In terms of alertness and cognitive performance, a slightly cooler environment may be ideal.

Along with her research group, Yonat Zwebner studied the impact of temperatures on consumers through several different experimental studies.[82] In one of the studies, research subjects were divided into two groups and exposed to temperatures that were either slightly higher or lower than the average room temperature. The low temperature was approximately +18 °C and the high one approximately +26 °C. One of the key findings was that research subjects exposed to the higher temperature were willing to pay significantly higher prices for products than subjects exposed to the lower temperature and presented with identical products. To simplify, it seems that higher temperatures make consumers more willing to spend money, whereas in cooler temperatures they are more likely to consider their decisions more carefully. Another study focused on online shopping. For this study, the researchers gathered two years' worth of data from an online price comparison portal. Through the platform, consumers in the country of the study (Israel) could compare prices and click through to the home page of a specific retail company to make the purchase. The researchers were particularly interested in these clicks, as they were thought to indicate intention to purchase. The research data contained more than 6.3 million of such purchase intentions, or clicks. The researchers aggregated the click data with precise daily temperature data in Israel for a two-year period, while controlling for other potential factors, such as holidays and similar periods, which could impact behaviour. The most statistically significant finding was that consumers' intentions to purchase on the price comparison portal increased as the outdoor temperature rose. Even though the study focused on the impacts of outdoor temperatures on the intention to purchase, the results can be thought to suggest that an increase in temperature in general tends to increase consumers' willingness to buy.

Determining an optimal temperature for various retail environments or shopping situations is more or less impossible although it is said that most people appear to be comfortable with the temperature of 22 °C.[83] What is important is that the retailers recognise that temperature does have an effect on consumer behaviour. The impacts may be particularly surprising if the temperature goes below or above what is thought to be the average.

---

[82] Zwebner et al. (2014).
[83] Cheema and Patrick (2012).

> **Canada Goose** has launched a "Cold Room" in some of their flagship stores to simulate freezing conditions. The Cold Room gets as cold as −25 °C. The idea of the Cold Room is to provide customers with an environment where they can test and experience Canada Goose clothing in the conditions for which they were designed.

Similarly to temperature, airflow can also be considered an atmospheric cue in the shopping environment. Izadi and her research group conducted a currently unique study on how the direction of the airflow influences the emotional states of consumers.[84] The researchers wanted to determine whether the impacts of airflow changed when the flow came from directly the front or back. The impact of the direction of the airflow on consumers' energetic activation was a particular focus. In this study, energetic activation refers to the degree to which people have energy and feel alive and vital. The study itself was based on carefully constructed experimental settings and surveys. The experiments were conducted both in laboratories and as fieldwork. In the experimental studies, research subjects were exposed to airflow from the front and the back (in the laboratory, the speed of the airflow was set to 1.3 m/s) while using various methods to determine the consumers' energetic activation and emotional states. The main finding was that when the airflow was frontal, it increased the subject's energetic activation, compared to airflow from behind. It was also discovered that people who were exposed to frontal airflow performed better in tasks that required creativity. The researchers attributed their findings largely to human physiology and the fact that our skin is more sensitive to airflow coming from the front than it is to airflow from the back. Consequently, frontal airflow is thought to increase energetic activation. This study is a good example of how just changing the direction of the airflow can influence consumers (Fig. 4.5).

4.2 Design Cues

Design cues are aesthetic and functional cues or elements in the retail environment which help the consumer understand the shopping context as a space and a set of functions.[85] Aesthetic cues include the general design of the store environment, the colour scheme and surface materials, while functional cues include the store layout, signage and aisle alignments. Whereas

---

[84] Izadi et al. (2019).
[85] Baker et al. (1994) and Baker et al. (2002).

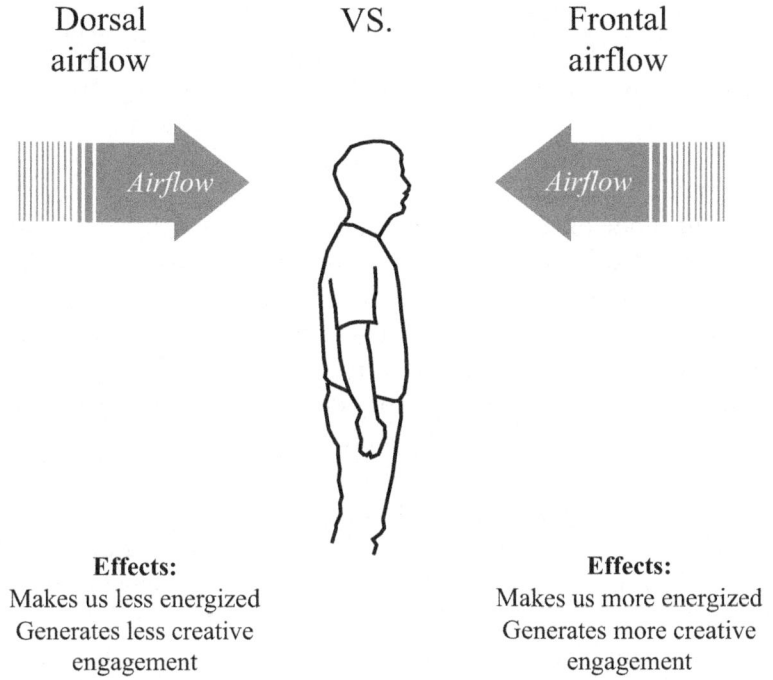

Fig. 4.5 Frontal airflow vs. dorsal airflow (Izadi et al., 2019)

ambient cues are primarily non-visual atmospheric cues, design cues strongly rely on vision in evoking customers' awareness.[86] Although design cues are observable, it is likely that many of the cues that come to our visual field are processed more or less unconsciously.

Store Design

> **DID YOU KNOW?**
> – Store design is a highly important instrument for conveying meanings and generating various responses among consumers.
> – Good proportions, balance, order and harmony make the store design more pleasant.
> – A complex environment may increase the interest of the store, but it comes with a risk of cognitive overload.

---

[86] Roggeveen et al. (2020).

> – Store design is an efficient method of communicating quality and price level. For example, a spacious environment and products placed further apart communicate high quality.

Visual stimuli, i.e., stimuli that are sensed through our eyes are argued to be a dominant mode of sensory information.[87] It is said that up to 80–90% of the cues provided by an environment are perceived visually.[88] This highlights the meaning of good store design in creating and maintaining consumer interest. Understood broadly, store design cues relate to the overall architectural design language of the store: what the store looks like as a whole from the outside and inside. At its best, store design can create an inviting and inspiring atmosphere that makes the store much more than just a place to make purchases.

Aesthetically pleasing and generally pleasurable store design is typically a combination of good proportions, balance, order and harmony.[89] Every object has its place and everything makes sense. Store environments that are easy to comprehend are typically experienced as pleasant.[90] For example, Garaus made an empirical study that demonstrated that "[…] harmony facilitates understanding of store environments and enables shoppers to process the store as a whole […] which in turn results in favorable consumer responses".[91] Reber mentions some design features that are likely to evoke pleasure:

- Symmetrical stimuli;
- Simple shapes with high contrast;
- Shapes with rounded edges; and
- Repeated visual stimuli.[92]

Although a store design that is easy to understand is critical in creating pleasure, we may find perfect symmetry and harmony boring. Thus, store design that is somehow complex may be a more efficient way to appeal to

---

[87] Hutmacher (2019).
[88] Kerfoot et al. (2003) and Lindström (2005).
[89] What can be considered aesthetically beautiful or pleasing is a topic that has been fiercely debated for more than two millennia (Kuisma, 2010). It is clear that no generally accepted definition exists. However, one understanding, established since antiquity, is that our aesthetic eye often finds symmetrical and harmonious things as pleasant (ibid.).
[90] Jang et al. (2018).
[91] Garaus (2017, p. 274).
[92] Reber (2011).

customers and evoke arousal among them.[93] Complex store design stimulates us because it requires cognitive effort to comprehend. The complexity of the store environment can be increased by adding different elements, colours and materials, or by positioning elements in the environment in an unusual way, for example. Ode et al. state that the complexity of the environment is mainly related to the richness and/or diversity of things to look at in the environment.[94] And as stated, the higher the complexity, the more excited we are.

The above means that there are two alternative principles for store design:

- Visual coherence (to evoke pleasure).
- Visual complexity (to evoke arousal).

That is, store design can aim at creating a neat and simple store environment which is pleasant and easy to comprehend, or it can aim at creating a store which is somehow complex and visually rich, and therefore interesting to customers.[95] In other words, the easier the implemented store design is to understand, the more we feel pleasure as customers, whereas more complex store design and the higher the required cognitive effort, the greater our arousal.[96] The differences between these two alternative design principles are illustrated in Fig. 4.6.

Naturally, in designing the store environment, the retailer should take into account both visual coherence and visual complexity. This is no easy task, and managing the complexity can be a particularly tricky issue. It is known that if complexity gets too high and the amount of cognitive resources required exceeds a certain level, it is likely that we just feel exhausted or anxious. In fact, the relationship between the attractiveness of the store environment and its visual complexity can be represented as an inverted U-shaped curve, meaning that individuals tend to prefer moderate complexity more than either low or high complexity.[97] Store environments with low levels of complexity are likely to be viewed as dull, while stores with high complexity are likely to cause cognitive overload and this, in turn, has a negative effect on the attractiveness of the store.[98] Dzebic summarises this by stating: "Highly uncertain, novel or complex stimuli are experienced as overly arousing and

---

[93] Murray et al. (2015) and Jang et al. (2018).
[94] Ode et al. (2010).
[95] Oh and Petrie (2012).
[96] Jang et al. (2018).
[97] Day (1967) and Ode et al. (2010); see also Berlyne (1974).
[98] Jang et al. (2018).

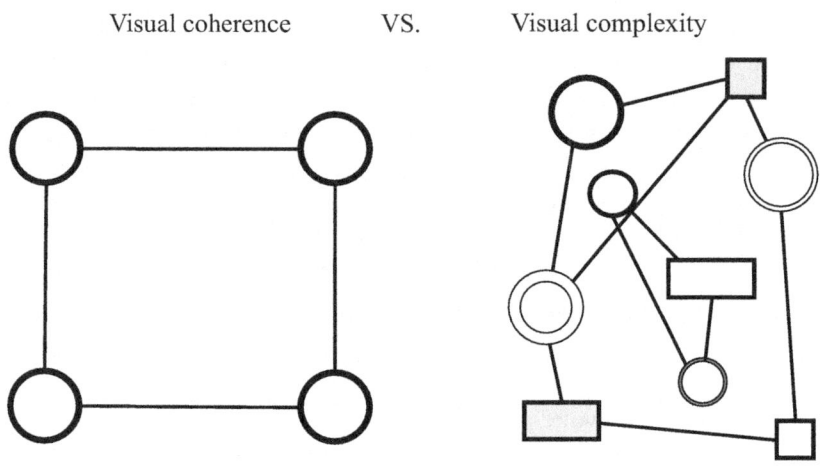

Fig. 4.6 Visual coherence vs. visual complexity

thus chaotic and unpleasant; on the other hand, redundant, familiar or simple stimuli lead to low levels of arousal and are once again experienced as unpleasant but now boring instead of chaotic".[99] The relationship between the attractiveness of the store environment and complexity is illustrated in the Fig. 4.7.

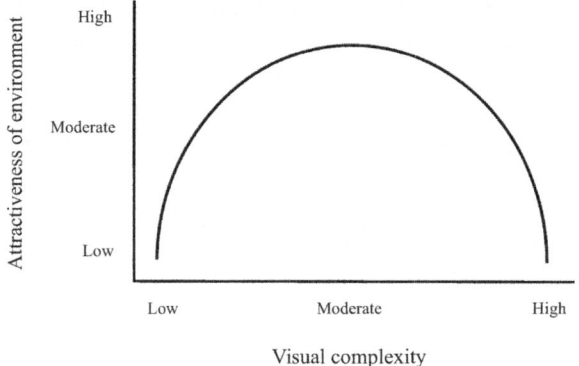

Fig. 4.7 The relationship between the attractiveness of environment and complexity

---

[99] Dzebic (2018, p. 4); see also Berlyne (1974).

> **Don Quijote**, or "Donki" is a Japanese chain of stores which are a cross between a discount store and a general store. It is tremendously popular among both Japanese customers and international tourists. Donki stores are typically jam packed, and have a unique charm, even though the general atmosphere can be chaotic. Shopping at Donki is an emotional experience, characterised by the joy of searching or rummaging. This feeling is enhanced by an arguably confusing product display, with products piled in huge heaps around the store, particularly on the entry floor. Donki stores are packed floor to ceiling with the most extraordinary variety of products, from sweets to toys and sports equipment.

We can conclude from the above that if a store wants to generate a shopping environment which is as pleasant and easy to understand as possible, a unified, harmonious and simple design language is likely to serve this goal better than more complex design. Meanwhile, if the goal is to specifically increase the arousal of the customers and generate an excited buzz, the store design should lean towards the visual richness and more complex design language—to a reasonable extent.[100] The final decisions on store design are naturally dependent on what kind of store is being designed, and how the store wants to position itself in the minds of consumers. The optimal store design will most likely be different for a fashion boutique and a grocery store.

Environmental psychologists Kaplan et al. have explored how aesthetics of outdoor environments affect human experience and based on their studies, they have proposed that besides coherence (e.g., unity, harmony and orderly) and complexity (e.g., diversity, variety, or richness), one should also look at the two other visual features of the environments and their effects on humans[101]:

- Legibility (to provide safety) and
- Mystery (to pull in).

Legibility refers to visual cues (e.g., landmarks and pathways) that facilitate and maintain orientation and movement within the environment. Legibility can be seen as a visual feature that provides safety when entering the environment, i.e., one knows the way and the way back. Meanwhile, a mysterious environment suggests that more information can be gained by moving deeper into the environment (e.g., there is a path that disappears from view or a bend in the road). The idea is that everything is not revealed at once. Mystery is a

---

[100] Spence et al. (2014).
[101] Kaplan (1987), Kaplan and Kaplan (1989), and Kaplan et al. (1989).

sort of promise that there is something more to explore. According to Kaplan et al., coherence and legibility together help individuals to understand and make sense of the environment, whereas complexity and mystery pull towards and encourage individuals to engage in exploration.[102] One could argue that legibility and mystery are issues that should be taken into account also in store design. Figure 4.8 illustrates four visual features of (store) environments and their effects on us.

It is also possible to categorise or label the styles of store design. In their study, Pecoraro and Uusitalo describe three distinct styles of store design.[103] A store can represent one of the following styles:

- Modern;
- Romantic; and
- Pragmatic.

Modern store design is based on minimalism, simplified shapes and open spaces, and it is characterised by the use of materials such as steel and glass. The modern store communicates expertise and scientific accuracy. Meanwhile, the romantic style is characterised by solutions that evoke a sense of

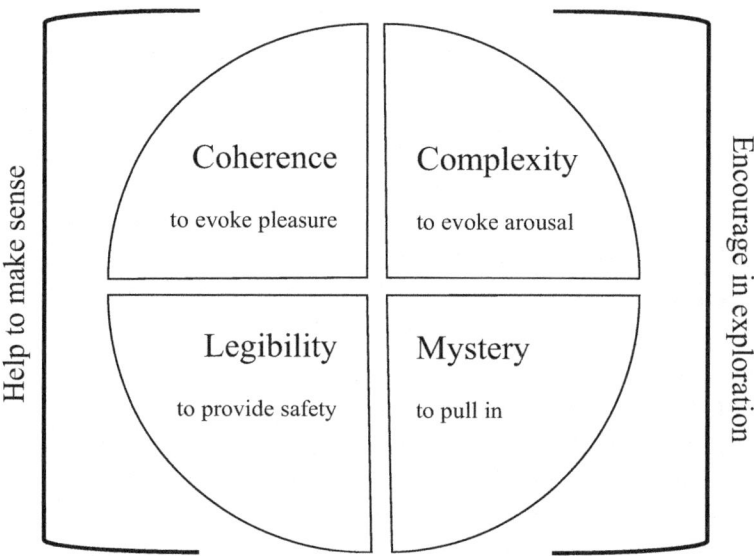

Fig. 4.8 Four visual features of environments (modified from Kaplan et al., 1989)

---

[102] Kaplan et al. (1989).
[103] Pecoraro and Uusitalo (2014).

authenticity, nostalgia and home-like coziness, leaning towards natural materials and traditional handicrafts. The romantic store is a socially stimulating place that responds to its customers' intrinsic social needs. Pragmatic store design is efficient and functional above all else. The pragmatic store has a rational and transparent layout and communicates convenience and efficiency. In their study, Pecoraro and Uusitalo established that stores using modern or romantic design could offer their customers intense emotional experiences, whereas stores focused on a pragmatic design and interested only in the efficient use of space would not necessary evoke any particularly emotional reactions in their clientele. On the other hand, Pecoraro and Uusitalo presume that pragmatic stores may be considered reliable shopping venues specifically because of their simplicity and functionality.

> **Zara Home** is a retail chain which sells furniture, lighting fixtures, textiles and interior accessories. The stores in the chain are aesthetically pleasing, and feature soft, natural colours that aim for a homey feel. The predominant material of the store interiors is wood. The atmosphere in the stores is relaxed, despite the extensive assortment of products on display.

As indicated above, store design is a very important part of the brand of the store, and can be used to generate various emotional responses among consumers but also to influence what kind of an image consumers generate of the store and what kinds of expectations they place on it. Studies have made the following findings:

- Round and circular shapes in the shopping environment evoke warmth and even friendliness, while angular shapes communicate competence and efficiency.[104]
- Curvilinear forms are often considered more approachable than rectilinear ones. Angular forms, especially when pointing downwards or towards us, may feel threatening, and can trigger an avoidance response.[105]
- A free-form layout is seen as evoking a prestige image with high-quality products, while grid layouts with predetermined pathways communicate a discount image with affordable products.[106]

---

[104] Liu et al. (2018).
[105] Spence (2020).
[106] Baker et al. (1994) and Baker et al. (2002).

- Adjusting the width of the aisles can also influence the image of the store. Wide aisles are associated with prestige shopping environments, while narrow aisles are associated with lower prestige.[107]

One specific design feature that designers refer to is the "cathedral effect". The cathedral effect is based on the notion that people tend to prefer high ceilings to low ones. High ceilings communicate freedom, while lower ceilings evoke feelings of confinement or restriction.[108] Spaces with high ceilings are thought to encourage people to explore and be more creative.[109] Thus, for some retail environments, high ceilings could be a way to inspire their customers and create a sense of freedom. Figure 4.9 demonstrates the cathedral effect.

Similarly, the choice of materials for in-store fixtures may also influence the impression the store generates. For example, the use of glass and chrome in clothing stores has been found to evoke positive reactions in customers. Kerfoot et al. found that when glass is used in combination with chrome,

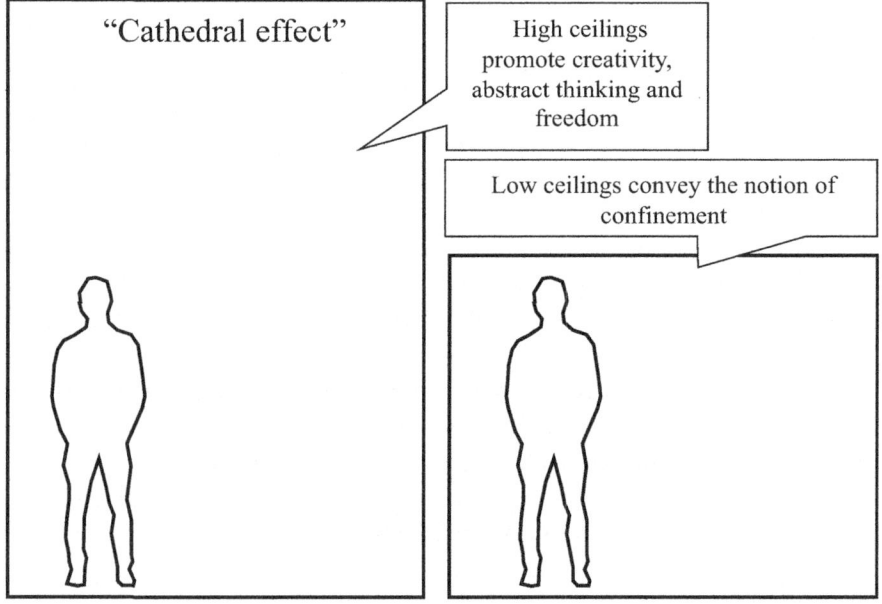

Fig. 4.9 The cathedral effect (Meyers-Levy & Zhu, 2007)

---

[107] Baker et al. (1994) and Gardner and Siomkos (1985).
[108] Meyers-Levy and Zhu (2007).
[109] Joyner (2020).

consumers think that displays look funky and fashionable.[110] Wooden floors and fixtures also create an image of quality and exclusivity, whereas vinyl and plastic typically generate the opposite impression. Additionally, loosely spaced products generally communicate both quality and a high-price point. On the other hand, some retailers might use power aisles, i.e., a configuration of a smaller number of products in larger quantities to create the impression that the products are offered at extremely low prices.[111]

> The technology company **Apple** is a good example of a business which maintains its image of innovation and quality through its flagship stores. The wide open spaces of Apple stores and the products displayed at a distance from one another communicate high quality. The store design is also very modern and minimalistic. Everything extraneous has been removed. The main colour of the stores is grey-white. The stores also primarily use glass and steel to emphasise the impression of quality. In fixtures, light-coloured wood is preferred.

Stores may also have specific areas that need to be designed with special care, as they may carry particular significance for the customers. Entryways and checkout areas may be very significant for the attractiveness of the store, and for promoting ease of shopping or leaving the store. In the world of clothing stores, Underhill points to fitting rooms as an additionally critical area.[112] According to Underhill, the fitting rooms of a clothing store may be the most important space in terms of the customers' purchasing decisions, and for this reason special attention should be paid to making the fitting rooms as pleasant as possible. One critical area we may not even think of as having an impact is customer toilets. According to a study by Piha, the (un)pleasantness of a customer toilet may greatly influence our shopping experience.[113]

Colours

> **DID YOU KNOW?**
> – Customers often find cool colours, such as blue and green, more pleasant than warm colours, such as red or yellow.

---

[110] Kerfoot et al. (2003).
[111] Smith and Burns (1996).
[112] Underhill (1999).
[113] Piha (2018).

> - A store environment with cool colours increases the customer's intentions to purchase, particularly for more expensive products.
> - Colours convey a great deal of significance, and the colour palette of the store can be used to influence the price and quality impression of the store.
> - Lighting affects how we perceive colours.

The most concrete, and therefore most researched, of the design cues in a store environment are its colours. Colours carry a great deal of different types of meanings, and it has been established that colours have a significant impact on us as customers. For example, colours influence how much we notice the store and the extent to which we want to approach it. It is claimed that our first impression of the store is largely based on colours.[114] Colours also influence how much time we spend in the store, and how likely we are to make impulse purchases.

The impacts of colours on our behaviour can largely be attributed to their connection to our emotions. It has been widely accepted that our feelings are affected by colours.[115] Certain colours have the ability to excite and arouse us whereas others have a more relaxing effect—for example, red is said to be more arousing than blue. These emotional reactions to colours tend to be surprisingly similar for men and women.[116]

There are many studies on this topic, with Bellizzi et al. making the following observations already in 1983:

- Cool, or short-wavelength, colours such as blue and green are considered relaxing and are thought to evoke tranquility. Consequently, these colours are likely to make us spend more time in the store.[117]
- Meanwhile, warm, or long-wavelength, colours such as red and yellow activate and increase our alertness but are also thought to be less attractive. This may lead to people leaving the store faster.

Even though warm colours such as red or yellow are often thought to be good for drawing attention and attracting customers while making them

---

[114] Singh (2006).

[115] It should be noted that colour stimuli are complex and should be described with respect to three distinct characteristics: hue, saturation and brightness (Brengman, 2002). Brengman (2002) argues that studies in a retail context typically take only the effects of colour hue into account, while the effects of saturation and brightness tend to be ignored completely. Thus, it can be said that there is a need for further studies to develop a more profound understanding of how colour may affect consumers.

[116] Valdez and Mehrabian (1994).

[117] Bellizzi et al. (1983).

4 Identifying Cues and Their Effects in a Retail Store

more susceptible to impulse purchases, studies suggest that the ability of these colours to evoke pleasure and to make the shopping more pleasant is debatable.

Bellizzi and Hite also found that a blue store environment was more pleasant to consumers than a red environment. Consumers wanted to approach a blue environment and avoid a red one. Possibly the most interesting finding in Bellizzi and Hite's research is that products displayed against a blue background evoked more decisions to purchase than those displayed against a red background.[118] One explanation for this might be that blue is a colour that communicates reliability. Thus, it is not wonder that it has been claimed that blue would be a particularly effective colour in a store environment when more expensive products are on display, but for more affordable products that require less deliberation from the consumer, warmer colours could be more effective.[119]

Babin and team conducted an experimental study on the impact of colours on consumers at a fashion store.[120] According to the results, a cool store colour (blue) was considered more pleasant than a warm one (orange). Blue also increased intentions to buy more than orange. However, the researchers found that the results changed significantly when lighting was considered. Cool colours are viewed positively in bright light, while warm colours are more positively received in softer lighting. According to the study, using soft lighting with an orange-toned interior cancels the negative impacts of orange. The most negative reactions were associated with the colour orange in bright lighting.

All in all, it could be said that cool colours (e.g., blue and green) appear to be systematically preferred over warm colours (e.g., red and yellow).[121,122] On the other hand, warm colours are seen to be more arousing than cool colours. In other words, colours like red and yellow are generally seen as stimulating and exciting, while colours like green and blue are perceived to be relaxing and calm.[123] The complexity of these effects means that retailers must carefully consider the meaning of colours in the retail environment.

---

[118] Bellizzi and Hite (1992).
[119] Bellizzi and Hite (1992) and Bellizzi et al. (1983).
[120] Babin et al. (2003).
[121] Brengman (2002) specified the effects of colours on pleasure by stating that extremely short-wavelength colours seem to be generally preferred, followed by the extremely long-wavelength colour red. According to Brengman (2002), yellow-green, yellow and orange appear to be generally disliked. Furhermore, Brengman (2002) pointed out that "pleasure-displeasure reactions to spectral colours appear to approximate a U-shaped function of wavelength, with yellows (green-yellow, yellow and red-yellow) at the bottom portion of the U".
[122] Valdez and Mehrabian (1994).
[123] Brengman (2002).

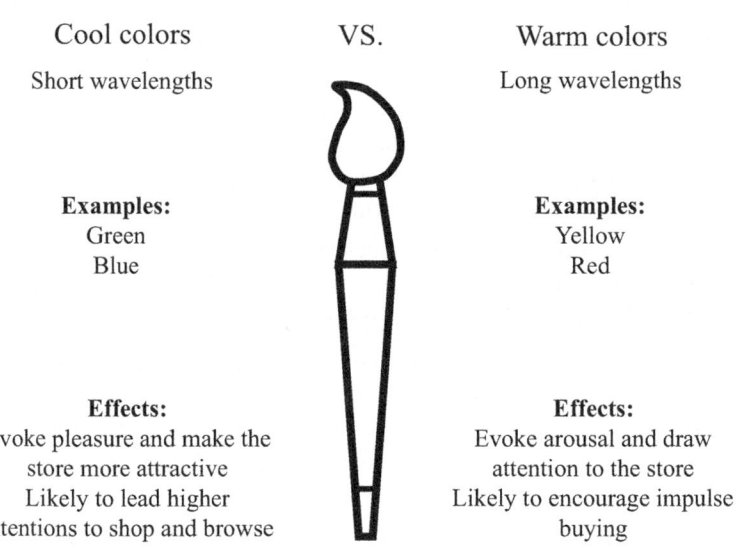

Fig. 4.10 Cool colours vs. warm colours (Bellizzi & Hite, 1992; Bellizzi et al., 1983)

While in some stores, there might be a need to use high-energy colours for increasing attention and excitement, in others calm colours should be used to induce relaxed feelings among customers (Fig. 4.10).

Colours can also impact how prestigious consumers consider a retail space to be, or the kind of price impression the store develops. As Aslam has emphasised, colours are powerful cues that influence perceptions about price and quality.[124] Examples of this include:

- Green communicates a high-quality shopping environment;
- Bright orange communicates affordable prices;
- Black communicates exclusivity;
- Grey is associated with professionalism;
- Burgundy communicates refinement and luxury;
- White communicates simplicity and cleanliness.[125]

The above indicates that colours in a store environment convey certain semantic meanings to us. Understanding these colour-meaning associations is not an easy task and retailers most possess considerable sensitivity to be aware of how consumers perceive and interpret colours in different social and cultural contexts. One widely used instrument to investigate these meanings

---

[124] Aslam (2006).
[125] Baker et al. (1994), Baker et al. (2002), Spence et al. (2014), and Hultén et al. (2009).

that colours communicate is the semantic differential, in which colours are rated on a series of bipolar adjective scales (e.g., good versus bad).[126] Studies based on the semantic differential have demonstrated, for example, that blue conveys meanings of security and comfort, while orange communicates distress and black is associated with power and strength.[127]

In addition to the overall background colours of the store, retailers should think carefully about colours across merchandise assortments. It is said that merchandise colour is a significant factor that affects consumers' perceptions of price and quality, and assists them in building image perceptions of the wider retail offering.[128]

> **Aesop**, a chain of stores selling skincare products and fragrances, is a good example of sensory marketing. The colour palette of Aesop stores is very uniform and well-thought-out to the smallest detail. Aesop stores are minimalistic in design, and products are displayed in extremely simple but clear ways. The materials of the fixtures are of high quality, and the lighting is carefully planned. Product packaging is simple, and exudes exclusivity and high quality. Naturally, customers may sample Aesop products in the stores.

Finally, colours are not experienced in isolation but rather in conjunction with others. As Schloss and Palmer stated: "[…] the aesthetic experience of any given colour is strongly influenced by its participation in combinations of two or more colour".[129] Although this is a highly complex matter, studies have been conducted on what kinds of colour combinations are liked or disliked (i.e., colour combination preferences) and whether different colour combinations are experienced to be harmonious or disharmonious (i.e., how strongly different colours in the combination belong together). One rather extensive study related to colour combinations was conducted by Schloss and Palmer. In their study, Schloss and Palmer investigated perceptual responses to colour pairs. In short, they found that people tend to prefer colour pairs that contain cooler colours and that have the same hue (hue refers to the dominant colour family). Also, people prefer contrast in lightness but not strong contrast in hue. Furthermore, Schloss and Palmer found that colour pair preference and colour pair harmony vary mainly as a function of hue similarity so that colour pairs with similar hues are both more preferred and more harmonious. All in all, the study revealed that preference and harmony

---

[126] Brengman (2002).
[127] Valdez and Mehrabian (1994).
[128] Kerfoot et al. (2003).
[129] Schloss and Palmer (2011, p. 551).

are closely related to one another. In addition, Schloss and Palmer studied how background colours affect people's preferences for the figural colours against which they are presented. The study revealed that people tend to like colours against strongly contrasting backgrounds. As Schloss and Palmer summarised their findings: "[...] warmer figures are preferred on cooler backgrounds, cooler figures are preferred on warmer backgrounds, and figures are generally preferred on backgrounds of contrasting lightness".[130] Although the study is extensive and helps to understand preferences and harmony of colour combinations, there is a need for further studies to explore how colour combination preferences might be influenced by the context such as the retail store. One can assume that the type of retail store (e.g., luxurious store vs. discount store) may have affected how colour combinations are experienced.

> **Loft** is a Japanese specialty store chain, offering a broad range of household goods. The product assortment leans heavily towards cosmetics and well-being products. Loft stores combine a yellow and black colour palette with a grey concrete or tile floor. This combination is both distinctive and trendy.

Exploring different colour combinations becomes even more complex when combinations are studied from a semantic point of view. According to Caivano: "[...] since colours have a semantic weight, produce emotions, have meanings, are used as signals, indicate situations, propose behaviours, communicate messages, etc., and all this can vary according to the way in which colours are combined and according to the context, it is also possible to consider colour combinations from a semantic point of view".[131] Understanding the semantic meanings of different colour combinations is very challenging. However, there is a framework, Kobayashi's Colour Image Scale, that helps in this semantic decoding.[132] This framework is presented in Fig. 4.12. In short, the framework is based on a two-dimensional scale where the axes correspond to the scales "hard-soft" and "cool-warm". The framework is rather extensive, matching 1170 three-colour combinations to 180 descriptive words. For example, the framework shows that if white is combined with red and blue, the association is "lively", while white combined with yellow and blue convey the meaning of "sporty". Or if different shades of brown are combined, the attached meaning is "rustic" but if brown is

---

[130] Ibid. (p. 568).
[131] Caivano (2015).
[132] Kobayashi (1991), Solli and Lenz (2010), and Horiguchi and Iwamatsu (2018).

combined with black and grey, the meaning turns into "quiet and sophisticated".[133] Kobayashi's Colour Image Scale is a tool that also helps retailers select colour combinations (Fig. 4.11).

> **Nespresso** stores seek to provide the ultimate coffee experience, and are an excellent example of a store that communicates with colours. Nespresso stores use colours in a very sophisticated way, allowing Nespresso to differentiate itself from the competition with an image of a luxury lifestyle. Nespresso's core colour palette features three colours: black, white and gold. Of these, black and white are a nearly inseparable combination in any form of marketing. In the stores, colourful coffee capsules complement the core palette. The colours of the capsules bring vibrancy to the store ambience. The skilful use of colours, combined with the open design of the interior, gives visitors a unique customer experience from the moment they step inside.[134]

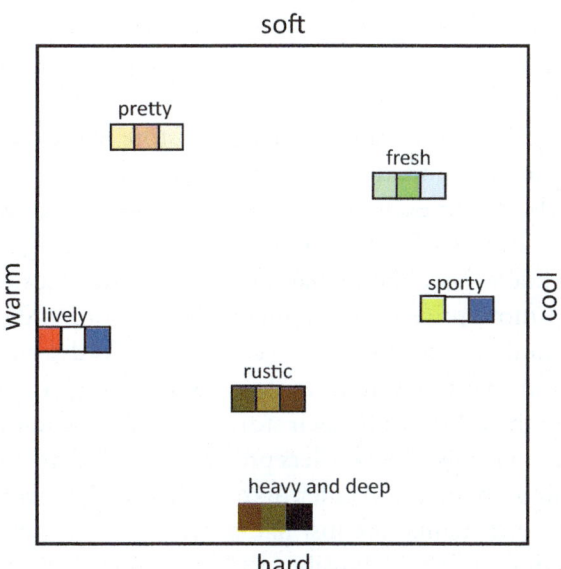

Fig. 4.11 Semantic space of colours and examples of three-colour combinations (Solli & Lenz, 2010; see also Horiguchi & Iwamatsu, 2018)

---

[133] Solli and Lenz (2010).
[134] Grigelova (2019).

Names, Signs and Symbols

> **DID YOU KNOW?**
> - A store's name can act as an information-rich cue of the store and its features.
> - The amount of information and the typeface design in the signage can influence consumers. For example, handwritten signs can create an impression of a human touch and enhance emotional attachment.

Consumers may observe various signs and symbols while shopping. These may also function as cues for the consumer, and may influence the conclusions they draw on the store. Nowadays it is more and more common that various in-store signs are digitised meaning that signs and their content can be changed or updated rather quickly and in some cases signs can include also dynamic content such as videos and images.

One might not even realise but just the name of the store can act as a cue that provides a tremendous amount of information to consumers.[135] At its best, the store name supports the planned strategic positioning and intended image of the store.[136] As Grewal et al. state, the store name represents a store's abstract, gestalt nature, and the name can affect the image of the store in consumers' minds.[137] For example, some store names such as Massimo Dutti, Charles & Keith or Saks Fifth Avenue can evoke an image of a luxurious environment, while others like Dollarama, Dollar Tree, Costco or Netto are likely to evoke a more price-oriented image. Some stores are named by their founders (e.g., John Lewis, Salvatore Ferragamo, Nordstrom or Filippa K) and this can be an effective way to build a connection with consumers on a human level. On the other hand, such store names can be less informative for customers. Thus, in some cases retailers prefer names that are more descriptive and say something about the retailer, like 7-Eleven, Wholefoods or Poundland. Sometimes store names are just names without any literal meaning like Lululemon, Lindex or IKEA. Possibly the best-known example of a brand name with no meaning is Häagen-Dazs. All in all, there are numerous options how to name the store and there are also numerous opinions of what are "good" and "bad" names. Whatever the name, retailers should remember that naming is a critical decision and the chosen name can convey a great deal of meaning. Just a single word can be a very powerful marketing tool

---

[135] Grewal et al. (1998).
[136] Robertson (1989).
[137] Grewal et al. (1998).

for retailers. Robertson gives some concrete tips that may help in naming decision.[138] According to Robertson, the name should be simple, distinctive and somehow meaningful. It is also important that the name evokes positive emotions and sounds pleasant.

An interesting finding related to names is that if the name is difficult to pronounce, it tends to evoke negative responses, such as a greater perceived risk and uncertainty.[139] As Song and Schwartz demonstrated, explanation for this effect can be found from fluency theory; fluently processed names tend to evoke positive responses whereas disfluently processed names are likely to generate negative evaluations. Based on this, retailers should consider how easy (or difficult) the name is to pronounce when choosing a name for their store.

An even more intriguing aspect of names and naming is sound symbolism (or phonetic effects). Sound symbolism refers to the relationships between sounds and meanings specifically the semantic meanings that the phonetic features of words convey to us.[140] The existence of sound symbolism is confirmed by several studies. For example, Klink made an empirical study on sound symbolism that demonstrated that brand names containing front vowels[141] (as opposed to back vowels) are perceived, for example, as smaller, lighter, milder, thinner, softer, faster, more feminine, lighter and prettier.[142] Furthermore, the same study showed that brand names containing fricatives[143] (as opposed to stops) are perceived as smaller, faster, lighter and also more feminine. Klink summarises his findings by stating that the meanings conveyed by brand sound can relate to tangible features such as size as well as intangible features such as speed. Furthermore, the relationship between sounds and meanings seems to hold not just for product categories but also for services. In fact, as Klink states, the brand sound as an extrinsic cue is particularly critical for services. Thus, service providers such

---

[138] Robertson (1989).
[139] Song and Schwarz (2009).
[140] Yorkston and Menon (2004).
[141] Klink (2000) specifies that vowel sounds where the highest point of the tongue is in the front of the mouth are "front vowels" while vowel sounds where the highest point of the tongue is in the back of the mouth are considered "back vowels". Examples of front vowels are words such as "bee, hit and test" whereas examples of back vowels are "food, home and dusk". Klink's actual study was conducted by utilising word-pairs that were identical except for the vowels and consonants being contrasted. Examples of these word-pairs are "detal-dutal", "esab-usab" and "geleve-goleve".
[142] Klink (2000).
[143] According to Encyclopedia Britannica, fricatives are consonant sounds produced by bringing the mouth into position to block the passage of the airstream, but not making complete closure, so that air moving through the mouth generates audible friction.

as retailers should think about the sound (phonetic effect) of their name carefully. Just the phonetic features of the name can lead to surprising effects among consumers.

It has also been theorised that discrete signage is associated with a refined retail environment, while more apparent signage communicates a more affordable price impression. Studies have also noted that the amount of information available in the signs influences consumer choice.[144] For example, if two products have identical value, consumers are more likely to pick the product with more information available.[145] Also, the colours and sizes of signs influence consumers. For example, if sale signs are red in colour and large in size, consumer attention increases significantly. However, it seems that the effect of increasing the size of a sign is only the square root of the increased area, e.g., increasing the size of a sign (such as an advertisement), fourfold will only attract two times as much attention.[146]

There are some extremely interesting studies on the effect the typeface of a sign or ad has on consumers and their choice behaviour, such as the study by Schroll et al.[147] The study is based on several experiments, which indicate that handwritten typefaces (as opposed to machine-written typefaces) led to more favourable product evaluations by consumers, and made it more likely they would choose a product.[148] The positive impact of a handwritten typeface was particularly prominent in products that the consumer had no special relationship with, whereas the handwritten typeface had no effect for products that the consumer was already emotionally attached to. The study also sought to explain why the handwritten typeface has this effect on consumers. The experiments showed that handwritten fonts made the products seem more human and increased the consumers' emotional attachment to them. According to the researchers, handwritten fonts convey a human touch, warmth and sensitivity. Similar results were reached by Liu et al.[149]

It should be noted that the idea that typefaces convey meanings is not a new one and there are in fact numerous studies on how certain typefaces affect us.[150] Researchers have particularly explored the psychological impact of typeface factors such as serifs, tails and line weights. Regarding the semantic qualities of typefaces, Childers and Jass state that "[…] one

---

[144] Turley and Milliman (2000).
[145] Patton (1981).
[146] Lee et al. (2015).
[147] Schroll et al. (2018).
[148] The following handwritten fonts were used in the experiments: DJB This is Me, Moon Flower and All Things Pink. The machine-written fonts used were Gill Sans, Helvetica and Futura.
[149] Liu et al. (2019).
[150] Choi and Kang (2013).

may view words as being 'dressed up' in the 'costume' of type styles. These costumes portray meaning independently of the words they clothe".[151] Brumberger has examined typeface studies and writes that some studies have found that typefaces that are lighter in weight (in terms of width and stroke thickness) are seen as delicate and feminine, while heavier (bold) typefaces are seen as strong and masculine.[152] As Choi and Kang point out, there are also studies that have demonstrated that the serif typeface (i.e., a font with tiny lines at the ends of each stroke) is considered to be more charming than non-serif typefaces.[153] There are many similar findings and in general, researchers have demonstrated that people are capable of perceiving consistent semantic meanings in typefaces.[154] Based on these studies, we could say that the choice of font for a store's signage or logo is far from insignificant no matter whether the sign itself is traditional or digitised. Typographic cues are likely to be particular important cues under low involvement conditions.[155]

Store Layout

> **DID YOU KNOW?**
> - The layout of the store influences how enjoyable consumers find their shopping experience.
> - Consumers prefer rotating to the right.
> - Consumers find open and free pathways pleasant.
> - Forced rotation increases impulse purchases.
> - Consumers have a very negative reaction to feeling like they are losing control of the shopping environment.
> - The store layout should not be changed too frequently to avoid interfering with the shopping habits of customers.

Research into the design cues in retail environments often points to the store layout as one of the most critical design cues for a pleasant shopping experience.[156] Among others, Ainsworth and Foster demonstrated in their study that the degree to which consumers find the store layout enjoyable has a significant impact on how much they enjoy the shopping experience as a

---

[151] Childers and Jass (2002, p. 95).
[152] Brumberger (2003).
[153] Choi and Kang (2013).
[154] Childers and Jass (2002).
[155] Ibid.
[156] Ludmila Bandeira et al. (2019).

whole.[157] So the more enjoyable the layout, the more enjoyable the shopping experience. This is not surprising, since the layout largely determines how easy it is to move around in the store and how easily different products or product areas can be located. This is to say that the layout must help the customer reach the goals they have set for their shopping. Related to in-store navigation, an interesting observation is that around 80% of a consumers' in-store time is used for navigation, while the remaining 20% is spent deciding which products to buy.[158]

Underhill posited that customers have a natural tendency to take the rightmost route in the store.[159] This means that when entering the store, customers unconsciously turn to the right and begin to go around the store in a counter-clockwise direction. This right-hand rotation has been attributed to the fact that the majority of people are right-handed, and therefore naturally begin their journey in the store to the right. Another aspect that Underhill raises is that when entering a store, the customer needs some space to descend into the store environment, and to tune their senses to receive the stimuli in the store. This is to say that the customer is not in a shopping mode immediately upon entering a store, and may even become irritated if they are confronted with merchandise at the entrance. Such things should naturally be considered when planning the store layout and positioning products in the store.

> **FamilyMart** is a Japanese convenience store chain, with stores located along significant thoroughfares, at metro stations and next to office buildings. FamilyMart stores are very small, and therefore have a limited range of products. However, the stores are also an impressive example of how the smallest retail space can be used to maximum advantage while enabling easy shopping. The shelves are also as low as possible so that there is a sense of space and good visibility to all parts of the store.

The basic layout of a store can be either free-form or a grid. The grid refers to layout where a lot of products are displayed on long aisles or rows in a well-organised and predictable fashion, whereas a free-form layout allows customers to browse and wander freely within the store. One layout option is also the "racetrack", a loop that guides customers to walk past every item within the store from entering to arriving at the checkout counter. Figure 4.12 illustrates these layout options.

---

[157] Ainsworth and Foster (2017).
[158] Otterbring et al. (2016).
[159] Underhill (1999).

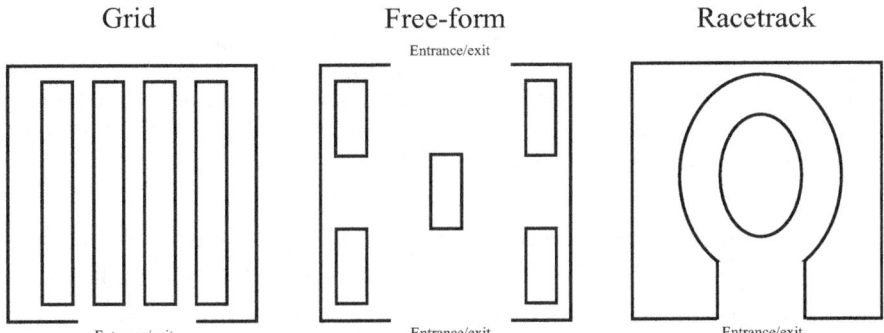

Fig. 4.12 Three basic retail store layout options

All of these layout options have their benefits and restrictions. Studies have made the following observations:

- A layout which offers space and free areas of movement will reduce consumers' stress levels in comparison with a grid layout that has forced routes.[160]
- A clear pathway through the store increases customers' propensity to browse and purchase more naturally than an ambiguously indicated pathway, or a layout with no pathway at all.[161]

Ebster and Garaus meanwhile emphasise that one key factor in store layout and in-store movement that influences the customer's shopping experience is whether the customer retains a sense of being in control of the shopping environment—whether the customer knows where they are and how they can move around in the environment, or whether something in the environment interferes with the customer's internal compass and at worst makes them feel they have lost control.[162] If customers feel that they are losing the sense of control, it may trigger very negative emotions, for example, the desire to leave the store. The retailer may seek to enhance this sense of control by separating different areas as clearly as possible, adding signage or other types of landmarks inside the store. Keeping shelves sufficiently low may also help the customers understand the store environment and how to move within it.

---

[160] Baker et al. (2002).
[161] Kerfoot et al. (2003).
[162] Ebster and Garaus (2011).

> The **Redi** shopping centre, located in Helsinki's Kalasatama district, received negative publicity after opening, as customers kept getting lost. The labyrinthine and curving corridors led to customers becoming disoriented, not knowing where they were or where they were going. Efforts have since been made to fix the problem with improved signage.

Ainsworth and Foster also point out that once customers have learned to use the chosen layout, the store should refrain from unnecessary changes to its design.[163] This is because customers appreciate permanence and knowing how to move through the store and find the items they need. If the layout of the store is changed frequently or without a sensible reason, this will only serve to annoy customers, and in the worst case, compel them to switch to another store. This is to say that it is unwise to meddle with the layout, if the intention is to generate positive shopping experience.

The general organisation level of the store environment is also a relevant factor. It is generally acknowledged that disarray and lack of tidiness in the store imply poor quality and low prices, whereas a well-organised and clean store generates an impression of high quality, and consequently, of higher prices. For example, Kerfoot et al. found that neat and sparse displays are associated with more expensive brands. The level of organisation also influences how consumers perceive product availability. Cosku et al. conducted a study on the topic, intended to understand the ways messy and crowded stores influence consumer behaviour.[164] The researchers were particularly interested in whether these factors trigger in-store hoarding or in-store hiding types of behavioural patterns. In-store hoarding means that the customer picks up a product and holds onto it, even if they are unsure whether they even want to purchase the product. In-store hiding, meanwhile, means that consumers hide products from others, so that they can later return and purchase the product. The results suggested that consumers have a higher tendency to hide products from others, or carry them around just in case, if the store is very messy or crowded. The researchers suggested that messy and crowded stores generate impressions of scarcity and competition between consumers, which then trigger the described behaviours.

> The Swedish furniture chain **IKEA** has gained immense popularity everywhere in the world. IKEA has become famous for its simple design, affordable prices

---

[163] Ainsworth and Foster (2017).
[164] Coskun et al. (2020).

> and innovative assembly system. IKEA is also known for its labyrinthine stores, which are laid out so that customers can only reach the exit once they have gone through the entire store. The purpose of this fixed-path layout is to make customers spend more time in the store and to increase the likelihood of impulse purchases.

4.3 Social Cues

Social cues relate to other people present in the retail environment, such as other customers and staff, as well as their number, body language, gestures and appearance. This is to say that when we shop, we are surrounded by other people and the social cues they transmit. Social cues may have a significant impact on us, since we have a natural tendency to observe and interpret other people.[165] It is also known that we tend to make fast and intuitive judgements of other people. For example, it is found that we need only 100 milliseconds to have a first impression of another person just by assessing the facial appearance.[166] Researchers have found that additional exposure time is not likely to change our initial impressions that much; additional time primarily increases confidence in our judgements.

Retail Store Employees

> **DID YOU KNOW?**
> – The number and service-mindedness of staff are critical factors for a positive shopping experience.
> – The smallest gestures may be very significant for customers.
> – The mood of staff tends to spread to customers.

The customer servants in the store have a tremendous impact on the kind of shopping experience we have and what we think about the store. According to one experimental study, when customers encounter several members of staff who are dressed formally and greet them, the customers will consider

---

[165] Halko and Hytönen (2014).
[166] Willis and Todorov (2006).

the store to have a high level of quality and service.[167] The same study established that social cues, such as having a sufficient number of staff who are neatly dressed, and who have a friendly demeanour and a customer-focused mindset led to customers developing a positive opinion of the store and liking the store as a shopping location.[168] Many other studies have also shown that friendly, helpful and professional customer service staff are a central factor for a pleasant customer experience.[169] It is well established that the smallest gestures made by customer-facing staff can be very significant for customers. For example, a store attendant offering a customer a shopping basket is a pleasant surprise for the customer, and often leads to them purchasing more products.[170] Similarly, greeting customers as they enter and making eye contact with them reduces shoplifting. Thus, gestures like eye contact or just a gentle smile constitute an integral part of interpersonal communication and social cues in a store environment. Against this backdrop, it may seem surprising that many retail companies have transitioned almost entirely to self-service shopping, and the number of store attendants has been cut to the minimum.

> **Isetan Mitsukoshi** is one of Japan's largest department store groups. Isetan Mitsukoshi department stores base their operations on the principle of hospitality, which can be seen in the department stores' desire to emphasise the importance of every moment shared with customers and in the pursuit of perfection in even the smallest details. One daily ritual which illustrates Isetan Mitsukoshi's hospitality is how the stores open to customers. The department stores open at 10:00 AM, and have turned this small matter into an event that shows great respect. The store's customer service staff, dressed in neat and well-fitting uniforms, open the doors at the exact time to the second, and then bow deeply towards the customers waiting outside. When customers walk in, employees working in different departments stand politely behind their counters and bow to customers as they pass their counter.

It should also be mentioned that empathy towards a personable customer servant may also influence a customer's purchasing decision. This is related to the observation that we have the capacity to interpret and understand the emotional states of others, and to experience empathy, particularly towards

---

[167] Baker et al. (1994).
[168] Kumar and Kim (2014) and Hofmann et al. (2021).
[169] Xu (2007).
[170] Underhill (1999).

people we find fair or pleasant.[171] According to Halko and Hytönen, as consumers we tend to make our decisions based on social factors. This means we are able to consider or speculate on the motivations of others while being quick to internalise the emotional states and feelings of others.[172] Somewhat relatedly, Pugh conducted a study which focused on how customer servants expressing emotions influenced the customers.[173] According to the study, if the customer servant expressed positive emotions towards the customer, for example by smiling and making eye contact, it also increased positive emotions in the customer and their positive opinions of the quality of the service. This phenomenon where feelings transfer from one person to the next is known as "emotional contagion". The tiniest gestures can be significant for emotional contagion, for example, the store attendant smiling when they greet the customer.[174] Related to this, Hofmann and her team made an interesting observation: customers recognise a smile even when the store attendant is wearing a mask.[175]

> **Hamleys** is a UK toy store chain which is known for its stores where shopping is an experience in many ways. A central role is given to the Hamleys store attendants, who joke with the customers, present the toys in fun ways and play with them. The happy store attendants send their customers home with a smile.

It should be remembered that the kinds of reactions the cues and signals from the store employees trigger in us are strongly influenced by the kinds of expectations we have for the service level of the store. It is a well-known thing that our expectations create a sort of standard against which we rate our experiences. When our expectations are met or exceeded, we become satisfied. Otherwise, we are dissatisfied. Our expectations are in turn influenced by our previous experiences of the store and its service level, along with all forms of communication and other information relating to the store that we have accumulated.[176]

---

[171] Halko and Hytönen (2014).
[172] Ibid.
[173] Pugh (2001).
[174] Puccinelli, Andrzejewski et al. (2013).
[175] Hofmann et al. (2021).
[176] Parasuraman et al. (1985).

Employee Clothing

> **DID YOU KNOW?**
> – The level of formality of staff clothing acts as a cue for consumers regarding the service quality in the retail environment. The formality of staff outfits also influences consumers' perceptions of store image.

One cue relating particularly to customer service has to do with the way staff are dressed. These days many workplaces have a very relaxed view of employee dress, and staff are rarely provided with detailed instructions on how to dress. This means that clothing at the workplace may be very informal and heterogeneous in style. However, formal dress of retail staff, particularly customer service staff, is an important cue, and formal uniforms may be used to communicate a particular level of service and quality for the customers. Yan and her team staged an experimental study to determine how the outfits of store attendants influenced customer service expectations and opinions on the store.[177] According to the study, the more formal the outfits of the staff, the more competent and professional they appeared. The study also showed that formal dress among staff increased positive opinions of the store as a whole. This means that having store employees dress with a certain level of formality is important, not just to set the employees apart from customers, but to communicate their professionalism on one hand and the overall brand of the store on the other. Shao et al. also emphasise the importance of having staff dressed appropriately.[178] They emphasised the fact that the way staff are dressed is a cue which communicates not just the competence of the staff or the level of customer service, but the company and its quality as a whole (Fig. 4.13).

> **Tokyu Hands** is a Japanese chain of speciality stores, focused on craft and DIY supplies. The stores have many departments, full of various crafting materials and tools. For example, there is a department dedicated entirely to various types of pens and pencils. However, one of the most interesting departments is the small carpentry workshop, which offers a wide variety of different sizes and types of planks and laths along with an extensive selection of tools and supplies from screws to nails. The department also features Tokyu Hands

---

[177] Yan et al. (2011).
[178] Shao et al. (2004).

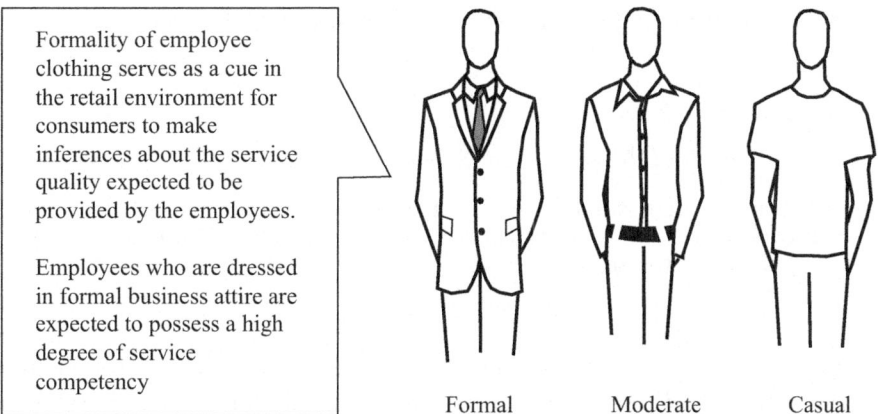

Fig. 4.13 Effects of employee clothing formality (Yan et al., 2011)

> carpenters, who can help customers saw the lumber into the desired shapes, or even craft them into whatever the customer may need. The neatly dressed carpenters are an example of customer service that communicates high quality, and above all, expertise.

In the future, we are sure to encounter digitised or AI-based customer service more frequently. There are already stores and hotels where customers are greeted by a customer service robot. Even though these robots are currently quite clumsy and can really only complete rudimentary and routine customer service tasks, it is likely that in the future they will be able to provide increasingly genuine customer service interactions, and solve increasingly individualised problems. Simultaneously, companies will begin to pay more attention to the appearance and gestures of the robots, and they will likely become more human-like. It is essential that we closely follow how customers react to these humanoid service robots and other new forms of customer service, and what kinds of meanings become associated with them.[179] In a retail environment, these new types of service may prove to be powerful atmospheric cues for customers, and may generate unexpected reactions among the clientele.

---

[179] Biswas (2019).

Social Presence of Others and Interpersonal Touch

> **DID YOU KNOW?**
> – If there are no other customers in the store, the lone customer will feel uncomfortable.
> – However, if there are too many other customers, and particularly if the customer comes into physical contact with them, they will become annoyed and may leave the store.

Studies have shown that the mere social presence of other customers may trigger a range of different emotional states. It is a common understanding that overcrowding in a store evokes negative emotions. One study based on social impact theory showed that if several other customers were in close proximity with them on the same aisle, the customers became annoyed. However, if the other customers were further away, there was no such effect. The same study established that the consumers had a negative reaction to situations where there were no other customers around. The least annoying situation for consumers was one where there was a single other customer nearby. In general, results indicate that we have a desire to belong and feel socially attached, but at the same time the presence of others can cause negative emotions. Research suggests that we all have a feeling of personal space around ourselves, and having others, such as other customers, come too close to our personal space may feel unpleasant or even threatening.[180] Such negative emotions may easily lead to us leaving the store altogether (Fig. 4.14).

Another study focused on how customers react if other customers inadvertently touch them.[181] The study was set in a real store environment, where a research assistant posing as a customer would casually touch other customers. The research assistant would quickly brush against the upper back of the customer. Both male and female research assistants were employed in the study. The study suggested that the customers who were touched by the research assistant gave a more negative review of the store, and spent less time in the store than customers who were not touched. This effect was particularly pronounced among both male and female customers when the research assistant was male. However, being touched by a female research assistant impersonating a customer also had a negative effect. The study shows that a retail setting where customers come to be in close proximity to each

---

[180] Halko and Hytönen (2014).
[181] Martin (2012).

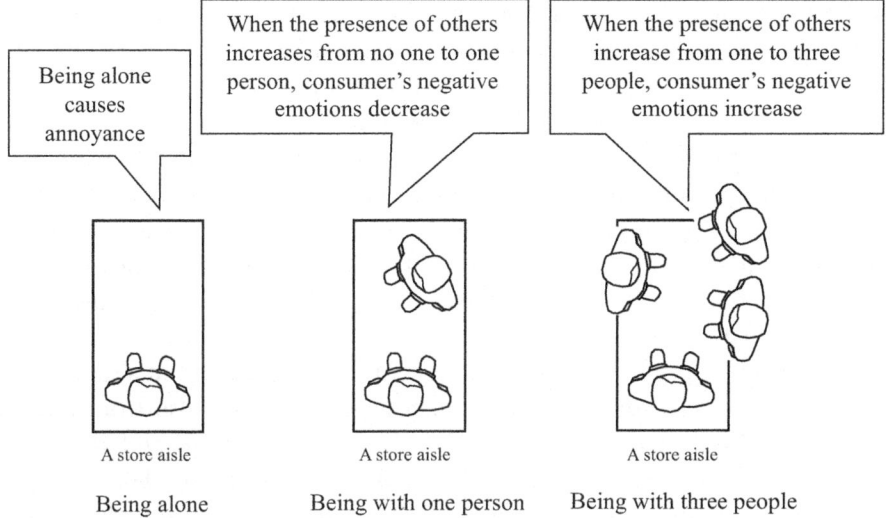

Fig. 4.14 The influence of a mere social presence (Argo et al., 2005)

other (particularly if physical touch is involved) may trigger negative reactions. Researchers speculate that one potential emotion that accidental touch may generate is "tense arousal" (as opposed to energetic arousal), which motivates consumers to avoidance behaviour. When designing the space, retail companies should strive to avoid generating intersections in the store where customers may come into unwanted physical contact with others. However, this is not possible to avoid in all retail stores.

Spontaneous Mimicry

> **DID YOU KNOW?**
> – The mere perception of another's postures, mannerisms, facial expressions and other behaviours automatically increases the likelihood that we will engage in that behaviour ourselves.

One of the most interesting impacts of social cues is spontaneous mimicry. For example, Chartrand and Bargh have studied the extent to which people mimic each other's gestures, positions, expressions and other body movements.[182] They conducted three experimental studies on the topic. The

---

[182] Chartrand and Bargh (1999).

key finding from the studies was that the research subject would unconsciously mirror the expressions and other movements of strangers. This was apparent, for example, in how the research subjects would rub their face, smile or shake their foot when their interlocutor did the same. The analyses conducted by the researchers showed that the imitation was not coincidental, but was evidence of a real phenomenon. The study posits that we have a natural tendency to mimic the gestures and movements of others automatically, without realising we are doing it. This phenomenon is known as the "chameleon effect". Other studies have made similar observations and come to similar conclusions.

Even though spontaneous mimicry has hardly been studied in a retail environment, it is a relevant socio-psychological phenomenon also from a retail perspective. People encounter many others while shopping, and they may imitate their behaviour without realising they are doing so. For example, what other customers put in their shopping baskets, or how they move inside the store, may guide the behaviour of a single consumer without their awareness.[183]

Queues and Crowding

> **DID YOU KNOW?**
> - Queuing in a store is generally viewed very negatively.
> - The norm of being efficient creates social pressure that are likely to lead to more negative affective experiences among customers.
> - In a crowded shopping environment, the customer is likely to base the shopping decisions more on emotions than on cognitive information processing and consideration.

One specific factor which often makes customers annoyed or even angry, is having to stand in line. The annoyance usually comes from queues to the cashier seeming to move too slowly, or if the customer perceives their queue to be moving more slowly than others. Long and slow cashier's queues are an atmospheric factor or cue which generally has a negative impact. As Underhill stated, the worst thing is that the negative emotion arising from queuing may overshadow an otherwise pleasant shopping experience.[184] For some people, long queues may even be a reason to not enter the store in the first place.

---

[183] One study on mimicry found that research subjects subconsciously chose the size of their ice cream order according to what size the person next to them was eating (Johnston, 2002).
[184] Underhill (1999).

Dahm et al. took a closer look at queuing in store, and particularly the related social pressures.[185] In their study, they point out that "[...] queues are governed by social norms that provide cohesion to the social system and that people are aware of and adhere to when they join a queue".[186] One specific norm that is related to queuing is "the norm of being efficient". According to Dahm et al., this norm creates social pressure in the queuing environment that, in turn, is likely to influence customers' affective reactions. The main finding of the study was that the negative emotions experienced by the consumers increased when the number of people behind them grew. The intensification of the negative emotions was particularly pronounced in the situation where the consumer reached the front of the queue and began to access the service they had waited for. In this situation, the consumer could experience significant social pressure from the people queuing behind them. The negative emotions increased with the increase in social pressure. The study emphasises that retail stores should find ways to minimise the negative impacts of queuing. This could mean rearranging the space so that people at the front of the queue cannot see the people behind them. The negative effects of queuing can also be mitigated by communicating to the customers that everyone will be served in turn. Self-service checkouts or self-scanning may also help with the problems relating to queuing. However, the specific type of the retail environment must always be considered when deciding which measures to deploy. What may work for one store may be a disaster for another. In any case, efforts should be made to make sure the checkout queues move as quickly as possible. This is very important for a positive shopping experience.

> **K-Citymarket Iso Omena** is a large hypermarket in Finland that received significant publicity when it launched a novel "slow checkout" service for its customers. The slow checkout is a designated checkout area where customers can easily load their items onto the belt and pack them without any rush after payment. The cashier can also take the time to chat with the customers. Customers who use the slow checkout know that the service is supposed to be slow—it is in fact the whole point. The slow checkout service has become popular among families with children and older people.

Meanwhile, Aydinly and her team studied how experiences of crowding influence the purchasing decisions of consumers inside a store.[187] The

---

[185] Dahm et al. (2018).
[186] Ibid. (p. 219).
[187] Aydinli et al. (2020).

researchers were primarily interested in the impacts crowding has on the composition of the shopping basket. The study used a massive dataset, comprising all purchases of 3,600 households for four weeks. This material was combined with a survey which the researchers used to determine how crowded the consumers felt during the four-week period in question. The main observation was that crowdedness increased emotional purchasing decisions, which was apparent in the composition of the shopping basket. According to the study, consumers shopping in a crowded store bought more hedonistic products and well-known brand products than when they were in a less-crowded store. The researchers posit that crowdedness is a distraction that reduces the cognitive capacity and information processing of consumers, which increases the impact of affective factors on the purchasing decision. This is to say that in a crowded shopping environment, the consumer relies more on their feelings than their cognitive information processing and judgement. According to the researchers, this is because affective purchasing behaviour is much easier and requires less effort than purchasing behaviour based on cognitive consideration.

Red Carpet Treatment

> **DID YOU KNOW?**
> – Conspicuously rewarding loyal customers, or the "red carpet treatment", delights those in the loyalty scheme, but often annoys bystanders. Thus, the red carpet treatment tends to have conflicting effects.

One specific social cue is related to how loyal customers, or VIPs, are considered in the shopping environment. Typically VIP customers are offered various special benefits, or a "red carpet" may even be laid out to communicate their status. For the customers in the loyalty scheme, these benefits may be very important, and visible rewards are likely to enhance their feeling of status and gratitude. At the same time, such benefits may serve as cues which radiate negative impacts on other customers.

Related to this, Steinhoff and Palmatier have conducted an interesting study specifically on the kinds of impacts conspicuous rewarding of customers in a loyalty scheme has on the loyal customers themselves as well as customers outside the scheme.[188] The customers not in the scheme were dubbed bystanders. One of the findings was that when bystanders perceived

---

[188] Steinhoff and Palmatier (2016).

themselves as being excluded from the rewards for loyal customers, they experienced unfairness. This impact was more intense the more visible the rewards in the loyalty scheme were. This means that when loyal customers were rewarded in front of bystanders, this generated significant feelings of unfairness among the bystanders. Even though loyal customers often enjoy being rewarded in front of other customers, such high-visibility rewarding can be thought of as a social cue which triggers negative feelings among bystanders. In line with Steinhoff and Palmatier, it can be argued that providing visible rewards to VIP customers (particularly at the expense of bystanders) may be a dangerous strategy even though it can enhance VIP customers' gratitude and status.[189]

The researchers explain the negative effects of visible rewards with the fact that the rewards may seem entirely arbitrary to bystanders who are not aware of the reason why loyal customers are being rewarded. According to Steinhoff and Palmatier, the negative feelings of bystanders can be reduced by clearly communicating the rules and reward system of the loyalty scheme. All in all, rewarding loyal customers requires considerable awareness of the situation and the ability to also consider the customers who are not in the loyalty scheme (Fig. 4.15).

> The luxury brand **Louis Vuitton** is famous not only for its expensive handbags, but also its impressive storefronts, with security people guarding the doors to let customers in one by one. The stores will only have a handful of customers at any given time, while there may be a long line of customers outside the door. By restricting access, the store can guarantee personal service and the opportunity to shop in peace, but above all, it generates an impression of exclusivity and desirability of the brand.

4.4 Haptic Cues and the Need for Touch

> **DID YOU KNOW?**
> - As a rule, customers have a strong need to know what a product feels like.
> - The opportunity to touch products while shopping increases purchase intentions.
> - The haptic characteristics of the product, such as weight, can be adjusted to evoke a specific image of quality.

---

[189] Ibid.

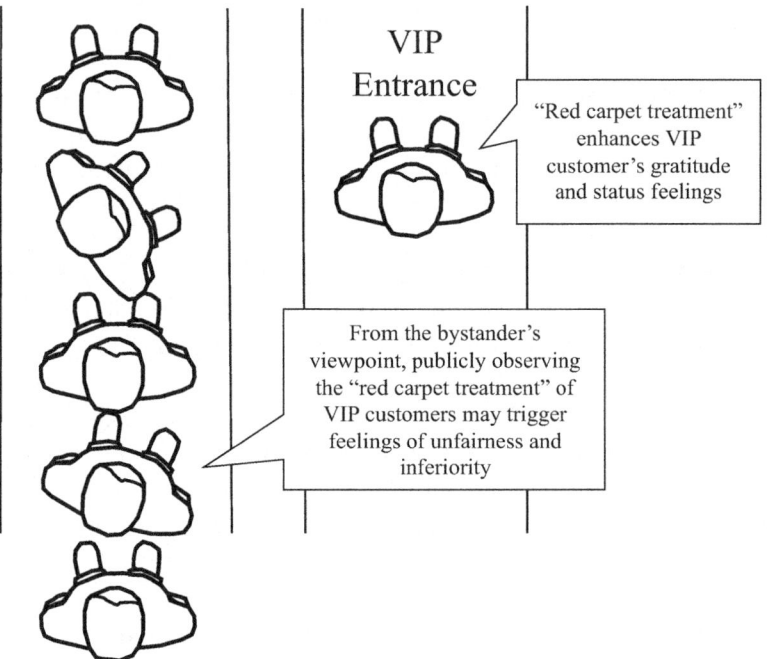

Fig. 4.15 The effects of red carpet treatment (Steinhoff & Palmatier, 2016)

– If the product has no particular material characteristics, the ability to touch the product has little impact on our choice.

Haptic cues are stimuli that we can perceive through our sense of touch. We may have haptic cues literally at our fingertips when we touch a product on a store shelf, for example. We can sense the softness or smoothness of the surface material, or the weight of the packaging. It is said that our sense of touch can provide us with important information on the product and its characteristics. Even though haptic cues are very concrete and tangible, we are rarely fully aware of their impact.

In their review article, Spence et al. state that when customers can physically touch the product, it significantly increases the likelihood that they will purchase it, and even their willingness to pay more for the product.[190] In similar vein, Underhill emphasises the importance of touching the products.[191] Underhill believes that we make most of our impulse purchases

---

[190] Spence et al. (2014).
[191] Underhill (1999).

because we have been able to physically touch or otherwise try the product while shopping. He emphasises that retailers should do everything in their power, including begging, to have their customers to touch and try the products while they shop. The biggest mistake would be to place products in glass display cases where customers cannot reach them. At the same time, it has been said that while consumers want to touch products, they may not want to buy a product that has been touched by others.[192] One example of this is that when buying a magazine, customers will often take a copy from the middle of the stack instead of the top one.

> **Virgin Megastore** is a retail chain selling electronics, toys, home décor items and many other consumer goods. Even though the product selection is wide, it is also highly curated. According to the chain, it primarily sells "serious fun" to its customers. A central part of the chain's business idea are its comfortable and inspiring stores, where products are well presented and freely available to customers to touch and test.

The study by McCabe and Nowlis is an excellent illustration of the significance of the haptic qualities and cues relating to products. They examined how a consumer's choice behaviour changes when they have the opportunity to touch a product, or when they are only given the product information as written descriptions or pictures.[193] The study featured products which were different both in terms of material and shape. The research subjects were presented with the products by providing (1) a written description, (2) a written description and a picture or (3) a written description and an opportunity to touch the product. The result was that if the product was of a pleasant material and could be touched, the likelihood that a consumer would choose it increased significantly in comparison to a situation where only a written description or a picture was provided. According to the researchers, products such as fluffy bath towels are best sold at brick-and-mortar locations, where consumers can touch them while shopping. If the product did not have any special material properties, the ability to touch it did not influence the consumers' choice behaviour. For such products, an online store may be an optimal retail channel.

Ranaweera and team also studied haptic cues and conducted several experimental studies to research the significance of haptic qualities for the formation of product impressions.[194] The study established that haptic cues

---

[192] Spence et al. (2014).
[193] McCabe and Nowlis (2003).
[194] Ranaweera et al. (2021).

relating to the surface structure (smooth vs. rough) and weight (light vs. heavy) influenced the product impressions among customers. For example, after touching a smooth product, consumers associated it with competence, sophistication and lower ruggedness. If the product felt heavy, it was more likely to be viewed as "more competent" than a lighter product. However, the researchers also found that the impact of haptic cues depended on the consumer's need for touch. Nevertheless, the study is still a good indication of the kinds of impressions a simple touch can evoke.

It has also been established that the heavier the product packaging, the higher the perceived quality and price.[195] One study that focused on the impact of the weight of a box of chocolates or a soda can/may have on the taste experiences of consumers showed that the weight of the packaging in both cases significantly influenced the experienced flavour intensity.[196,197] The central finding was that the more heavy the packaging, the more intense consumers found the flavour of the product. This means that just the weight of the packaging can change the impressions customers glean of the product, even if no factual changes are made to the product itself. Other studies have had similar results.[198]

The significance of our sense of touch is also well described in the experiments conducted by Ludwig and Simner, where they studied what colours people associate with objects they touch.[199] For the experiment, the researchers created 18 objects with different haptic stimuli. The objects differed in roughness, hardness and roundness. In the study, the research subjects touched the objects in a random order without seeing them. It was emphasised that they should not guess the colour of the object they were touching, but to choose the colour that they associated with the touch sensation. They found that the more smooth, soft and round the material, the more intensely it was associated with bright colours. Smoothness and softness were also thought of as being colourful. Certain objects were clearly associated with a particular colour. For example, hard materials were associated with black, rough surfaces with brown and soft ones with yellow and pink. All in all, the researchers found that people systematically link certain tactile sensations with specific visual experiences. This also describes the effects touching an object may have.

---

[195] Piqueras-Fiszman et al. (2011).
[196] In the research setting, the lighter box of chocolates weighed 184 grams and the heavier 234 grams, while the lighter soda weighed 287 grams and the heavier 347 grams.
[197] Kampfer et al. (2017).
[198] Piqueras-Fiszman et al. (2011) and Piqueras-Fiszman and Spence (2011, 2012).
[199] Ludwig and Simner (2013).

Jha et al. have conducted an interesting study on the impact of haptic cues on our behaviour in a retail setting. The researchers tested the impacts of haptic cues by using a store discount card.[200] Two haptic cues were investigated in the study: weight and softness of the discount card.[201] Four different cards were made for the study, with different weights and different levels of softness. In the study, a heavier store discount card was used more. There was a similar link with softness: the softer the card, the more it was used. This is an excellent illustration of how tiny haptic-related changes can result in different behavioural reactions.

All in all, the importance of haptic information is something that the retailer should be aware of. We as consumers like to touch the products and in many cases we have a burning need to know what the surface material of an object, such as a wallet, feels like on our fingertips, or what a garment feels like against our skin.[202] We cannot experience this feeling by looking at the product; we must hold it in our hands or put it on to feel these qualities. The ability to physically touch the product and experience its tactile characteristics is likely to have a significant impact on what we think about the product and whether we want to buy it. Hultén et al. compare a touch experience to a handshake that affects our impression of the other person.[203] In many cases, the ability to experience the product with our hands is a prerequisite for our purchasing decision. The ability to touch, even briefly, can also lead to impulse buys.

4.5 Merchandise-Related Cues

Merchandise-related cues are cues which we encounter when examining the merchandise on store shelves and selecting products. Merchandise-related cues relate to the quality of the products and the number of options. Merchandise arrangement is a central merchandise-related cue. We know that

---

[200] Jha et al. (2020).
[201] One store discount card was light and hard (printed on paper which was 0.4064 mm thick and laminated). The second was light and soft (0.4064 thickness, unlaminated). The third was heavy and hard (1.016 thickness, laminated) and the fourth heavy and soft (1.016 thickness, unlaminated). In every other sense, all four cards were identical.
[202] It should be noted that the importance of haptic information varies from one individual to the next. For some consumers the ability to receive haptic information is a critical issue, while for others the ability to touch is not as important. Peck and Childers (2003) have developed a metric known as the Need for Touch (NFT) to illustrate these individual differences. Put simply, persons higher in NFT tend to seek haptic information and to use it as they make product evaluations.
[203] Hultén et al. (2009).

very minor shelf-space solutions can increase the desirability of a product. Merchandise-related cues can also be used to influence impressions of the store more broadly.

You Are What You Sell

> **DID YOU KNOW?**
> - A high-quality product selection strengthens the overall quality impression of the store.
> - The consumer's gaze is drawn most intensely to well-known and strong brands.
> - Country of origin is a critical quality cue for consumers.

Ailawadi and Keller have suggested that the position a store holds in the minds of consumers is strongly influenced by the brands the retailer offers.[204] In short, the better quality the brands on offer, the more quality the store is thought to possess. Ailawadi and Keller aptly summed this as "you are what you sell". Thus, the brands sitting on the store shelves can be seen as an important quality cue, based on which consumers evaluate both the product selection of the store and the store and its quality as a whole.[205] Particularly, for stores that aim to build high-end image of themselves, having the right brands on the shelves can be a critical factor or cue.

The way brands drive our attention was shown in the study conducted by Bialkova et al., which used eye-tracking cameras to establish that in a retail environment, the gaze of consumers is most intensely drawn to the most popular or well-known brands. The study also found that consumers look at popular brands for longer.[206] This means that the eye of the consumer scans the shelves for well-known or familiar brands and attaches to them more easily than other options. And the more attention the brand gets, the more likely the branded product is to be purchased. Understanding this brand effect is crucial for retailers and manufacturers as well. Based on this, placing less-known brands next to the most popular brands could be an efficient tactic for drawing customers' attention to these more unfamiliar brands and boosting their sales.

---

[204] Ailawadi and Keller (2004).
[205] Graciola et al. (2020).
[206] Bialkova et al. (2020).

> NK, or **Nordiska Kompaniet**, is a Swedish department store with a product selection based on high-quality and well-curated products and brands. The store features the most famous top brands and the latest fashion trends. Products and brands are organised on the shop-in-shop principle, meaning that each department of the store is almost its own brand store with its own features, while generating a quality impression of the department store as a whole.

One specific merchandise-related quality cue which comes up in studies again and again is the country of origin. For example, Aboah and Lees found in their research that the country of origin is an extremely critical quality cue for consumers.[207] Teas and Agarwal made a similar observation when they established that the country of origin of a product has a significant impact on the quality impression.[208] Meanwhile, Wall et al. found that the country of origin can be even more important than price as a quality cue.[209] Particularly when customers are unfamiliar with the product, they tend to use the country of origin as a cue to form their opinion about the product and its quality.[210]

> **Kyrö Distillery Company** is a Finnish rye distillery that produces award-winning gin (Kyrö Gin, formerly known as Napue) and single malt rye whiskey (Kyrö Malt Rye Whisky) in an old dairy in Isokyrö, Finland. When Kyrö Distillery started to sell its products to foreign markets like the UK or Japan, Kyrö realised that its brand recognition outside of Finland was virtually zero. To solve this brand recognition problem, Kyrö launched a novel campaign that emphasised its country of origin. The main theme of the campaign was to highlight that Kyrö Distillery is "Brutally Finnish". The campaign exceeded all expectations, leading to a significant increase in brand recognition and product sales.[211]

You Get What You Pay For

> **DID YOU KNOW?**
> – A high-price level generates expectations of high quality.
> – Gimmicky price reductions may lower the quality impression.

---

[207] Aboah and Lees (2020).
[208] Teas and Agarwal (2000).
[209] Wall et al. (1991).
[210] Laroche et al. (2005).
[211] https://www.we-are-lure.com/work/kyroe-brutally-finnish/.

> – Consumers' perceptions of a store's price level are very permanent.

Price is very often perceived by consumers as an extrinsic quality cue.[212] We have all heard the phrase "you get what you pay for". Simply put, this means that a high price is thought to indicate high quality, while low prices suggest low quality. This is based on the general belief that high-quality products are more expensive to manufacture, and therefore cost more on the market.[213] However, the correlation of price and quality may be entirely fictitious, and a high price is no guarantee of actual high quality. This was nicely shown in Hilke Plassmann's study where the brains of research subjects were scanned as they tasted three wines with different prices. The study revealed that the subjects' brains registered the wines differently, with neural signatures indicating a preference for the most expensive wine. In actuality, all of the wine given to the subjects was the same.[214]

The connection of price to expected or experienced quality can be viewed both in terms of individual products and the store as a whole. The correlation between price and perceived quality has been established in studies such as the one by Teas and Agarwal.[215] Erdem et al. also found that price is a very important quality cue, and that playing around with price reductions may erode the quality impression of the brand.[216] Meanwhile, Kerin et al. have identified the significance of price as a quality cue at the store level, even though they especially emphasised the importance of the overall shopping experience on the formation of quality impressions.[217] Similarly, Graciola et al. established that consumer perceptions of a store's price level contribute to the impression of the store. Diallo et al. pointed out that low prices do not automatically mean that the store is thought of as low quality.[218] Low prices may indicate an efficient business model and, hence, high quality. The importance of the price may also decrease with the presence of a great number of

---

[212] Stafford (1969) and Wheatly and Chiu (1977).
[213] Teas and Agarwal (2000).
[214] Source: Harrell (2019).
[215] Teas and Agarwal (2000).
[216] Erdem et al. (2008).
[217] Kerin et al. (1992).
[218] Diallo et al. (2015).

other cues.[219] Hamilton and Chernev have posited that consumers' impressions of a store's price level are very permanent. Once the consumer has made up their mind about the price level of the store, it is very difficult to change.[220]

The Number of Alternatives and the Compromise Effect

> **DID YOU KNOW?**
> - Retailers can serve customers who want variety by increasing the number of available options, but an increase in product options does not automatically lead to higher demand.
> - In some cases, merely changing the perceived variety of an assortment can affect consumption quantities.
> - The choice-making process under extensive-choice conditions is experienced as enjoyable but often also difficult and frustrating. A large number of options may trigger the choice overload effect.
> - When presented with a range of options, consumers tend to choose the middle one.

Consumers may also be influenced by varying the number of available options. Research frequently discusses variety-seeking behaviour among consumers, and how the increase of product options may address this need for variety.[221] For example, Ailawadi and Keller have suggested that increasing the number of options serves variety-seeking consumers in particular, and makes the store more attractive for them.[222] They specified that as the perceived assortment of brands, flavours and sizes increases, consumers with variety-seeking behaviour are likely to perceive greater utility. Consumers with uncertain future preferences will also feel they have more flexibility in their choices.

> **K-Citymarket Kupittaa** in Finland is known for its unique assortment strategy that aims to offer a great variety of products under each category. One specific category with an enormous number of options is beer. The store offers more than 700 different brands for its beer-loving customers. In addition to the global and national megabrands, there are many local craft beer brands, and

---

[219] Dodds and Grewal (1991).
[220] Hamilton and Chernev (2013).
[221] McAlister and Pessemier (1982) and Morales et al. (2005).
[222] Ailawadi and Keller (2004).

> even signature beers named after the store staff. In total, the beverage section has around 4,000 different products, including different package sizes.

Kahn and Wansink conducted an interesting study on how the assortment structure can be designed in different ways to influence consumer demand. They focused particularly on how the (dis)order of the assortment structure influences demand when the number of options is increased.[223] The researchers found that if the assortment structure is disorganised or otherwise confusing, introducing new options (such as new flavours) does not lead to a particular increase in demand, whereas adding options to assortments which are well-organised increases demand significantly. Thus, organised assortments are likely to have a positive effect on consumption quantities when actual variety is increased, whereas increasing more options in a disorganised manner is not likely to increase consumption. One of the most interesting findings of this study was that consumption quantities are also influenced by the perceived variety of an assortment.[224] In other words, the mere perception of high variety can increase consumption even in a situation where actual variety is unchanged. As Kahn and Wansink summarised their study: "[…] When consumers perceive the variety of an assortment as high, they are more likely to consume more product than when variety is perceived as lower— even when actual variety is held constant".[225] According to the study, this perceived variety may increase demand for products. The ability to maneuver with perceptions is important for retailers, as actually increasing product variety is typically associated with significant additional costs.

One specific issue related to extensive assortments is the choice overload effect.[226] Simply put, it is argued that extensive assortments might lead to cognitive overload, and may therefore actually decrease the likelihood of purchase.[227] Choice overload means the difficulty or even discomfort associated with choice when the number of options increases significantly. Consumers may feel very uncertain about their choice if the number of options is excessively high. The choice overload effect may lead to the

---

[223] In the study, the (dis)organisation of the assortment structure was manipulated so that the products selected for the study were either organised into clear uniform groups by colour or flavour, or randomly mixed so that the colours and flavour options were in disarray.

[224] Kahn and Wansink (2004).

[225] Ibid. (p. 531).

[226] Iyengar and Lepper (2000).

[227] Ailawadi and Keller (2004).

consumer not making a choice to purchase at all, or regretting the choice later. This is to say that extravagant increases to product variety may not always result in positive impacts among consumers. Scheibehenne et al. point out that the threat of choice overload can be diminished by making categories easy to navigate and improving ease of comparison of different options.[228] Ailawadi and Keller, in turn, suggest that retailers can cut choice sets without seriously affecting consumer perceptions, as long as retailers pay attention to the most popular brands, the organisation of the assortment and the availability of diverse product attributes.[229]

Simonson and Tversky have made an interesting observation relating to the number of options and our choice behaviour. Namely that the attractiveness of an individual product increases if it is the middle option, and decreases if it is on either extreme side.[230] This is generally known as the extremeness aversion effect, which means that consumers tend to avoid extremes and choose the middle option.[231] For example, consumers are typically not keen to choose the product with the highest quality and the highest price or the lowest quality and the lowest price from the choice set, but instead they prefer the option that is located in the middle of these extremes. In general, consumers are likely to think that the intermediate option has "good enough quality" with a reasonable price (at least when compared to extreme options). However, it should be noted that in their empirical study, Simonson and Tversky found that extremeness aversion seems to apply only to quality but not to price (i.e., consumers find the lowest quality more aversive than the highest price). This may indicate that quality is perceived as a more important feature than price. Nevertheless, the existence of this choice behaviour model also means that retailers may influence the popularity of a specific product by varying the number of options and particularly by adding or decreasing available extreme options. At its best, extremeness aversion can be used as a method for predicting consumer choice. However, extremeness aversion does not explain our choices in all situations. As Simonson and Tversky pointed out, extremeness aversion is likely to have less impact in situations in which consumers have well-established preferences and purchase habitually.[232]

---

[228] Scheibehenne et al. (2010).
[229] Ailawadi and Keller (2004).
[230] Simonson and Tversky (1992).
[231] Neumann et al. (2016).
[232] Simonson and Tversky (1992).

Product Display and Shelf Position

> **DID YOU KNOW?**
> - The best shelf position is between our eye and waist levels, approximately 130–135 centimetres from the floor.
> - Consumers believe that expensive and high-quality brands are located on the top shelves, while cheaper brands are on lower shelves. Also, products that are located on the right-hand side of a display are perceived to be more expensive than those on the left-hand side.

It is well known that the manner of presentation or merchandise arrangement can affect consumers' purchase behaviour. For example in department stores, clothes may be presented hanging, folded, on display rails or on mannequins. In their study, Kerfoot et al. found that hanging was viewed as the most attractive presentation method by consumers whereas the use of display rails was perceived more negatively.[233] They also found that the use of mannequins generated a positive response among consumers. Grocery stores, in turn, try to appeal to customers by placing fresh products with bright colours in the front of the shop. Some grocery stores even build eye-catching pyramid-shaped fresh fruit displays to catch the consumers' attention and entice them to visit the store.

> **Waitrose & Partners** is a British supermarket chain that is known for its modern and bright in-store design and impressive product displays. Waitrose & Partners have built their upmarket reputation above all by investing in extensive counters dedicated to meat and fish, patisserie, sushi or cheese and deli products, along with must-see wine departments. Some stores also feature in-store tasting and wine bars. For many customers, Waitrose & Partners is more than a regular supermarket chain, it is a whole luxurious lifestyle. The stores are so iconic that in the UK, the "Waitrose effect" means that opening a new Waitrose & Partners store is likely to increase nearby property prices.

One particular issue which has fascinated researchers for years is where on the shelves a product should be placed to make sure it is noticed and placed in the shopping basket. This question is crucial for retailers, but also individual suppliers and manufacturers. If the product is placed in the wrong location, customers may not notice it, resulting in low sales. Meanwhile, a product in a good shelf location is more easily noticed, which may lead to considerable increases in sales. But what exactly is a good shelf location?

---

[233] Kerfoot et al. (2003).

Chandon and team have used eye-tracking studies to find that products located close to the centre of the shelf are more easily noticed than products towards the sides of the shelf.[234] According to the study, the likelihood a product is noticed drops dramatically when it is moved from the centre to the side. Products in the lower left corner were least noticed. Meanwhile, Drèze et al. found that the best shelf position is between our eye and waist level, approximately 130–150 centimetres from the floor, while the worst positions are on the lowest shelves, or conversely very high up, above our natural gaze.[235] According to this study, moving a product to the correct vertical position may increase sales up to nearly 40%. Chandon et al. demonstrated that placing a product close to the centre of the shelf on an upper shelf instead of a lower one increases the likelihood that the product will be noticed and consequently selected.[236] The study also established that the likelihood of a product being noticed is ultimately largely determined by how much shelf space it is given, meaning how many identical products are placed side by side (this is also known as the product having multiple facings). The study established that when the number of facings increased from four units to eight, the likelihood of the product being noticed increased nearly 30%. However, the study also suggested that if the number of facings was further increased by four, to twelve, the likelihood of the product being noticed only increased by extra 7%. This means that the correlation of shelf space and the likelihood of the product being noticed is not entirely linear.

The position of the product on the shelf may also evoke various associations relating to the product's price and quality. For example, Valenzuela and Raghubir have made an interesting observation that consumers believe more expensive and high-quality brands to be located on top shelves, while cheaper brands are relegated to lower shelves.[237] Products in the middle of the shelf are thought to have a superior price-quality ratio. In similar fashion, Barone et al. demonstrated that low (vs. high) locations promote lower-price estimates.[238] Barone et al. argue that the price location effect is based on the "down = less" and "up = more" metaphorical beliefs that consumers are likely to hold. Another study indicated that products located on the right-hand side of a display are perceived as more expensive than to those on the left-hand side.[239] This is explained by the fact that people are frequently exposed to

---

[234] Chandon et al. (2007).
[235] Drèze et al. (1994).
[236] Chandon et al. (2009).
[237] Valenzuela and Raghubir (2009).
[238] Barone et al. (2020).
[239] Cai et al. (2012).

sets of numbers or rulers on which small numbers are to the left of large numbers, and thus there is a learned association between right position and larger numerical values (i.e., higher prices). Sunaka et al. in turn made an interesting finding that when consumers consider the lightness (in terms of weight) of the products, they tend to choose light (vs. dark) coloured products that are located in the upper shelf positions.[240] Taken together above discussion, just the positioning of the product on the shelf can serve as a quality and price cue for the consumer. Overall, the position of the product on the shelf influences not just how likely the product is to be noticed and selected, but also the kinds of impressions that are associated with it (Fig. 4.16).

It should be emphasised that deciding on the amount of shelf space or position for a product may be very difficult, as space is usually limited, as are good shelf positions. Planning optimal shelf maps requires that the retailer is able to use product- and category-specific sales data and other similar information, while possessing a comprehensive understanding of the preferences and choice tendencies of consumers. Positioning products also requires an eye for visual design and composition. Impressive product displays may be an important way for a store to differentiate itself. All in all it is key that product positioning is not decided based on hard sales data alone. The

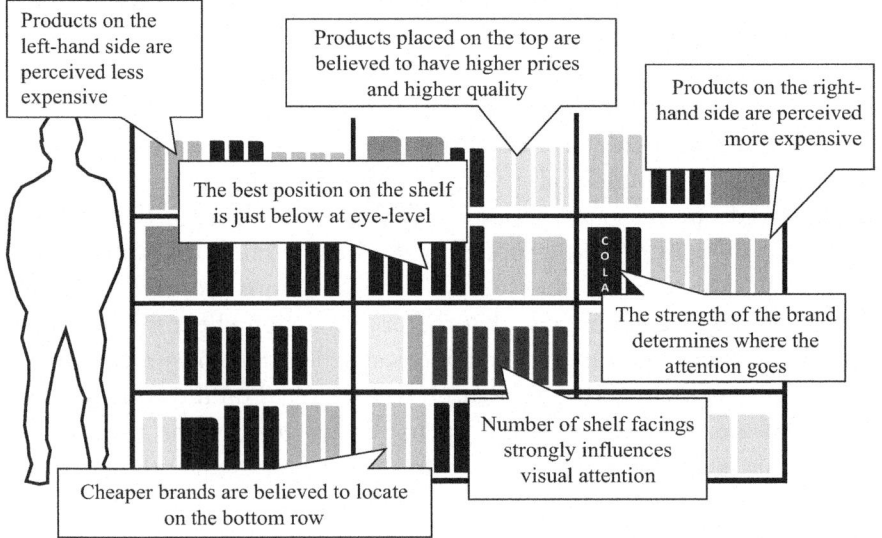

Fig. 4.16 Shelf-space cues

---

[240] Sunaga et al. (2016).

retailer must understand the myriad impacts product positioning may have, including those relating to impressions.

> **Uniqlo** is a Japanese clothing chain, with a concept of offering high-quality everyday clothes which are simple and relaxed, but also affordable. Uniqlo exclusively sells its own brands. Brick-and-mortar locations are important for Uniqlo both as a retail channel and in building its brand. The stores are simple, but often very pleasant shopping environments with spacious lobbies and wide corridors. Meticulously designed product displays are also part of the Uniqlo store image. Even jeans are folded in a specific way to ensure the desired display.

The Scarcity Principle

> **DID YOU KNOW?**
> – Limited availability and high popularity of a product increase the willingness to buy among customers.
> – The presence of purchase restrictions may result in higher sales.

In the retail industry, it is common for consumers to be lured with cues that relate to either the limited availability or great popularity of products. Scarcity has been found to increase the desirability and appreciation of products. High popularity, meanwhile, tells consumers that the product is much sought-after on the market and that the product is associated with very little risk, as many other consumers have already bought it. Cialdini and Goldstein, among others, have noted that cues that communicate scarcity through phrases like "limited time only" are very efficient methods for influencing consumers.[241] They attribute this to the fact that we have a natural tendency to consider a thing with limited availability or which only exists in small quantities to be somehow better than something that is readily available. Cialdini and Goldstein have dubbed this the scarcity principle. One could say that in a store environment scarcity creates a sense of urgency around a product offering and persuades consumers to act fast. The fear of missing out is a strong motivator and can drive us to make spontaneous purchases without an evaluation of actual need.

Das et al. conducted a study which focused on the impact of limited availability and high popularity on consumers' intention to buy for two products

---

[241] Cialdini and Goldstein (2002).

of very different types.[242] The product types were hedonic and utilitarian. A hedonic product provides experiences and pleasure whereas utilitarian product provides practical and rational benefits. The study was conducted by arranging the research subjects randomly into various groups and exposing them to "limited edition" (scarcity) or "best seller" (popularity) messages, so that the phrases related to either a hedonic or utilitarian product. The research team found that "limited edition" cues, which communicate scarcity, increased the consumers' willingness to buy when the product was hedonic and related to pleasure-seeking. Meanwhile, for ordinary utilitarian products, the consumers' willingness to buy was boosted by "best seller" cues, which communicate high popularity among shoppers. Based on this research, Das et al. determined that "limited edition" cues enhance the experienced uniqueness of hedonic products, while "best seller" cues reduce the experience of risk associated with the purchasing of utilitarian products (Fig. 4.17).

> **Amazon 4-star** stores, a retail concept already discontinued by Amazon.com, had an innovative idea for their assortments. Amazon 4-star stores exclusively carried products that were rated 4 stars and above on Amazon.com. In other words, all products that were on sale were "the best of the best" products, ranging from consumer electronics to books and home items. The stores also

Fig. 4.17 Scarcity cue vs. popularity cue (Das et al., 2018)

---

[242] Das et al. (2018).

> offered categories like "Most-Wished-For", "Trending around the local area" and "Frequently bought together".[243]

Inman's team conducted four experimental studies to determine how the presence of restrictions influences consumers and their purchasing behaviour.[244] Ways of restricting consumers' opportunities for purchasing include, e.g., reducing the number of products an individual consumer may buy (i.e., purchase limit), or by restricting the period of time during which the consumer may take advantage of an offer (i.e., time limit). In their study, the researchers found that setting purchasing restrictions had a significant positive impact on sales of the product. One of the studies established that product sales could more than double if the retailer set restrictions to purchasing the products, for example, by using phrases such as "no more than 3 per customer". It seems that restrictions make an offer or deal very attractive for consumers. Particularly in the absence of other cues, a restriction announced by the retailer seems to lead the consumers to believe that the deal being offered is good and worth taking advantage of. All in all, the researchers proposed that restrictions on purchasing could be a very efficient promotional tool for a store.

> **Stockmann**, the Finnish chain of department stores, has an annual sale campaign known as Hullut Päivät ("Crazy Days"), which is a good example of how customers can be influenced both through price reductions and restrictions on purchases. When a discount is only valid for a very short period of time, the customers feel like they are encountering a unique offer and most seize the opportunity, or miss the deal of a lifetime. During Hullut Päivät, consumers are also given the impression that there are few products available.

Product Packages

> **DID YOU KNOW?**
> – Features of product packages like shape, colour or weight can serve as significant cues to simplify and speed up how consumers judge and choose products in a store.

---

[243] Introducing Amazon 4-Star (2018).
[244] Inman et al. (1997).

- For unpackaged food products, aesthetics is one of the main attributes that consumers use as unconscious cues of quality.

Research has shown that factors or cues relating to package design may have significant impacts on the kinds of impressions consumers associate with a product. For many marketers, package design is one of the most important tools to attract consumer attention and communicate information about a product and its features at the moment of choice. Chen et al. have emphasised that package design can serve as a heuristic to speed up how we categorise and choose brands and products.[245]

Thus, it is not surprising that there is a growing body of research on how packaging affects consumers' evaluations and choice. For example, researchers have found that a tall, slim package shape creates the perception of higher brand status to a significantly greater extent than a package that is short and wide.[246] According to the researchers, the explanation behind this finding is that consumers tend to transfer norms from their interpersonal relationships to guide their brand assessments. Another study suggested that angular packaging is associated with higher prices than rounded packaging.[247] The same study also demonstrated that consumers have a more positive attitude towards the angular packages compared to the round packages. In general, it is said that angular shapes convey meanings of toughness and strength, whereas rounded shapes have softer meanings such as friendliness and harmony.

In grocery stores, many food products across various categories are displayed without packaging. These unpackaged food products also have cues that signal, for example, safety and quality. It has been said that aesthetics is one of the main attributes that consumers use as unconscious cues of quality when purchasing unpackaged food products.[248] Consumers often think that aesthetically perfect foods are safe and high-quality (i.e., "beauty-is-good" thinking), whereas aesthetically imperfect foods like ugly fruits or vegetables are related to food hazards (i.e., "ugly-is-risky" thinking). However, not all consumers are cautious of imperfect food products. As Castagna et al. demonstrated, individuals with an abstract mindset tend to see beyond the aesthetics of imperfect foods, and hence are more open to purchasing such foods.[249]

---

[245] Chen et al. (2020).
[246] Ibid.
[247] Becker et al. (2011).
[248] Castagna et al. (2021).
[249] Ibid.

Product-level cues are also closely connected to various haptic cues, such as what the packaging material feels like, or how heavy it is. For example, Krishna et al. state that for many products and brands, haptic perceptions are the dominant input for determining the quality of products.[250] Weight is a particularly important quality cue. Product-level haptic cues are discussed in more detail in Sect. 4.4.

Packaging-related cues are often thought to be primarily the responsibility of manufacturing companies. While this is largely true, it is also clear that retailers must also pay increasing attention to product-level design cues as stores' private labels become more common. Similarly, individual product-level cues such as product packages may radiate impacts more broadly to the store as a whole and the associated overall impressions. An individual product or product packaging may have an impact beyond its size specifically in the realm of impressions.

4.6 Pricing-Related Cues

Pricing-related cues are primarily various ways of communicating the price of a product, or a special offer.[251] They are typically intended to convince the consumer at the moment of choice of the fact that a specific deal or offer is particularly good and worth taking. Pricing-related cues may also influence the kind of quality impression a consumer has of the store as a whole.[252]

Odd-Ending Pricing Versus Even Pricing

> **DID YOU KNOW?**
> - Odd-ending pricing increases demand, but they may generate an impression of low quality.
> - Even pricing is seen as a sign of high quality.

Possibly the most well-known price-related cue relates to odd-ending pricing. Odd-ending pricing means "99-prices", setting prices at numbers that are just below an even number (e.g., €99 or €4.99). Among others,

---

[250] Krishna et al. (2010).
[251] For a comprehensive review of various psychological pricing principles, see Larson (2014). In his review, Larson divides pricing principles into four categories: framing, congruency, context and signalling.
[252] Krishna et al. (2002).

Gendall has studied the impacts of such odd-ending prices for three different products.[253] The prices for the products were originally 4, 7 and 50 dollars. Gendall was interested in seeing how demand for the products changed when the prices were changed to end in 95 or 99 (e.g., 3.95 or 3,99). In short, Gendall's main finding was that demand for each of the three products increased with both styles of pricing, but for the cheaper products (priced at 4 and 7 dollars) the 99-price increased demand more than the 95-price, whereas for the more expensive product (priced at 50 dollars) the 95-price generated more demand than the 99-price. According to this study, 99-end pricing seemed to see the most impactful pricing model for cheaper products, while 95-pricing is most effective for more expensive ones. Whether the retailer chooses 95- or 99-end pricing, the main takeaway should be that setting prices just a little under an even number is likely to increase demand.

In general the positive impacts of such odd-ending pricing is explained by the fact that consumers read the price from left to right, leading to them observing and remembering the first number of the price better than the rest of the numbers.[254] For this reason, the consumer may feel that a price of €2.99 is significantly cheaper than a price of €3.00, even though the actual price difference is just a single cent. Consequently, the first digit of a price tag holds great significance for the consumer and may be the deciding factor in whether they choose to pick the product for their basket or not. However, it should be borne in mind that while odd-ending pricing may increase demand for the products, it may simultaneously suggest lower quality or create an impression of the location being a discount store. It has been suggested that stores seeking to generate impressions of high quality prefer even pricing, as that is considered an indicator of higher quality than odd-ending pricing.[255] Even pricing might also offer convenience for the customers because "round prices" are typically more quickly processed (i.e., easier to calculate and make estimates with) compared to odd-ending or precise prices. In other words, even pricing reduces the amount of time and cognitive effort that is needed to process the price information.[256] Thus, as Wieseke et al. state, even pricing can be one way to serve convenience-conscious customers who want to make their purchase decisions fast without any extra mental effort. Figure 4.18 demonstrates odd-ending pricing and even pricing.

---

[253] Gendall (1998).
[254] Coulter (2001).
[255] Schindler and Kibarian (2001).
[256] Wieseke et al. (2016).

A mug for **9,99 €** 　　　　　　A mug for **10,00 €**

Odd-ending pricing 　　　　　　Even pricing

Fig. 4.18 Odd-ending pricing vs. even pricing

> **Daiso** is Japan's leading 100-yen discount store that uses even pricing instead of 99-end pricing, even though their main competitive edge is low prices. Furthermore, despite being a discount store chain, Daiso stores are very pleasant and tidy shopping environments with high product availability and clear and well-planned displays. The product assortment ranges from kitchen goods to toys, stationery, storage solutions and home decor.

Absolute Versus Relative Price Discounts

> **DID YOU KNOW?**
> - For high-price products, a price discount framed in absolute terms is seen as more significant than the same price reduction framed in percentage terms, whereas for low-price products, a price discount framed in percentage terms is considered more significant than those framed in absolute terms.

In addition to odd-ending pricing, researchers have studied whether discounts should be indicated as percentages (e.g., 15% off) or absolute values (e.g., €25 off). Chen et al. focused on this issue in their study.[257] The research group conducted an experimental study in which research subjects were placed in an imaginary shopping situation. The research subjects were asked to imagine a situation where they had already decided to purchase a computer of a particular brand (worth $1,795) or a memory disk (worth $7.95). The subjects were then presented with an offer in which they could also buy a superior, but also 25% more expensive computer (worth $1 995)

---

[257] Chen et al. (1998).

or disc (worth $9.95). If they chose to buy the more expensive computer or disk, they would be given a 10% discount. For some research subjects, the discount was given as a percentage, and for other, as absolute values. The actual monetary value of the discounts was identical. The researchers were interested to see which of the presented offers (discount as a percentage or as an absolute value) would seem to offer more savings, or be perceived as a better offer by the research subjects. After the study, the researchers found that for the more expensive product, the research subjects considered the offer indicated in absolute value to be better, or they thought it provided more savings than the offer indicated as a percentage. For the less expensive product, the result was reversed, and the offer indicated as a percentage was seen as better than the one indicated as an absolute value. These results seem to show that for more expensive products, a discount indicated as an absolute value has more impact on the consumers and their perception of savings, while for more affordable products, a discount indicated as a percentage has more impact. All in all, the study is a good example of how just the way a discount is marked can serve as a significant cue for consumer behaviours (Fig. 4.19).

> Finland's largest discount store chain **Tokmanni** is an example of a retail chain whose pricing structure demonstrates various psychological pricing-related cues, from odd-ending pricing to listing discounts either as percentages or as values in euros, depending on the monetary value of the product. Tokmanni will typically advertise its cheapest products with percentage discounts, and more expensive products with discounts in euros (e.g., "Save 50€").

Premiums Versus Price Cuts

> **DID YOU KNOW?**
> - A premium promotion (a free gift) generates lower purchase effects than a price cut, even when the premium is judged to be equivalent to the price cut.

Foubert and team conducted a study on whether retailers could more effectively influence consumers by making a minor price cut, or by offering a free product of the same value with purchase (a premium promotion).[258]

---

[258] Foubert et al. (2018).

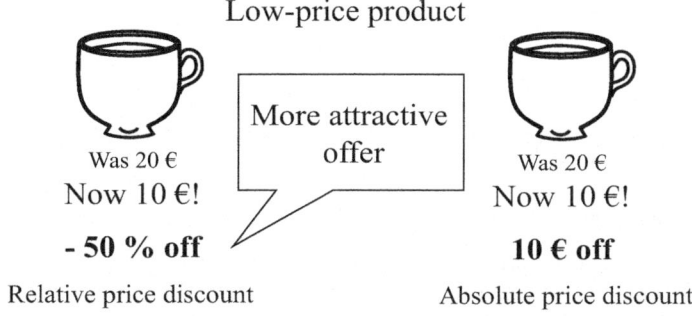

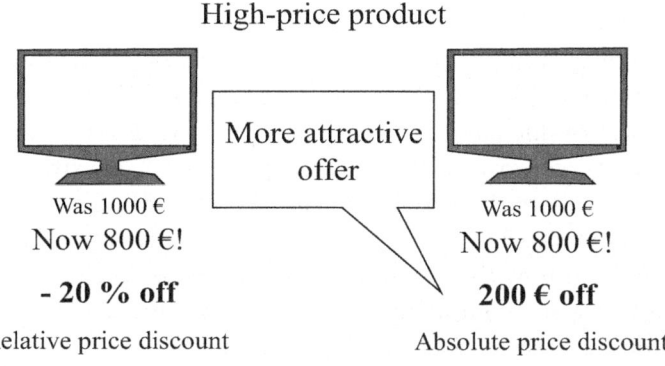

Fig. 4.19 Absolute vs. relative price discounts (Chen et al., 1998)

The study examined the impacts of these two factors on the consumers' decision to buy. More than 2,000 people participated in the study. People who actively participate in the grocery purchases of their household were recruited for the study. In short, the result was that a price cut has a stronger impact than a premium promotion, even when their monetary value was considered identical. This was true both for the products selected and the number of products purchased. A similar impact was apparent for nearly all of the products studied. Researchers also found that it made no difference what the free gift in the premium promotion was, or whether it was related to the product being purchased or not. Based on this study, we can say that a price cut has a more significant impact on consumers' choice behaviour than a free gift with an identical monetary value. This is true at least in the grocery segment. However, as Foubert et al. emphasise, managers need to consider the costs of price cuts too. Even though premium promotions seem to be less effective than equivalent price cuts, premiums may cost less than price cuts and thus, can in some cases be a more profitable promotion technique than price-based incentives.

Within- Versus Between-Store Price Promotion Cues

> **DID YOU KNOW?**
> – Between-store cues are an effective way to convince a customer that the deal being offered is good. This works only when the cues are concrete in nature. Cues which are abstract or vague may confuse the consumer or raise suspicions.

A common way of marketing a product on sale is to tell the consumer what the same product would cost at a competing store, or what it cost previously. Krishnan et al. conducted a study on the topic to determine which method is more effective; comparing the reduced price in an advertisement to the price in a nearby store (between-store cue), or comparing the reduced price in an advertisement to a previous price (within-store cue).[259] The researchers wanted to find out how the consumer is influenced by the target of the price comparison (price at a competing store vs. previous price). The experimental studies established that comparing the discounted price of a product to the price at a competing store had a bigger impact than comparing it to a previous price. When the price of the product was compared in an advertisement to the price in a competing store, the consumer considered the deal to be better, and was less interested in shopping around for an even lower price. However, Krishnan et al. emphasised the importance of making sure the comparison was concrete. Comparing with a competing nearby store must be done in very concrete and specific terms. Excessively abstract or vague price comparisons with competitors only serve to confuse the consumer and cause suspicion (Fig. 4.20).

Red Versus Black Prices

> **DID YOU KNOW?**
> – Male consumers tend to perceive greater savings when a price is shown in red instead of black.

---

[259] Krishnan et al. (2006).

4 Identifying Cues and Their Effects in a Retail Store

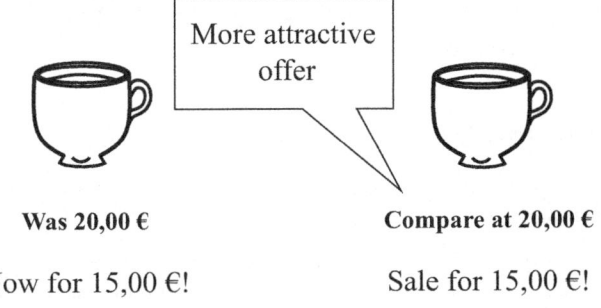

Fig. 4.20 Within- vs. between-store price promotion cues (Krishnan et al., 2006)

Retailers often like to use the colour red to indicate savings. Related to this, Puccinelli et al. conducted an interesting study and assessed the impact of red versus black prices on consumers' perceptions of savings.[260] The researchers wanted to find out whether the consumer felt they were saving more money when they bought a product with a red price tag or one with a black price tag.[261] The study had a particular focus on whether this opinion varied by gender. According to the results, male consumers felt they were saving more when the prices of the products were indicated in red instead of black in advertisements. The researchers believe this to be attributable to men using the red colour as a heuristic cue or a shortcut, leading them to believe a price indicated in red would be somehow a better offer than a price indicated in black, even when the actual prices were identical. Red also evokes positive feelings in men, which can be a contributing factor to why the colour red seems to indicate greater savings. The colours did not have a significant impact among women. According to the researchers, women are in a sense immune to impacts like this, as they tend to examine advertisements more closely than men. Among men, the impact of the colour red also became less pronounced as their level of involvement increased. Puccinelli et al. pointed

---

[260] Puccinelli, Chandrashekaran et al. (2013).

[261] The research participants were shown shop advertisements of toasters and microwave ovens. The advertisements given to the participants differed only in that the prices of the products were listed in either red or black. Otherwise they were entirely identical. After looking at the advertisements, participants had to evaluate how good they thought the offers were. To determine this, they were presented with statements, such as "I would save a great deal of money if I shopped at this store".

out that people are more likely to use heuristic cues to form judgements only in low involvement contexts.

Price Presentation Order

> **DID YOU KNOW?**
> – When differing brand options are presented in descending price order, consumers are likely to choose higher-price option, while presenting options in ascending price order makes consumers tend to choose lower-priced options.

Just whether differing brand options are presented in descending or ascending price order can affect consumers' choices. For example, Suk et al. demonstrated that it is most profitable to present prices to customers in a descending rather than an ascending order.[262] To be more specific, when differing brand options are presented in descending price order, consumers tend to choose higher-price options, while when brands are presented in ascending order, consumers are likely to choose lower-priced options. This is called "the price order effect". Suk et al. observed this effect across a wide array of research contexts. As Suk et al. elaborated, one explanation for this effect is that the brand options that are located on the top of a list act as reference values (reference points) for those other options that appear towards the bottom. Consequently, as consumers tend to use the options on the top as reference points, they are also likely to choose higher-price options in a descending price order (because reference value is high). In an ascending price order, this goes the other way around; consumers tend to choose lower-priced options because reference value (i.e., value on the top) is low.

Bagchi and Davis in turn explored an interesting question that when consumers consider a package price, which presentation order is more appealing; price first (e.g., 29€ for 70 items) or item quantity first (e.g., 70 items for 29€)[263]? Based on their three studies, Bagchi and Davis concluded that if calculating unit price becomes difficult, it is best to present quantity before price. However, Bagchi and Davis emphasised that presentation order should not be varied without proper testing. In general, the study

---

[262] Suk et al. (2012).
[263] Bagchi and Davis (2012).

indicates that consumers tend to anchor on the first piece of information that is provided to them, and this information is likely to affect their judgements.

Multiple-Unit Price Promotions

> **DID YOU KNOW?**
> – Multiple-unit pricing can generate a significant increase in sales compared to single-unit pricing.

It is well known that many customers tend to buy large quantities of products when exposed to various multiple-unit price promotions (quantity anchors) at the point-of-purchase. These volume promotions may increase buying even when the actual unit price is not changed with increased purchasing quantities. For example, the multiple-item offer "3 mugs for 15€" can stimulate consumers much more than single-item offer "1 mug for 5€". This kind of effect was found by Wansink et al. who demonstrated in their study that multiple-unit pricing can produce a significant increase in baseline sales compared to single-unit pricing.[264] The effect was found across numerous product categories. This finding indicates that just creating an image of the multiple-unit price being a great deal affects our choice behaviour. One can assume that multiple-unit pricing works primarily when involvement is low and consumers rely on heuristic decision-making (Fig. 4.21).

In their other studies, Wansink et al. also found that purchase quantity limits (such as "limit of 4 per person") increased sales (see also the chapter on the scarcity principle), and an explicit product quantity anchor (such as "Buy 18 Snickers bars for your freezer") increased consumers' purchase quantity intentions.[265] An interesting finding was that this explicit product quantity anchor increased purchase intentions even without a discount. Thus, the study conducted by Wansink et al. indicates that just a suggestive selling slogan at the point-of-purchase can boost sales even when the price is not discounted. This also means that shoppers and their purchase quantities can be affected without expensive marketing efforts.

---

[264] Wansink et al. (1998).
[265] Ibid.

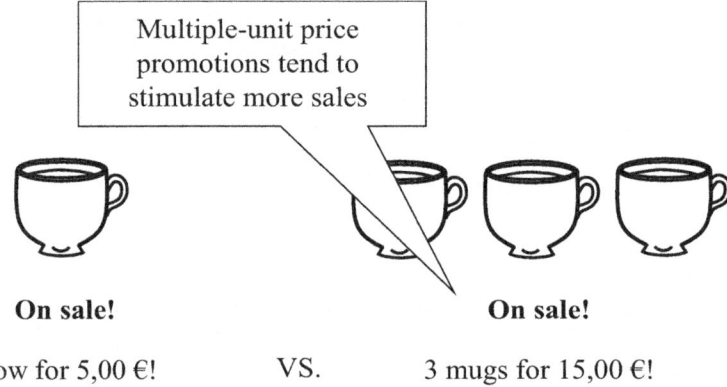

Fig. 4.21 Multiple-unit pricing (Wansink et al., 1998)

Setting Purchasing Goals and the Goal-Gradient Effect

> **DID YOU KNOW?**
> - Consumers are often encouraged to buy more with the help of various rewards (goals), and consumers may accelerate their purchasing as they progress towards the reward.

It is well known that our purchasing behaviour can be guided by rewards or purchasing goals. This is a common trick in retailing, and most loyalty programmes are based on the human psychology of rewards. Rewards that can affect us can be, for example, monetary-based rewards (e.g., "Buy five ice creams, get one free") or more abstract status-based rewards (e.g., "Red carpet treatment"). The most advanced programmes in retailing may have several tiers (such as Silver, Gold and Platinum levels) to enhance loyalty and, of course, to motivate customers to continue buying and purchasing more from the retailer. But what is truly interesting is that our tendency to approach a goal (e.g., the next reward) increases with proximity to the goal. Researchers have dubbed this the goal-gradient effect, which means that an individual's motivation to act increases or accelerates when they approach their goal (or they perceive themselves to be approaching the goal). One of the most important studies on this topic is Kivetz et al. from 2006.[266] The research team conducted a series of various experiments to determine the existence of the

---

[266] Kivetz et al. (2006).

goal-gradient effect. The studies were conducted in a real café among real customers. The research settings were carefully prepared.

In the first setting, the researchers gave café customers stamp cards which would give the customers a free coffee after they had collected ten stamps. The goal was to track how quickly the customers collected the ten stamps for their free coffee, and most importantly, whether the customers accelerated their purchases to get stamps when they approached their goal, a free coffee. The researchers collected nearly a thousand stamp cards, representing approximately 10,000 purchase transactions. The main finding was that the customers did, in fact, accelerate their purchases the closer they got to their free coffee. More specifically, the inter-purchase time (the time between one stamped purchase and the next one) decreased as the customer approached the goal. The researchers found that the difference between the first inter-purchase time and the last one was 0.7 days. This means that once the stamp card was filling up, the customers would get their last stamp approximately 20% faster than when they began collecting the stamps. On average, customers spent 24.6 days to gain ten stamps. The researchers calculated that if the frequency of the stamps had remained stable from the beginning, the collection of ten stamps would have taken 29.4 days. Thanks to the stamp card and the related goal-gradient effect, customers purchased two extra coffees per month, if compared to a situation where the stamp card was not present.

There was also another field study on the topic. The researchers gave some customers a stamp card which would give them a free coffee after collecting ten stamps, and other customers a stamp card which required 12 stamps for a free coffee. However, the 12-stamp card already had two stamps. This means that both customer groups had an identical number of stamps (ten) to collect for a free coffee. Interestingly, the people whose cards came with two stamps collected the necessary stamps more quickly than customers whose cards were not pre-stamped. Specifically, the customers with the ten-stamp card spent 15.6 days to gain a free coffee (i.e., to gain ten stamps), whereas customers with the twelve-stamp card with two stamps spent 12.7 days to gain a free coffee (i.e., to gain ten stamps). This means that the customers with the twelve-stamp card collected the necessary ten stamps three days (or 20%) faster than the customers with the ten-stamp card.

The researchers attribute this to illusionary goal progress. This means that the customer is given the impression that the distance to the goal is shorter than it is. As demonstrated in the study, if the goal is considered to be closer (whether or not this is actually the case), the customer will accelerate their behaviour. In other words, just the impression of the goal being close makes consumers change their behaviour. The research group also found that once the goal was reached, the consumers deaccelerated.

These findings are significant, and a good illustration of how very small things can result in big changes in consumer behaviour. Using the goal-gradient effect is a very subtle form of influencing, based on an in-depth understanding of the psychological processes of consumers.

4.7 Summary

This chapter has demonstrated that the store environment can be seen as a set of stimuli containing cues that may affect consumers' internal evaluations and ultimately their actual behaviour. Cues are generally understood as sensory stimuli (e.g., scents, light or sound) that we can sense during our stay in the store. Internal evaluations, in turn, refer basically either to our emotional responses or cognitive evaluations. Feeling happy or being excited can be seen as examples of emotional responses to cues that we sense, while changes in our attitudes, impressions or expectations can be seen examples of cognitive evaluations that cues may trigger in our mind. The effects may also bypass our internal evaluations, like in the case of subtle scents. Taken together, one can say that cues that we can sense with our sensory organs such eyes, nose and ears can affect how we feel, think or behave in a retail store during our shopping journey.

Furthermore, as this chapter has shown, the cue diversity in any given store is extremely extensive, encompassing the full range of cues from very abstract or even hidden ambient factors to very concrete and visible merchandise- and pricing-related cues. At the same time, this diversity means that there are cues that are likely to affect us from the background while some cues are related more directly to the moment of choice. One could say that some cues have a very persuasive style, whereas others are more subtle and have an indirect effect on us. It is also important to note that from a marketing perspective, some cues can be used to achieve immediate reactions among customers, such as impulse purchases, while others are to be used as long-term brand building tools. Thus, the nature of cues and their role in the retailer's business varies significantly.

One specific issue that the chapter has emphasised is related to the semantic meanings that cues convey to us. For example, colours are typically cues that convey specific meanings. Some interior design cues such as high ceilings or curvilinear forms can also communicate certain things to customers. In a similar vein, the weight of a product or tall and slender packages can indicate something to us. Some of the meanings that cues convey are rather obvious and perceived more or less in a similar manner among customers (like orange indicating low prices) but other meanings can be more complex and difficult to decode (like the meanings of shapes). Some intended meanings can be also interpreted differently between different groups (e.g., young vs. older consumers). Furthermore, meanings might change when cues are combined and interpreted as a whole. It is clear that understanding the meanings that cues actually convey is not the easiest task, but it is necessary for retailers to deploy the right cues in the right place at the right time.

This chapter has introduced cues as "cue-by-cue" or "sense-by-sense" style, but in real-life situations cues work in pairs or in other cue combinations. This highlights the fact that the retail store is multisensory in nature and we are affected by multisensory cues when we shop there. This is something that we delve into in Chapter 5.

Self-Reflective Questions
- When you walk into a store, what is the first thing you notice?
- What kinds of cues make you approach the store? What kinds of cues make you avoid the store?
- What kind of store do you think is aesthetically beautiful or pleasant? What kind of store design or colour palette appeals to you?
- On the basis of what kind of observations do you conclude that a store is very high-quality or affordable?
- What things annoy you or make you bored while shopping in a store?
- When you buy a product for the first time, how do you judge whether the product in question has good quality? What might raise your doubts about the quality of the product?
- What is the meaning of being able to touch the product? How important is it to you that you can feel the product or its packaging on your fingertips or in the palm of your hand?
- What kinds of products do you typically buy as impulse purchases?
- How do you feel and behave when you enter either an empty store or a very crowded environment?

> **Decision-Based Questions**
>
> - As a store manager, how would you name your store? What kinds of meanings does your chosen name seek to convey?
> - As a store manager, how would you use cues to attract consumers passing by and entice them to visit the store?
> - As a store manager, how would you use cues to encourage or guide customers to look around and browse the products in the store?
> - As a store manager, how would you use cues to lengthen the time that customers spend in the store?
> - As a store manager, how would you use cues to make the visit at the store as enjoyable as possible?
> - As a store manager, how would you use cues to increase unplanned impulse purchases?
> - As a store manager, how would you use cues to draw the customers' attention towards a certain product or category in the store?

References

Aboah, J., & Lees, N. (2020). Consumers use of quality cues for meat purchase: Research trends and future pathways. *Meat Science, 166*, 108142.

Ailawadi, K., & Keller, K. (2004). Understanding retail branding: Conceptual insights and research priorities. *Journal of Retailing, 80*, 331–342.

Ainsworth, J., & Foster, J. (2017). Comfort in brick and mortar shopping experiences: Examining antecedents and consequences of comfortable retail experiences. *Journal of Retailing and Consumer Services, 35*, 27–35.

Areni, C., & Kim, D. (1993). The influence of background music on shopping behavior: Classical versustop-forty music in a wine store, In L. McAlister & M. L. Rothschild (Eds.), *NA—Advances in Consumer Research* (Vol. 20, pp. 336–340). Provo, UT: Association for Consumer Research.

Areni, C., & Kim, D. (1994). The influence of in-store lighting on consumers' examination of merchandise in a wine store. *International Journal of Research in Marketing, 11*, 117–125.

Argo, J. J., Dahl, D. W., & Manchanda, R. V. (2005). The influence of a mere social presence in a retail context. *Journal of Consumer Research, 32*, 207–212.

Arshamian, A., Gerkin, R. C., Kruspe, N., Wnuk, E., Floyd, S., O'Meara, C., Garrido Rodriguez, G., Lindström, J. N., Mainland, J. D., & Majid, A. (2022). The perception of odor pleasantness is shared across cultures. *Current Biology, 32*, 2061–2066.

Aslam, M. (2006). Are you selling the right colour? A cross-cultural review of colour as a marketing cue. *Journal of Marketing Communications, 12*, 15–30.

Aydinli, A., Lamey, L., Millet, K., ter Braak, A., & Vuegen, M. (2020). How do customers alter their basket composition when they perceive the retail store to be crowded? An empirical study. *Journal of Retailing, 97*, 207–216.

Babin, B., Hardesty, D., & Suter, T. (2003). Color and shopping intentions: The intervening effect of price fairness and perceived affect. *Journal of Business Research, 56*, 541–551.

Bagchi, R., & Davis, D. F. (2012). 29 for 70 items or 70 items for 29? How presentation order affects package perceptions. *Journal of Consumer Research, 39*, 62–73.

Baker, J., Grewal, D., & Parasuraman, A. (1994). The influence of store environment on quality inferences and store image. *Journal of the Academy of Marketing Science, 22*, 328–339.

Baker, J., Levy, M., & Grewal, D. (1992). An experimental approach to making retail store environmental decisions. *Journal of Retailing, 68*, 445–460.

Baker, J., Parasuraman, A., Grewal, D., & Voss, G. (2002). The influence of multiple store environmental cues on perceived merchandise value and patronage intentions. *Journal of Marketing, 66*, 120–141.

Barone, M. J., Coulter, K. S., & Li, X. (2020). The upside of down: Presenting a price in a low or high location influences how consumers evaluate it. *Journal of Retailing, 96*, 397–410.

Becker, L., van Rompay, T. J., Schifferstein, H. N., & Galetzka, M. (2011). Tough package, strong taste: The influence of packaging design on taste impressions and product evaluations. *Food Quality and Preference, 22*, 17–23.

Bellizzi, J. A., Crowley, A. E., & Hasty, R. W. (1983). The effects of color in store design. *Journal of Retailing, 59*, 21–45.

Bellizzi, J. A., & Hite, R. E. (1992). Environmental color, consumer feelings, and purchase likelihood. *Psychology & Marketing, 9*, 347–363.

Berlyne, D. E. (1974). The new experimental aesthetics. In D. E. Berlyne (Ed.), *Studies in the new experimental aesthetics: Steps towards an objective psychology of aesthetic appreciation* (pp. 1–25).

Bialkova, S., Grunert, K., & van Trijp, H. (2020). From desktop to supermarket shelf: Eye-tracking exploration on consumer attention and choice. *Food Quality and Preference, 81*.

Biswas, D. (2019). Sensory aspects of retailing: Theoretical and practical implications. *Journal of Retailing, 95*, 111–115.

Biswas, D., Lund, K., & Szocs, C. (2019). Sounds like a healthy retail atmospheric strategy: Effects of ambient music and background noise on food sales. *Journal of the Academy of Marketing Science, 47*, 37–55.

Balkwill, L.-L., Thompson, W. F., & Matsunaga, R. (2004). Recognition of emotion in Japanese, Western, and Hindustani music by Japanese listeners. *Japanese Psychological Research, 46*, 337–349.

Brengman, M. (2002). *The impact of colour in the store environment: An environmental psychology approach*. Faculty of Economics and Business Administration, Ghent University.

Brumberger, E. R. (2003). The rhetoric of typography: The persona of typeface and text. *Technical Communication, 50*, 206–223.

Cai, F., Shen, H., & Hui, M. K. (2012). The effect of location on price estimation: Understanding number-location and number-order associations. *Journal of Marketing Research, 49*, 718–724.

Caivano, J. (2015). Color combination. In M. R. Luo (Ed.), *Encyclopedia of color science and technology* (pp. 1–8). Springer.

Caldwell, C., & Hibbert, S. (1999). Play that one again: The effect of music tempo on consumer behaviour in a restaurant. In B. Dubois, T. M. Lowrey, & L. J. Shrum, M. Vanhuele (Eds.), *E-European advances in consumer research* (Vol. 4, pp. 58–62). Provo, UT: Association for Consumer Research.

Castagna, A., Pinto, D., Mattila, A., & de Barcellos, M. (2021). Beauty-is-good, ugly-is-risky: Food aesthetics bias and construal level. *Journal of Business Research, 135*, 633–643.

Chandon, P., Hutchinson, J. W., Bradlow, E. T., & Young, S. H. (2007). Measuring the value of point-of-purchase marketing with commercial eye-tracking data. In M. Wedel & R. Pieters (Eds.), *Visual marketing: From attention to action* (pp. 225–258). Mahwah, NJ: Lawrence Erlbaum Associates.

Chandon, P., Hutchinson, J. W., Bradlow, E. T., & Young, S. H. (2009). Does in-store marketing work? Effects of the number and position of shelf facings on brand attention and evaluation at the point of purchase. *Journal of Marketing, 73*, 1–17.

Chartrand, T. L., & Bargh, J. A. (1999). The chameleon effect: The perception—Behavior link and social interaction. *Journal of Personality and Social Psychology, 76*, 893–910.

Cheema, A., & Patrick, V. M. (2012). Influence of warm versus cool temperatures on consumer choice: A resource depletion account. *Journal of Marketing Research, 49*, 984–995.

Chen, H., Pang, J., Koo, M., & Patrick, V. (2020). Shape matters: Package shape informs brand status categorization and brand choice. *Journal of Retailing, 96*, 266–281.

Chen, S. S., Monroe, K. B., & Lou, Y. (1998). The effects of framing price promotion messages on consumer's perceptions and purchase intentions. *Journal of Retailing, 74*, 353–372.

Childers, T. L., & Jass, J. (2002). All dressed up with something to say: Effects of typeface semantic associations on brand perceptions and consumer memory. *Journal of Consumer Psychology, 12*, 93–106.

Choi, S. M., & Kang, M. (2013). The effect of typeface on advertising and brand evaluations: The role of semantic congruence. *The Journal of Advertising and Promotion Research, 2*, 25–52.

Cialdini, R., & Goldstein, N. (2002). The science and practice of persuasion. *The Cornell Hotel and Restaurant Administration Quarterly, 43*, 40–50.

Coskun, M., Gupta, S., & Burnaz, S. (2020). Store disorderliness effect: Shoppers' competitive behaviours in a fast-fashion retail store. *International Journal of Retail & Distribution Management, 48*, 763–779.

Coulter, K. S. (2001). Odd-ending price underestimation: An experimental examination of left-to-right processing effects. *Journal of Product and Brand Management, 10*, 276–292.

Custers P., de Kort Y., IJsselsteijn, W., & de Kruiff M. (2010). Lighting in retail environments: Atmosphere perception in the real world. *Lighting Research & Technology, 42*, 331–343.

Dahm, M., Wentzel, D., Herzog, W., & Wiecek, A. (2018). Breathing down your neck!: The impact of queues on customers using a retail service. *Journal of Retailing, 94*, 217–230.

Das, G., Mukherjee, A., & Smith, R. (2018). The perfect fit: The moderating role of selling cues on hedonic and utilitarian product types. *Journal of Retailing, 94*, 203–216.

Day, H. (1967). Evaluation of subjective complexity, pleasingness, and interestingness for a series of random polygons varying in complexity. *Perception and Psychophysics, 2*, 281–286.

De Luca, R., & Botelho, D. (2019). The unconscious perception of smells as a driver of consumer responses: A framework integrating the emotion-cognition approach to scent marketing. *AMS Review, 11*, 145–161.

Diallo, M. F., Coutelle-Brillet, P., Rivière, A., & Zielke, S. (2015). How do price perceptions of different brand types affect shopping value and store loyalty? *Psychology of Marketing, 32*, 1133–1147.

Dodds, W., & Grewal, D. (1991). Effects of Price, Brand, and Store Information on Buyers' Product Evaluation. *Journal of Marketing Research, 28*, 307–331.

Drèze, X., Hoch, S. J., & Purk, M. E. (1994). Shelf management and space elasticity. *Journal of Retailing, 70*, 301–326.

Dzebic, V. (2018). *Emotions and the environment: The variable effect of environmental complexity on pleasure and interest*. UWSpace.

Ebster, C., & Garaus, M. (2011). *Store design and visual merchandising: Creating store space that encourages buying*. Business Expert Press.

Erdem, T., Keane, M. P., & Sun, B. (2008). A dynamic model of brand choice when price and advertising signal product quality. *Marketing Science, 27*, 1111–1125.

Eroglu, S. A., Machleit, K. A., & Chebat, J.-C. (2005). The interaction of retail density and music tempo: Effects on shopper responses. *Psychology & Marketing, 22*, 577–589.

Foubert, B., Breugelmans, E., Gedenk, K., & Rolef, C. (2018). Something free or something off? A comparative study of the purchase effects of premiums and price cuts. *Journal of Retailing, 94*, 5–20.

Garaus, M. (2017). Atmospheric harmony in the retail environment: Its influence on store satisfaction and re-patronage intention. *Journal of Consumer Behaviour, 16*, 265–278.

Gardner, M. P., & Siomkos, G. J. (1985). Toward a methodology for assessing effects of in-store atmospherics. In R. J. Lutz (Ed.), *NA—Advances in consumer research* (Vol. 13, pp. 27–31). Chicago: Association for Consumer Research.

Garlin, F. V., & Owen, K. (2006). Setting the tone with the tune: A meta-analytic review of the effects of background music in retail settings. *Journal of Business Research, 59*, 755–764.

Gendall, P. (1998). Estimating the effect of odd pricing. *Journal of Product & Brand Management, 7*, 421–443.

Graciola, A. P., Toni, D. D., Milan, G. S., & Eberle, L. (2020). Mediated-moderated effects: High and low store image, brand awareness, perceived value from mini and supermarkets retail stores. *Journal of Retailing and Consumer Services, 55*.

Grewal, D., Krishnan, R., Baker, J., & Borin, N. (1998). The effect of store name, brand name and price discounts on consumers' evaluations and purchase intentions. *Journal of Retailing, 74*, 331–352.

Grigelova, N. (2019). *Nespresso brand book*. https://issuu.com/nel.grigelova/docs/nespresso_brand_book_

Halko, M.-L., & Hytönen, K. (2014). Sosiaalinen ympäristö ja kuluttajien käyttäytyminen. *Kansantaloudellinen Aikakauskirja, 110*, 466–476.

Hamilton, R., & Chernev, A. (2013). Low prices are just the beginning: Price image in retail management. *Journal of Marketing, 77*, 1–20.

Harrell, E. (2019). Neuromarketing: What you need to know. *Harvard Business Review*.

Hofmann, V., Stokburger-Sauer, N., Wanisch, A., & Hebborn, H. (2021). Masked smiles matter—Employee verbal expertise and emotion display during COVID-19. *The Service Industries Journal, 41*, 107–137.

Holland, R. W., Hendriks, M., & Aarts, H. (2005). Smells like clean spirit: Nonconscious effects of scent on cognition and behavior. *Psychological Science, 16*, 689–693.

Horiguchi, S., & Iwamatsu, K. (2018). From Munsell color system to a new color psychology system. *Color Research & Application, 43*, 827–839.

Hultén, B., Broweus, N., & van Dijk, M. (2009). *Sensory marketing*. Palgrave Macmillan.

Hunter, P. G., Schellenberg, E. G., & Schimmack, U. (2010). Feelings and perceptions of happiness and sadness induced by music: Similarities, differences, and mixed emotions. *Psychology of Aesthetics, Creativity, and the Arts, 4*, 47–56.

Hutmacher, F. (2019). Why is there so much more research on vision than on any other sensory modality? *Frontiers in Psychology, 10*, 2246.

Imada, K. (2021). *You can now stream Muji's in-store music at home for free*. https://www.timeout.com/tokyo/news/you-can-now-stream-mujis-in-store-music-at-home-for-free-052521. Accessed 23 January 2023.

Inman, J. J., Peter, A. C., & Raghubir, P. (1997). Framing the deal: The role of restrictions in accentuating deal value. *Journal of Consumer Research, 24*, 68–79.

Introducing Amazon 4-Star. (2018). https://www.aboutamazon.com/news/retail/introducing-amazon-4-star. Accessed 17 September 2023.

Iyengar, S. S., & Lepper, M. R. (2000). When choice is demotivating: Can one desire too much of a good thing? *Journal of Personality and Social Psychology, 79*.

Izadi, A., Rudd, M., & Patrick, V. M. (2019). The way the wind blows: Direction of airflow energizes consumers and fuels creative engagement. *Journal of Retailing, 95*, 143–157.

Jakubowski, K., & Francini, E. (2023). Differential effects of familiarity and emotional expression of musical cues on autobiographical memory properties. *Quarterly Journal of Experimental Psychology., 76*, 2001–2016.

Jang, J. Y., Baek, E., Yoon, S. Y., & Choo, H. J. (2018). Store design: Visual complexity and consumer responses. *International Journal of Design, 12*, 105–118.

Jha, S., Balaji, M., Peck, J., Oakley, J., & Deitz, G. (2020). The effects of environmental haptic cues on consumer perceptions of retailer warmth and competence. *Journal of Retailing, 96*, 590–605.

Johnston, L. (2002). Behavioral mimicry and stigmatization. *Social Cognition., 20*, 18–35.

Joyner, S. (2020). *The psychology of high ceilings and creative work spaces*. Archinect. https://archinect.com/features/article/150193563/the-psychology-of-high-ceilings-and-creative-work-spaces

Kahn, B., & Wansink, B. (2004). The influence of assortment structure on perceived variety and consumption quantities. *Journal of Consumer Research, 30*, 519–533.

Kampfer, K., Leischnig, A., Björn, S. I., & Spence, C. (2017). Touch-flavor transference: Assessing the effect of packaging weight on gustatory evaluations, desire for food and beverages, and willingness to pay. *PLoS One, 12*.

Kaplan, R., & Kaplan, S. (1989). *The experience of nature—A psychological perspective*. Cambridge University Press.

Kaplan, R., Kaplan, S., & Brown, T. (1989). Environmental preference: A comparison of four domains of predictors. *Environment and Behavior, 21*, 509–530.

Kaplan, S. (1987). Aesthetics, affect, and cognition: Environmental preference from an evolutionary perspective. *Environment and Behavior, 19*, 3–32.

Kellaris, J., & Rice, R. (1993). The influence of tempo, loudness, and gender of listener on responses to music. *Psychology and Marketing, 10*, 15–29.

Kemp, E. A., Williams, K., Min, D.-J., & Chen, H. (2019). Happy feelings: Examining music in the service environment. *International Hospitality Review, 33*, 5–15.

Kerfoot, S., Davies, B., & Ward, P. (2003). Visual merchandising and the creation of discernible retail brands. *International Journal of Retail & Distribution Management, 31*, 143–152.

Kerin, R. A., Jain, A., & Howard, D. J. (1992). Store shopping experience and consumer price-quality-value perceptions. *Journal of Retailing, 68*.

Kivetz, R., Urminsky, O., & Zheng, Y. (2006). The goal-gradient hypothesis resurrected: Purchase acceleration, illusionary goal progress, and customer retention. *Journal of Marketing Research, 43*, 39–58.

Klink, R. R. (2000). Creating brand names with meaning: The use of sound symbolism. *Marketing Letters, 11*, 5–20.

Kobayashi, S. (1991). *Color image scale*. Kodansha International.

Krishna, A. (2012). An integrative review of sensory marketing: Engaging the senses to affect perception, judgment and behaviour. *Journal of Consumer Psychology., 22*, 332–351.

Krishna, A., Briesch, R., Lehmann, D., & Yuan, H. (2002). A meta-analysis of the impact of price presentation on perceived savings. *Journal of Retailing, 78*, 101–118.

Krishna, A., Elder, R., & Caldara, C. (2010). Feminine to smell but masculine to touch? Multisensory congruence and its effect on the aesthetic experience. *Journal of Consumer Psychology, 20*, 410–418.

Krishnan, B. C., Biswas, A., & Netemeyer, R. G. (2006). Semantic cues in reference price advertisements: The moderating role of cue concreteness. *Journal of Retailing, 82*, 95–104.

Kuisma, O. (2010). *Kauneus*. Ensyklopedia Logos. Filosofia.fi.

Kumar, A., & Kim, Y.-K. (2014). The store-as-a-brand strategy: The effect of store environment on customer responses. *Journal of Retailing and Consumer Services, 21*, 685–695.

Laroche, M., Papadopoulos, N., Heslop, L. A., & Mourali, M. (2005). The influence of country image structure on consumer evaluations of foreign products. *International Marketing Review, 22*, 96–115.

Larson, R. B. (2014). Psychological pricing principles for organizations with market power. *The Journal of Applied Business and Economics, 16*, 11–25.

Lee, H. K., Yoon, S., Lee, J. Y., Kim, H. B., Kwon, H. J., Kang, H., Hur, H. J., Lee, M., & Jun, D. (2015). The effects of sale signs on consumer intentions to visit a store. *Journal of Global Fashion Marketing, 6*, 20–32.

Lindström, M. (2005). *BRAND sense: Building powerful brands through touch, taste, smell*. Free Press.

Liu, S. Q., Choi, S., & Mattila, A. S. (2019). Love is in the menu: Leveraging healthy restaurant brands with handwritten typeface. *Journal of Business Research, 98*, 289–298.

Liu, S., Bogicevic, V., & Mattila, A. (2018). Circular vs. angular servicescape: "Shaping" customer response to a fast service encounter pace. *Journal of Business Research, 89*, 47–56.

Ludmila Bandeira, L. B., de La Martinière Petroll, M., Damacena, C., & Knoppe, M. (2019). Store atmosphere and impulse: A cross-cultural study [Store atmosphere and impulse]. *International Journal of Retail & Distribution Management, 47*, 817–835.

Ludwig, V., & Simner, J. (2013). What colour does that feel? Tactile–visual mapping and the development of cross-modality. *Cortex, 49*, 1089–1099.

Martin, B. (2012). A stranger's touch: Effects of accidental interpersonal touch on consumer evaluations and shopping time. *Journal of Consumer Research, 39*, 174–184.

Mattila, A. S., & Wirtz, J. (2001). Congruency of scent and music as a driver of in-store evaluations and behavior. *Journal of Retailing, 77*, 273–289.

McAlister, L., & Pessemier, E. (1982). Variety seeking behavior: An interdisciplinary review. *Journal of Consumer Research, 9*, 311–322.

McCabe, D., & Nowlis, S. (2003). The effect of examining actual products or product descriptions on consumer preference. *Journal of Consumer Psychology, 13*, 431–439.

Meyers-Levy, J., & Zhu, R. (2007). The influence of ceiling height: The effect of priming on the type of processing that people use. *Journal of Consumer Research, 34*, 174–186.

Milliman, R. E. (1982). Using background music to affect the behaviour of supermarket shoppers. *Journal of Marketing, 46*, 86–91.

Milliman, R. E. (1986). The influence of background music on the behavior of restaurant patrons. *Journal of Consumer Research, 13*, 286–289.

Morales, A., Kahn, B., McAlister, L., & Broniarczk, S. M. (2005). Perceptions of assortment variety: The effects of congruency between consumers' internal and retailers' external organisation. *Journal of Retailing, 81*, 159–169.

Morrin, M., & Ratneshwar, S. (2000). The impact of ambient scent on evaluation, attention, and memory for familiar and unfamiliar brands. *Journal of Business Research, 49*, 157–165.

Morrin, M., & Ratneshwar, S. (2003). Does it make sense to use scents to enhance brand memory? *Journal of Marketing Research, 40*, 10–25.

Murray, J., Elms, J., & Teller, C. (2015). Consumer perceptions of higher and lower-level designed store environments. *The International Review of Retail, Distribution and Consumer Research, 25*, 473–489.

Neumann, N., Böckenholt, U., & Sinha, A. (2016). A meta-analysis of extremeness aversion. *Journal of Consumer Psychology, 26*, 193–212.

North, A. C., Hargreaves, D. J., & McKendrick, J. (1997). In-store music affects product choice. *Nature, 390*.

Oakes, S. (2003). Musical tempo and waiting perceptions. *Psychology & Marketing, 20*, 685–705.

Ode, Å., Hagerhall, C., & Sang, N. (2010). Analysing visual landscape complexity: Theory and application. *Landscape Research, 35*, 111–131.

Oh, H., & Petrie, J. (2012). How do storefront window displays influence entering decisions of clothing stores? *Journal of Retailing and Consumer Services, 19*, 27–35.

Otterbring, T., Wästlund, E., & Gustfasson, A. (2016). Eye-tracking customers' visual attention in the wild: Dynamic gaze behavior moderates the effect of store familiarity on navigational fluency. *Journal of Retailing and Consumer Services, 28*, 165–170.

Parasuraman, A., Zeithaml, V. A., & Berry, L. (1985). A conceptual model of service quality and its implications for future research. *Journal of Marketing, 49*, 41–50.

Park, N.-K., & Farr, C. A. (2007). The effects of lighting on consumers' emotions and behavioral intentions in a retail environment: A cross-cultural comparison. *Journal of Interior Design, 33*, 17–32.

Patton, W. E. (1981). Quantity of information and information display type as a predictor of consumer choice of product brands. *Journal of Consumer Affairs, 15*, 92–105.

Peck, J., & Childers, T. L. (2003). Individual differences in haptic information processing: The "Need for Touch" scale. *Journal of Consumer Research, 30*, 430–442.

Pecoraro, M., & Uusitalo, O. (2014). Exploring the everyday retail experience: The discourses of style and design. *Journal of Consumer Behaviour, 13*, 429–441.

Piha, S. (2018). *Evolutionary psychology for consumers: Awareness of ultimate explanations as a self-reflective tool for consumer empowerment* (Doctoral dissertation). University of Turku.

Piqueras-Fiszman, B., & Spence, C. (2011). Do the material properties of cutlery affect the perception of the food you eat? An exploratory study. *Journal of Sensory Studies, 26*, 358–362.

Piqueras-Fiszman, B., & Spence, C. (2012). The weight of the container influences expected satiety, perceived density, and subsequent expected fullness. *Appetite, 58*, 559–562.

Piqueras-Fiszman, B., Harrar, V., Alcaide, J., & Spence, C. (2011). Does the weight of the dish influence our perception of food? *Food Quality and Preference, 22*, 753–756.

Puccinelli, N., Andrzejewski, S., Markos, E., Noga, T., & Motyka, S. (2013). The value of knowing what customers really want: The impact of salesperson ability to read non-verbal cues of affect on service quality. *Journal of Marketing Management, 29*, 356–373.

Puccinelli, N., Chandrashekaran, R., Grewal, D., & Suri, R. (2013). Are men seduced by red? The effect of red versus black prices on price perceptions. *Journal of Retailing, 89*, 115–125.

Pugh, S. D. (2001). Service with a smile: Emotional contagion in the service encounter. *The Academy of Management Journal, 44*, 1018–1027.

Ranaweera, A., Martin, B., & Jin, H. (2021). What you touch, touches you: The influence of haptic attributes on consumer product impressions. *Psychology & Marketing, 38*, 183–195.

Reber, R. (2011). Processing fluency, aesthetic pleasure, and culturally shared taste. In A. P. Shimamura, & S. E. Palmer (Eds.), *Aesthetic science: Connecting minds, brains, and experience* (2011; online ed., 19 January 2012). Oxford Academic.

Robertson, K. (1989). Strategically desirable brand name characteristics. *Journal of Consumer Marketing, 6*, 61–71.

Roggeveen, A. L., Grewal, D., & Schweiger, E. B. (2020). The DAST framework for retail atmospherics: The impact of in- and out-of-store retail journey touchpoints on the customer experience. *Journal of Retailing, 96*, 128–137.

Roschk, H., & Hosseinpour, M. (2020). Pleasant ambient scents: A meta-analysis of customer responses and situational contingencies. *Journal of Marketing, 84*, 125–145.

Scheibehenne, B., Greifeneder, R., & Todd, P. (2010). Can there ever be too many options? A meta-analytic review of choice overload. *Journal of Consumer Research, 37*, 409–425.

Schifferstein, H., & Blok, S. (2002). The signal function of thematically (in)congruent ambient scents in a retail environment. *Chemical Senses, 27*, 539–549.

Schindler, R., & Kibarian, T. (2001). Image communicated by the use of 99 endings in advertised prices. *Journal of Advertising, 30*, 95–99.

Schloss, K. B., & Palmer, S. E. (2011). Aesthetic response to color combinations: Preference, harmony, and similarity. *Attention, Perception, & Psychophysics, 73*, 551–571.

Schroll, R., Schnurr, B., & Grewal, D. (2018). Humanizing products with handwritten typefaces. *Journal of Consumer Research, 45*, 648–672.

Shao, C. Y., Baker, J., & Wagner, J. A. (2004). The effects of appropriateness of service contact personnel dress on customer expectations of service quality and purchase intention: The moderating influences of involvement and gender. *Journal of Business Research, 57*, 1164–1176.

Simonson, I., & Tversky, A. (1992). Choice in context: Tradeoff contrast and extremeness aversion. *Journal of Marketing Research, XXIX*, 281–295.

Singh, S. (2006). Impact of color on marketing. *Management Decision, 44*, 783–789.

Smith, P., & Burns, D. J. (1996). Atmospherics and retail environments: The case of the "power aisle"". *International Journal of Retail & Distribution Management, 24*, 7–14.

Smith, P. C., & Curnow, R. (1966). Arousal hypothesis" and the effects of music on purchasing behavior. *Journal of Applied Psychology, 50*, 255–256.

Soars, B. (2009). Driving sales through shoppers' sense of sound, sight, smell and touch. *International Journal of Retail & Distribution Management, 37*, 286–298.

Solli, M., & Lenz, R. (2010). *Color semantics for image indexing*. CGIV 2010 final program and proceedings. Society for Imaging Science and Technology.

Song, H., & Schwarz, N. (2009). If it's difficult to pronounce, it must be risky: Fluency, familiarity, and risk perception. *Psychological Science, 20*, 135–138.

Spangenberg, E., Crowley, A., & Henderson, P. (1996). Improving the store environment: Do olfactory cues affect evaluations and behaviors? *Journal of Marketing, 60*, 67–80.

Spangenberg, E. R., Sprott, D. E., Grohmann, B., & Tracy, D. L. (2006). Gender-congruent ambient scent influences on approach and avoidance behaviours in a retail store. *Journal of Business Research, 59*, 1281–1287.

Spence, C. (2020). Senses of place: Architectural design for the multisensory mind. *Cognitive Research: Principles and Implications, 5*, 46.

Spence, C., Puccinelli, N. M., Grewal, D., & Roggeveen, A. L. (2014). Store atmospherics: A multisensory perspective. *Psychology & Marketing, 31*, 472–488.

Stafford, J. (1969). The price-quality relationship: An extension. *Journal of Marketing Research, 6*.

Steinhoff, L., & Palmatier, R. W. (2016). Understanding loyalty program effectiveness: Managing target and bystander effects. *Journal of the Academy of Marketing Science, 44*, 88–107.

Suk, K., Lee, J., & Lichtenstein, D. R. (2012). The influence of price presentation order on consumer choice. *Journal of Marketing Research, 49*, 708–717.

Summers, T., & Hebert, P. (2001). Shedding some light on store atmospherics: Influence of illumination on consumer behavior. *Journal of Business Research, 54*, 145–150.

Sunaga, T., Park, J., & Spence, C. (2016). Effects of lightness-location congruency on consumers' purchase decision-making. *Psychology & Marketing, 33*, 934–950.

Sweeney, J. C., & Wyber, F. (2002). The role of cognitions and emotions in the music-approach-avoidance behavior relationship. *Journal of Services Marketing, 16*, 51–69.

Teas, R., & Agarwal, S. (2000). The effects of extrinsic product cues on consumers' perceptions of quality, sacrifice, and value. *Journal of the Academy of Marketing Science., 28*, 278–290.

Turley, L. W., & Milliman, R. E. (2000). Atmospheric effects on shopping behavior: A review of the experimental evidence. *Journal of Business Research, 49*, 193–211.

Underhill, P. (1999). *Why we buy: The science of shopping*. Simon & Schuster.

Valdez, P., & Mehrabian, J. (1994). Effect of color on emotions. *Journal of Experimental Psychology: General, 123*, 394–409.

Valenzuela, A., & Raghubir, P (2009). Center of orientation: Effect of vertical and horizontal shelf space product position. In A. L. McGill & S. Shavitt (Eds.), *NA—Advances in consumer research* (Vol. 36, pp. 100–103). Duluth, MN: Association for Consumer Research.

Wall, M., Liefeld, J., & Heslop, L. A. (1991). Impact of country-of-origin cues on consumer judgments in multi-cue situations: A covariance analysis. *Journal of the Academy of Marketing Science, 19*, 105–113.

Wansink, B., Kent, R. J., & Hoch, S. J. (1998). An anchoring and adjustment model of purchase quantity decisions. *Journal of Marketing Research, 35*, 71–81.

Ward, P., Davies, B. J., & Kooijman, D. (2007). Olfaction and the retail environment: Examining the influence of ambient scent. *Service Business, 1*, 295–316.

Wheatly, J., & Chiu, J. (1977). The effects of price, store image, and product and respondent characteristics on perceptions of quality. *Journal of Marketing Research, XIV*, 181–186.

Wieseke, J., Kolberg, A., & Schons, L. M. (2016). Life could be so easy: The convenience effect of round price endings. *Journal of the Academy of Marketing Science, 44*, 474–494.

Willis, J., & Todorov, A. (2006). First impressions: Making up your mind after a 100-Ms exposure to a face. *Psychological Science, 17*, 592–598.

Xu, Y. (2007). Impact of store environment on adult generation Y consumers' impulse buying. *Journal of Shopping Center Research, 14*, 39–56.

Yalch, R., & Spangenberg, E. (1990). Effects of Store music on shopping behavior. *Journal of Consumer Marketing, 7*, 55–63.

Yalch, R., & Spangenberg, E. (2000). The effects of music in a retail setting on real and perceived shopping times. *Journal of Business Research, 49*, 139–147.

Yan, R., Yurchisin, J., & Watchravesringkan, K. (2011). Does formality matter? Effects of employee clothing formality on consumers' service quality expectations and store image perceptions. *International Journal of Retail & Distribution Management, 39*, 346–362.

Yi, F., & Kang, J. (2019). Effect of background and foreground music on satisfaction, behavior, and emotional responses in public spaces of shopping malls. *Applied Acoustics, 145*, 408–419.

Yorkston, E., & Menon, G. (2004). A sound idea: Phonetic effects of brand names on consumer judgments. *Journal of Consumer Research, 31*, 43–51.

Zhou, C., & Yamanaka, T. (2018). How does congruence of scent and music affect people's emotions. How does congruence of scent and music affect people's emotions. *International Journal of Affective Engineering, 17*, 127–136.

Zwebner, Y., Lee, L., & Goldenberg, J. (2014). The temperature premium: Warm temperatures increase product valuation. *Journal of Consumer Psychology, 24*, 251–259.

5

The Multisensory Nature of a Retail Store and Joint Effects of Cues

5.1 From Unisensory to Multisensory Approaches

The physical retail setting is a multisensory environment which addresses many of our senses simultaneously. This means that we are exposed to many different cues while shopping. As we move through a store, our senses are constantly collecting information on visual stimuli, scents and sounds, even if we are not consciously aware of it. Thus, the multisensory nature of our perception highlights the fact that cues should not be considered independently, but rather as a whole. As the retail environment is multisensory in nature, it is important to understand how cues work together, and what kinds of joint effects[1] the cues we encounter may have.

> The cosmetics chain **Lush** is an example of a retail company which conducts most of its customer influencing through sensory stimulation. Visiting a Lush store is an intensely multisensory experience. The stores combine a black-and-white colour scheme with natural wood and feature many enjoyable scents, with colourful products of various shapes sporting amusing names arranged in impressive displays. Customers can touch and try the products when shopping at a Lush store, and testing the products has been made very easy. Store staff also encourage customers entering the store to try the products.

---

[1] In this book, the term "joint effect" is used to describe the effects that occur when two or more cues (e.g., music and scents) work in combination.

It is rather clear that traditional sense-by-sense approaches, where the focus is on just one sense at a time, have significant limitations and shortcomings in multisensory environments such as retail stores. Thus, it is not surprising that researchers have become more and more interested in how our senses work together, and how our mind collates the information provided by our senses. The way we process information in multisensory environments is often explained by focusing on multisensory integration and cross-modal sensory interaction.

5.2 1 + 1 + 1 = 4

The general understanding is that the multisensory nature of the retail store forms a strong base for positive shopper perceptions and behaviour.[2] In other words, the retailer can offer enjoyable and satisfying shopping experiences and might even evoke "wow" moments for their customers if they create stimulating multisensory store environments. While empirical research on multisensory experiences is still rather limited, studies so far would appear to suggest that configurations of multisensory stimuli in a retail store are generally a positive thing, i.e., the richer the sensory experiences, the more positive the outcomes.[3]

In more theoretical terms, one could say that to interact effectively with a multisensory retail environment, our brains integrate and combine various kinds of information from multiple sources into a coherent and meaningful percept.[4] This is termed multisensory integration. Yau et al. give a clear definition of multisensory integration by writing that it refers to "[…] the process by which inputs (information) from two or more sensory modalities are combined by the nervous system to form a stable and coherent percept of the world. Multisensory integration enhances our ability to perceive and understand our environment, enabling us to move and interact with objects in our surroundings".[5] One could say that multisensory integration is critical for our perception of the store environment and understanding of it as a whole. By integrating information from different senses, for example, combining visual information with sounds and scents, we are able to create unique perceptual experiences in the store environment. The multisensory

---

[2] See, e.g., Helmefalk and Hultén (2017).
[3] See e.g., Mattila and Wirtz (2001), Imschloss and Kuehnl (2017), and Helmefalk (2017).
[4] Werner and Noppeney (2010) and Holmes et al. (2009).
[5] Yau et al. (2015, p. 1).

integration could even be called the thing that ultimately shapes our impressions and shopping experiences while we are at the store. Thus, the way we integrate sensory information largely affects how we perceive the store and how we shop. For example, whether we perceive a store as a trendy, affordable or high quality is based on the fusion of information in our mind.

An interesting feature of multisensory integration is that cues in the shopping environment which engage our senses may have a much stronger impact on us when used together than they would when used individually.[6] This effect is called the "superadditive multisensory response". Spence et al. specify that a superadditive response occurs: "[…] when presenting two or more sensory inputs simultaneously gives rise to a response (behavioural or neural) that is significantly greater than the impact of the individual signals".[7] More broadly speaking, this is a sign of "multisensory enhancement", meaning essentially that synergistic effects arise when various sensory cues are processed and integrated in our mind.[8]

However, superadditivity is not something that automatically appears in a multisensory environment. Based on studies in the area of multisensory integration, superadditivity is likely to arise when sensory cues occur at the same time and place and the cues are relatively weak but congruent.[9] Cue congruence in particular is seen as prerequisite for enhanced responses in a physical retail setting (this is discussed later in more detail).[10] Greater multisensory integration and potentially enhanced responses are also related to stimuli with low intensity (the principle of inverse effectiveness).[11] Figure 5.1 describes the basic idea of multisensory integration and multisensory enhancement.

Such a superadditive multisensory response was observed in a study that focused on the impacts of three distinct but congruent cues on consumer shopping behaviour.[12] The cues selected for the study were scent, background music and a visual cue. The visual cue was a set of three-metre red curtains placed behind the product shelf, the background music was jazz and there was a faint scent deployed via a hidden diffuser. In other words, each of the selected cues stimulated a specific sense of the customer. The study was carried out over 12 weeks in the lighting department of a furniture store. The main finding was that when all three cues were used simultaneously,

---

[6] Helmefalk (2017) and Spence et al. (2014).
[7] Spence et al. (2014, p. 481).
[8] Stein et al. (2009) and Stanford and Stein (2007).
[9] Holmes and Spence (2005), Calvert and Thesen (2004), Stanford et al. (2005), and Spence et al. (2014).
[10] Spence et al. (2014).
[11] Stein et al. (2020) and Senkowski et al. (2011).
[12] Helmefalk and Berndt (2018).

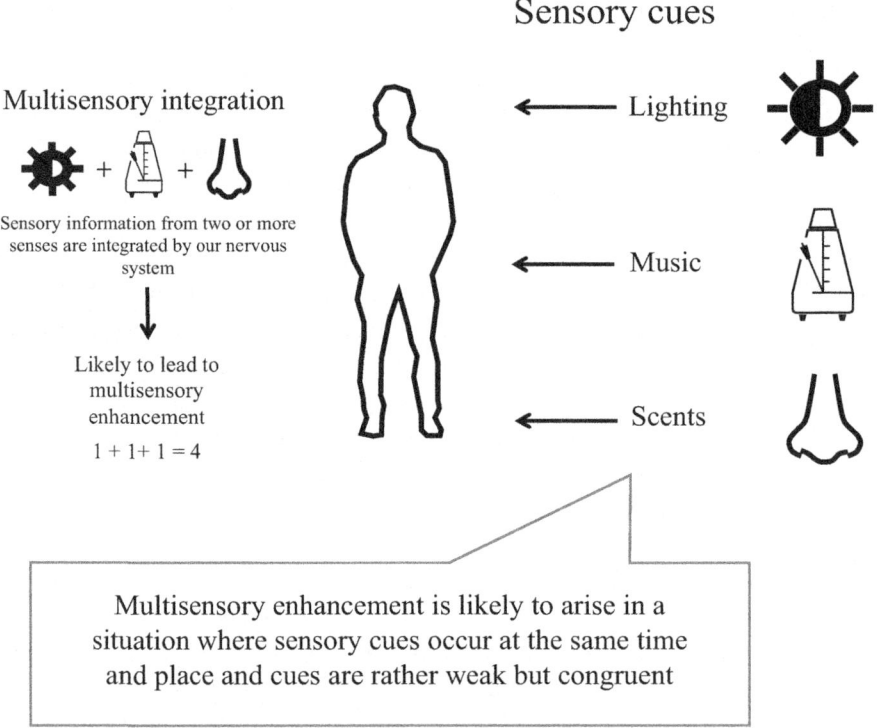

Fig. 5.1 Multisensory integration and multisensory enhancement (e.g., Spence et al., 2014; Stein & Stanford, 2008; Stanford et al., 2005)

they had a bigger impact than when the consumer was only exposed to one of the cues. According to the study, exposure to all three cues (constituting a congruent multisensory cue) significantly increased the amount of purchases and the time spent in the store. The researchers found that consumers were up to three times more likely to buy a product when all three cues were used simultaneously when compared to other cue settings that were tested. This demonstrates how great an impact cues can have when used together.

Although empirical studies such as the one described above are scarce in the field of retailing, multisensory integration has been more extensively studied in the field of neuroscience. In short, neuroscientific studies have demonstrated that multisensory integration enhances performance in several perceptual and behavioural domains.[13] One good example of multisensory integration and enhanced responses is related to learning. Our ability to learn has been found to be better when we are exposed to a multisensory experience

---

[13] Stein and Stanford (2008) and Stein et al. (2020).

(e.g., training with auditory–visual stimuli).[14] There are also studies that have demonstrated that our responses to multisensory experiences tend to be faster and more accurate than responses to the stimuli presented in isolation.[15] One could say that the general message of these studies is that "two is better than one".

Thus, we could sum up above discussion on multisensory integration with the help of the playful formula $1 + 1 + 1 = 4$. This means that in an optimal situation, different cues support or complement each other, and together generate a synergistic join effect which is more than the actual sum of the individual cues. In the multisensory retail environment, enhanced responses can mean, for example, longer visits at the store, more browsing or more purchased products as well as enhanced store images or more enjoyable and engaging shopping experiences. Thus, it is not surprising that sensory marketing in retail environments often highlights the importance of engaging all the senses in order to affect our perceptions and shopping behaviour.[16] The coming years will hopefully bring more academic research on multisensory integration and its synergistic effects in a retail setting.

> In his highly influential book on sensory branding, Martin Lindström gives an example of the industry that has managed to build a rather unique multisensory product. That is the automobile industry. According to Lindström, a car is completely controlled multisensory environment. A car engages almost all our senses in numerous ways; from the control panel feels, to the shape and design of the car, to the fabric of the seats, to the sounds of the doors and engine, and to the new car smell. Thus, just sitting into a new car can be a holistic multisensory experience.[17]

5.3 Sensory Overload and Degraded Responses

The joint effect of cues may also be negative, meaning that in some cases multiple cues may cause a degraded response. It has been established that using an excessive number of cues can overstimulate our minds. At its core, overstimulation means that we cannot process all of the information provided by our senses. It is a well-known fact that our capacity to perceive and process information is limited. Thus, using cues very intensively carries the risk of

---

[14] Shams and Seitz (2008).
[15] Tang et al. (2016).
[16] Helmefalk (2017).
[17] Lindström (2005).

sensory overload.[18] In a retail environment, an overstimulated customer may become annoyed and leave the store.

> Some old-style bazaars or open-air markets can be very sensory-rich environments that feature a great deal of noise, huge crowds, colourful surroundings and strong smells. While there are customers who greatly enjoy exploring these kinds of environments, some may become anxious because such multisensory environments are just too overwhelming and overstimulating for them.

Sensory overload is the outcome of too much stimulation. This happens easily if too many high-arousal cues are introduced simultaneously. For example, Homburg et al. found that three high-arousal cues can trigger sensory overload and cause negative responses among consumers.[19] In a similar fashion, Doucé and Adams found that adding a third high-arousal cue is likely to lead to sensory overload in a shopping environment.[20] Doucé and Adams specify that sensory overload seems to occur under the condition that the third high-arousal cue is processed by the visual or auditory sense. Based on the findings of Homburg et al. and Doucé and Adams, one could say that introducing even very few high-arousal cues in a store environment can lead to sensory overload and degraded responses. High-arousal cues could include fast-paced music and certain colours, such as orange and red. Visual complexity may also evoke high levels of arousal and ultimately sensory overload.[21] Figure 5.2 illustrates a possible high-arousal cue combination that could cause sensory overload.

It should be borne in mind, however, that the number of cues we can process simultaneously ultimately varies by individual. Whereas one person may enjoy a large number of different sensory stimuli, another may feel anxious in a similar situation. Age may be a factor in determining how many cues a customer can tolerate. For younger people, a cue-rich environment may not be a problem, and they may even seek out environments that provide maximum sensory stimulation, but older customers may have a negative response to a very small number of cues.[22] As a general rule of thumb, one could say that the retailer should rely more on "less is more" thinking than "more is more" when setting cues in a retail environment.

---

[18] Spence et al. (2014).
[19] Homburg et al. (2012).
[20] Doucé and Adams (2020).
[21] Jang et al. (2018).
[22] Spence et al. (2014).

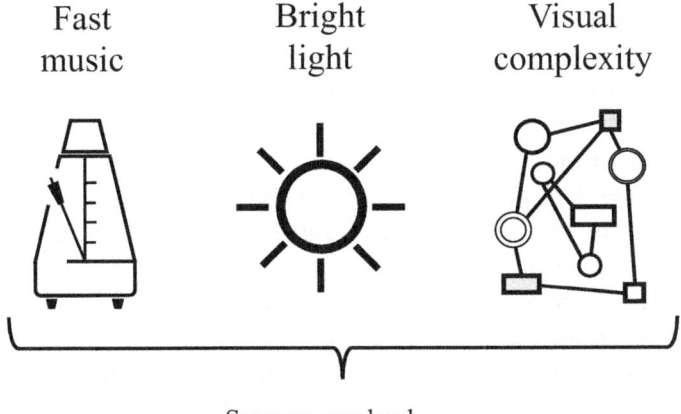

Fig. 5.2 High-arousal cues and sensory overload

5.4 Cross-modal Interaction

Our understanding of the different ways in which our senses interact in multisensory environments is increasing. The most well-known concept describing how our senses interact is cross-modal interaction. In short, cross-modal interaction means that our perception of certain sensory inputs, like texture, odour or flavour, can be altered by other sensory inputs, like visual perception.

There are numerous studies demonstrating cross-modal interaction. For example, Chylinski et al. found that the way we perceive texture arises from a cross-modal interaction involving colour and the actual texture.[23] The texture may feel very different when combined with different colours. Certain colours are also associated with specific tastes and flavours. For example, it has been established that just the colour of a fizzy drink may affect whether it tastes sweet or sour.[24] According to one study, when the yellow colour of a soda can was made 15% more saturated, consumers reported that it tasted more lemony, even though the flavour had not changed.[25] Visual information can also affect odour intensity.[26] One study demonstrated that if hand soap is in a red package instead of a white one, consumers considered its scent to be significantly more intense, even if the soap was identical.[27] Furthermore, the

---

[23] Chylinski et al. (2015).
[24] Koch and Koch (2003).
[25] Spence and Velasco (2018).
[26] Zellner and Kautz (1990) and Gilbert et al. (1996).
[27] Gatti et al. (2014).

influence of visual perception on auditory perception (e.g., perceived loudness) is well documented in previous studies.[28] For example, bright lights are found to make sounds seem louder, while dim lights lead to experiencing sounds as softer.[29] Thus, it can be said that our visual perception affects how we process non-visual information.

It has also been found that smell plays an important role in how we perceive other sensory inputs.[30] For example, odour–oral cross-modal interactions tend to affect our flavour perceptions when we taste wines.[31] Smell can also impact our haptic perceptions in meaningful ways.[32] Certain odours can even affect how much pain we feel (i.e., tactile sensation).[33] These very brief examples highlight the fact that information received from one sense has the potential to affect how we perceive information from another. Figure 5.3 illustrates the cross-modal effect with a very simple example; just changing the brightness of lighting (visual perception) might affect how loud we perceive the sounds in the environment (auditory perception).

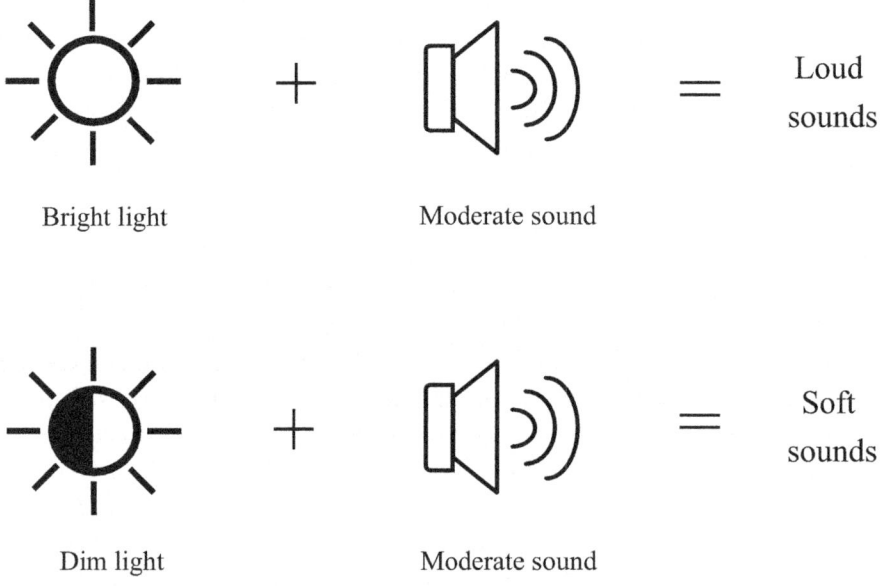

Fig. 5.3 A simplified example of cross-modal effects

---

[28] McGurk and MacDonald (1976) and Odgaard et al. (2004).
[29] Marks (1987).
[30] Velazquez et al. (2020).
[31] Pittari et al. (2020).
[32] Krishna et al. (2010).
[33] Spence (2022).

Spence et al. provide some simple examples of cross-modal effects in a retail setting[34]: As we know, bright orange usually indicates low prices, but if the colour appears in a store which smells intensely of citrus, the scent may change the meaning of the colour from cheap prices to a sense of freshness. Similarly, an atmospheric scent which is enjoyable in a quiet room may smell significantly less pleasant in a red-coloured room with loud background music. There are many other examples of potential cross-modal effects in the store environment. Chylinski et al. have pointed out that just the background colour of the retail store might affect our non-visual perceptions.[35] All in all, cross-modal sensory interaction might shape our shopping experiences in surprising ways.

The likelihood of unexpected cross-modal effects is high if the sensory cues are not somehow complementary in nature or they communicate very different meanings to customers. Thus, a logical association, or semantic match, between different cues should be ensured when setting in-store cues. This creates harmony in the store environment and ensures that the store as a whole conveys the meanings that it supposed to. Furthermore, if there are strong cross-modal associations between different cues (e.g., colours and odours), it is likely that they will generate enhanced responses among consumers.[36] If there is a severe mismatch or conflict between cues, the outcome may be chaotic or just weird from the viewpoint of customers.

To sum up, cross-modal interaction is a highly interesting phenomenon in multisensory environments. It refers to the blending of sensory inputs in our minds and the ways in which one sensory input (like colour) can shape how other sensory inputs (like texture or odours) are perceived. According to Spence, cross-modal effects tend to occur regardless of whether the cues (sensory inputs) are meaningfully related to each other.[37] Cross-modal interaction has been attributed to physiochemical and cognitive mechanisms that connect to our previous experiences and learning.[38]

For retailers, understanding cross-modal effects is crucial in developing balanced multisensory store environments that evoke the intended responses among consumers. However, cross-modal interaction is a largely unexplored topic in real store environments and the need for further research is significant.

---

[34] Spence et al. (2014).
[35] Chylinski et al. (2015).
[36] Demattè et al. (2006) and Marks (1987).
[37] Spence (2022).
[38] Velazquez et al. (2020).

5.5 Cue Congruence

Cue congruence is perhaps the most important concept in sensory marketing research.[39] Cue congruence refers to the situation where different sensory cues, like music and scent, are coherently aligned and they communicate or convey similar things to consumers. From the perspective of the customers, the cues match.[40]

Cue congruence in a store environment can take many forms. Specifically, cue congruence can be related to intended emotional responses or it can be semantic. First of all, congruence can refer to the emotional reactions that cues aim to evoke in us. For example, if the store introduces high-arousal music (e.g., fast music) and high-arousal scent (e.g., grapefruit) simultaneously, the sensory cues are in congruence.[41] Thus, a match between cues in terms of their stimulating qualities (or, more broadly, the emotional dimension) is one form of cue congruence. Secondly, congruence can also be related to the semantic meanings or associations that cues convey. For example, Krishna et al. state that cue congruence is about the fit of the semantic associations among the characteristics of sensory inputs.[42] In other words, if the associations or meanings that cues carry are in line with each other and can be interpreted in a similar fashion, there is cue congruence. In practice, a semantic match can mean, for example, that the store plays Top 20 music (in-store feature associated with a discount image) and features bright lighting (in-store feature associated with a discount image).[43] A feminine scent and smooth haptic qualities also constitute a semantic match, as Krishna et al. established.[44] In sum, if cues are generating similar emotions in us or they convey similar semantic associations or meanings to us, there is cue congruence. It is clear that to align cues in congruent manner, retailers must be well aware of the emotional responses that cues evoke and the semantic meanings that cues are likely to convey.

Cue congruency remains a relatively little researched topic.[45] Thus far, studies have mainly focused on understanding the joint effects of two

---

[39] Spence et al. (2014) and Helmefalk (2017).
[40] Krishna et al. (2010) and Imschloss and Kuehnl (2017).
[41] Homburg et al. (2012).
[42] Krishna et al. (2010).
[43] Baker et al. (1994).
[44] Krishna et al. (2010).
[45] Helmefalk (2017) and Spence (2020).

different cues. One such study, conducted by Imschloss and Kuehnl, examined the joint effects of music and haptic cues (flooring materials).[46] The study found that when the in-store flooring material and the background music were congruent, e.g., a soft flooring material was combined with calm music, research subjects developed more positive attitudes towards the products than when the cues were incongruent. Cue congruence also had a positive impact on intention to purchase. Another study found similarly that when the scent and music were congruent in terms of their arousal qualities, consumers rated the environment in much more positive terms than when the cues in the environment were in conflict.[47] Chang et al. demonstrated in their study that the semantic association between colour and music leads to more favourable brand attitudes in a store environment.[48] Helmefalk and Hultén also found a positive effect of multisensory congruent cues on shoppers' emotions and purchase behaviour.[49] In terms of joint effects at the product level, it has been found that when the scent and the haptic and tactile properties of the product are congruent, consumers will review the product in more positive terms.[50] All of these examples emphasise that cue congruence is likely to lead to positive responses in us. As Spence et al. pointed out: "Generally speaking, ensuring that various sensory cues are congruent is a good idea".[51]

> **Tsutaya** is a Japanese bookstore chain founded in 1983 in Osaka. Tsutaya has become known for its exceptionally beautiful stores that appeal to customers with their minimalist aesthetics and relaxed atmosphere. The store materials are of the highest standard and match each other perfectly. For example, the stores heavily feature hardwood and glass. The floors are polished concrete. Tsutaya bookstores also have pleasant green areas and often feature an adjacent cozy cafe. The most spectacular locations in the Tsutaya chain are named **Tsutaya Electrics** stores, where the bookstore's product selection is combined with additional electronic products and a high-quality curated design.

Regardless of the type of congruence, or even the type of the store, the positive impact of cue congruence on consumers is attributed to the fact that

---

[46] Imschloss and Kuehnl (2017).
[47] Mattila and Wirtz (2001).
[48] Chang et al. (2012).
[49] Helmefalk and Hultén (2017).
[50] Krishna et al. (2010).
[51] Spence et al., (2014, p. 480).

cues that fit together generate an image of a coherent, balanced and consistent environment.[52] Researchers also emphasise the fact that congruent cues are easier to comprehend, which reduces the cognitive load associated with perception, while generating the impression among the consumers that there is nothing suspicious about the shopping environment or situation. In other words, cue congruence signals that "everything is right and going well".[53] In terms of fluency theory, it can be said that ease of processing the environment signals a positive state of affairs and absence of threat.[54] This makes consumers have more self-confidence at the moment of purchase, which is in turn likely to encourage them to make more purchases. All in all, the premises of processing fluency offer a solid theoretical explanation why cue congruence tends to make the store more pleasant for consumers.[55]

5.6 Cue Incongruence

It is generally understood that people tend to prefer harmony and consistency in their lives and avoid inconsistency when possible.[56] Even though cue congruence is therefore a positive factor in principle, complete harmony and order may also render the shop environment uninteresting or uninspiring, if generally enjoyable, for the customer. Too much harmony without any "errors" might just not resonate with consumers. Customers may even consider an environment with full congruence among cues as boring, and not bother to explore the store more closely. As Jang et al. noted that "an excessively monotonous environment could make consumers lose interest and feel bored".[57] It is a well-known fact that we as consumers are curious and have a need to seek out new and inspiring experiences. Cue incongruence is one way to meet this need.

In some settings or in certain types of stores, it may be advisable to disrupt cue congruence to some degree and to increase complexity in the environment in order to heighten consumer arousal and interest to explore.[58] Cue incongruence means that there is a certain mismatch between cues and the store is more or less non-harmonious and therefore stimulating or even

---

[52] Oh and Petrie (2012).
[53] Imschloss and Kuehnl (2017).
[54] Forster et al. (2016).
[55] Reber (2011), Garaus (2017), Imschloss and Kuehnl (2017), and Jang et al. (2018).
[56] Spangenberg et al. (2006).
[57] Jang et al., (2018, p. 115).
[58] Spence et al. (2014).

surprising for customers. While extreme incongruity is rarely a good idea for retailers, moderate incongruity might be beneficial. For example, if the goal is to draw attention and generate general interest, some amount of complexity and cue incongruence may be effective. In such a case, the senses of the customers are intentionally stimulated in surprising, even absurd ways, while maintaining control of the cues. Incongruent stimulation could mean, for example, combining high-arousal cues (e.g., bright lighting) to cues that evoke pleasure (e.g., slow music). Or the store could introduce cues that are semantically somehow opposite to each other. Just non-matching colours may be enough to evoke arousal. There are many options for creating an incongruent or complex store environment.[59] The key is just to do things in an unusual way.

Managing cue incongruence is very challenging and comes with clear risks. It is well established that if an environment becomes too incongruent, e.g., because it combines several different shapes, colours, materials and design elements in an inconsistent manner, the consumer reactions can be intensely negative, particularly in terms of how pleasant they consider the environment to be.[60] Thus, poorly managed cue incongruence may overstimulate consumers and cause cognitive overload among them. This, in turn, is likely to lead to avoidance behaviour. The retailer must be particularly sensitive to the ability of its customers to receive cues which go in different directions or are diametrically opposed to one another, if such cues are to be deployed.

5.7 The Seesaw Effect in a Multisensory Retail Environment

Our ability to absorb various sensory cues such as colours, sounds and scents in concert is a fundamental feature of our nervous system and helps us function in a variety of situations. At its best, encountering multiple cues can lead to enhanced responses, and at its worst, degraded responses. For example, multisensory experiences can make our shopping journey more enjoyable or, alternatively, too many cues can just drive us to confusion. Cue (in)congruence is the critical issue. Our responses tend to vary depending on whether the cues that we perceive are congruent or incongruent. From the viewpoint of a retailer, managing cue congruence is a very important, and very challenging, task. Managing cue congruence (or, more broadly, sensory

---

[59] Garaus (2017).
[60] Oh and Petrie (2012) and Dzebic (2018).

marketing) is about creating optimal configurations of all in-store elements in a way that makes the store easy to process and evokes pleasure, while simultaneously satisfying the consumers' curiosity and generating genuine interest to explore the store.

The challenge of managing the joint effects of cues could be described as a seesaw as depicted in Fig. 5.4, in which cue congruence increases how pleasant the environment is, but decreases the customers' arousal levels and interest to explore, while cue incongruence increases the customers' arousal levels and interest to explore, but reduces the pleasantness of the store.[61] Of course, in reality, the seesaw effect is not that straightforward. For example, for some consumers, congruent and pleasant store environments may also be highly exciting.[62] However, the seesaw effect shows us how difficult it can be for a retailer managing a multisensory environment and its various sensory cues.

To be more specific, the overall seesaw effect in a multisensory store environment can be described and explained in the following way:

- Cue congruence increases the pleasantness of the store but decreases overall arousal and interest to explore: A coherent and harmonious store where everything is in the right place and belongs together helps us make sense of and comprehend the store environment as a whole, and hence, generates positive feelings such as pleasure and self-confidence in us, but at the same time it tends to make things boring or predictable, diminishing our interest to browse the store even when the individual cues are arousing.
- Cue incongruence decreases the pleasantness of the store but increases overall arousal and interest to explore: Complexity and a lack of coherence or harmony raise our attention and make the store exciting or mysterious, pulling us in, but at the same time it might confuse us and ultimately cause uncertainty and feelings of unpleasantness.

Based on the above, it could be said that there is a certain trade-off regarding pleasantness and overall arousal when managing cue (in)congruence in a retail setting. Both dimensions of experience are very important and necessary, but which one should the retailer prefer when seeking to create and maintain approach behaviour? The pleasantness of the store (achieved by cue congruence) or customers' arousal and interest to explore (achieved by cue incongruence)?

---

[61] Day (1967), Jang et al. (2018), and see also Berlyne (1974).
[62] Kuppens (2008).

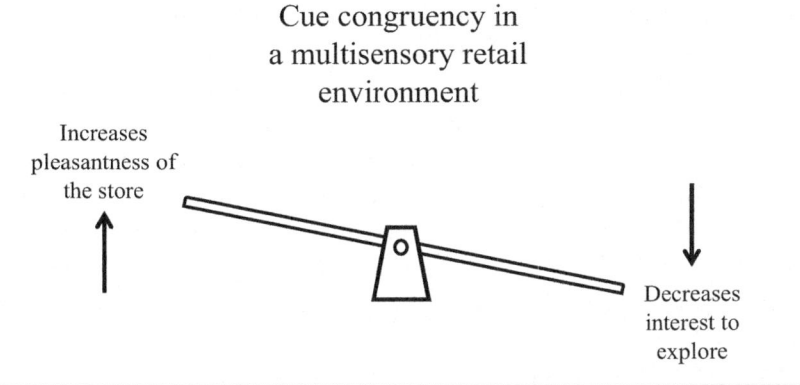

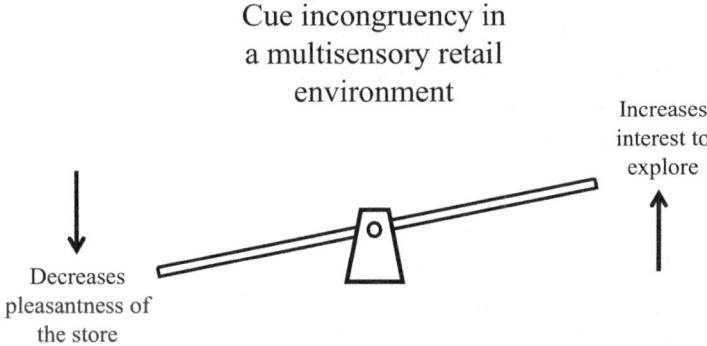

Fig. 5.4 Seesaw effect in a multisensory retail environment

5.8 Summary

One of the main advantages of physical retail stores is that they can stimulate all our senses at once and produce multisensory experiences. However, the multisensory nature of retail stores makes explaining the effects of cues rather complex and requires profound understanding of how our senses interact and work together. In particular, one should be familiar with issues such as multisensory integration and cross-modal interaction.

As studies have indicated, consumers tend to respond differently to cue combinations than to an individual stimulus.[63] Generally speaking, the joint effects or cue combinations are likely to lead to greater responses among customers, such as more purchases or longer visits at the store, but in some cases the joint effects can cause negative outcomes, for example in the form

---

[63] Helmefalk and Berndt (2018).

of sensory overload. Whether the joint effects lead to positive or negative outcomes is related to the level of cue congruence. The more congruent the cues, the more pleasant the store is likely to be. If the store is experienced as pleasant, various positive effects on shopping behaviour are likely to occur.[64] However, from the viewpoint of customers' overall arousal and interest to explore the store, some degree of cue incongruence may be also needed. In general, researchers and retailers have become increasingly aware of the joint effects of cues, including the meaning of cue (in)congruence. However, there is still very little empirical research on specific cue combinations and their joint effects.[65]

Understanding joint effects is an important starting point to studying the multisensory nature of retail stores—but it is not enough. In order to fully explain how cues affect us, we must be aware of various individual and situational factors that might either accelerate or inhibit the effects of cues. In academic terms, there are certain response moderators that help to explain why cues affect as they do, and why some customers might respond to cues very differently than other customers.[66] Chapter 6 takes a closer of these factors.

Self-Reflective Questions
- What is the sense that you trust most when making assessments?
- Describe a retail environment that you consider pleasant.
- Describe a retail environment that you consider exciting.
- What kind of retail setting makes you say "WOW"?
- What kind of retail setting makes you bored?
- How do you feel about complexity in a retail store?
- What kind of retail setting is too overwhelming to you?
- What kinds of cues do you think have a natural match with each other, and what kinds of cues are likely to be in conflict?
- What kind of retail setting do you consider ideal?

Decision-Based Questions
- As a store manager, how would you take advantage of the multisensory nature of your store?

---

[64] Kaltcheva and Weitz (2006).
[65] Spence (2020).
[66] Bitner (1992) and Roggeveen et al. (2020).

- As a store manager, what kinds of cue combinations would you use and what kinds of combinations would you avoid?
- As a store manager, how would you try to improve the multisensory enhancement among customers?
- As a store manager, how would you use cues to make your store pleasant but also arousing at the same time?
- As a store manager, how would you try to avoid sensory overload in a store environment? What sort of cues or cue combinations might lead sensory overload among customers?

References

Baker, J., Grewal, D., & Parasuraman, A. (1994). The influence of store environment on quality inferences and store image. *Journal of the Academy of Marketing Science, 22*, 328–339.

Berlyne, D. E. (1974). The new experimental aesthetics. In D. E. Berlyne (Ed.), *Studies in the new experimental aesthetics: Steps towards an objective psychology of aesthetic appreciation* (pp. 1–25). Hemisphere Publishing Corporation.

Bitner, M. J. (1992). Servicescapes: The impact of physical surroundings on customers and employees. *Journal of Marketing, 56*, 57–71.

Calvert, G. A., & Thesen, T. (2004). Multisensory integration: Methodological approaches and emerging principles in the human brain. *Journal of Physiology-Paris, 98*, 191–205.

Chang, Y., Nara., & Yun. L. (2012). The effect of semantic congruence between color and music on product evaluation. In *AP—Asia-Pacific Advances in consumer research* (Vol. 10; pp. 354–356). Association for Consumer Research.

Chylinski, M., Northey, G., & Ngo, L. V. (2015). Cross-modal interactions between color and texture of food. *Psychology & Marketing, 32*, 950–966.

Day, H. (1967). Evaluation of subjective complexity, pleasingness, and interestingness for a series of random polygons varying in complexity. *Perception and Psychophysics, 2*, 281–286.

Demattè, L., Sanabria, D., & Spence, C. (2006). Cross-modal associations between odors and colors. *Chemical Senses, 31*, 531–538.

Doucé, L., & Adams, C. (2020). Sensory overload in a shopping environment: Not every sensory modality leads to too much stimulation. *Journal of Retailing and Consumer Services, 57*. https://doi.org/10.1016/j.jretconser.2020.102154

Dzebic, V. (2018). *Emotions and the environment: The variable effect of environmental complexity on pleasure and interest*. UWSpace.

Forster, M., Leder, H., & Ansorge, U. (2016). Exploring the subjective feeling of fluency. *Experimental Psychology, 63*, 45–58.

Garaus, M. (2017). Atmospheric harmony in the retail environment: Its influence on store satisfaction and re-patronage intention. *Journal of Consumer Behaviour, 16*, 265–278.

Gatti, E., Bordegoni, M., & Spence, C. (2014). Investigating the influence of colour, weight, and fragrance intensity on the perception of liquid bath soap: An experimental study. *Food Quality and Preference, 31*, 56–64.

Gilbert, A. N., Martin, R., & Kemp, S. E. (1996). Cross-modal correspondence between vision and olfaction: The color of smells. *The American Journal of Psychology, 109*, 335–351.

Helmefalk, M. (2017). *Multi-sensory cues in interplay and congruency in a retail store context: Consumer emotions and purchase behaviors*. Linnaeus University Dissertations No 297/2017.

Helmefalk, M., & Berndt, A. (2018). Shedding light on the use of single and multi-sensory cues and their effect on consumer behaviours. *International Journal of Retail & Distribution Management., 46*, 1077–1091.

Helmefalk, M., & Hultén, B. (2017). Multi-sensory congruent cues in designing retail store atmosphere: Effects on shoppers emotions and purchase behavior. *Journal of Retailing and Consumer Services, 38*, 1–11.

Holmes, N., & Spence, C. (2005). Multisensory integration: Space, time and superadditivity. *Current Biology, 15*, 762–764.

Holmes, N. P., Calvert, G. A., & Spence, C. (2009). Multimodal integration. In M. D. Binder, N. Hirokawa, & U. Windhorst (Eds.), *Encyclopedia of neuroscience*. Springer.

Homburg, C., Imschloss, M., & Küehnl, C. (2012). *Of dollars and senses—Does multisensory marketing pay off?* University of Mannheim.

Imschloss, M., & Kuehnl, C. (2017). Don't ignore the floor: Exploring multisensory atmospheric congruence between music and flooring in a retail environment. *Psychology & Marketing, 34*, 931–945.

Jang, J. Y., Baek, E., Yoon, S. Y., & Choo, H. J. (2018). Store design: Visual complexity and consumer responses. *International Journal of Design, 12*, 105–118.

Kaltcheva, V. D., & Weitz, B. A. (2006). When should a retailer create an exciting store environment? *Journal of Marketing, 70*, 107–118.

Koch, C., & Koch, E. C. (2003). Preconceptions of taste based on color. *The Journal of Psychology, 137*, 233–242.

Kuppens, P. (2008). Individual differences in the relationship between pleasure and arousal. *Journal of Research in Personality, 42*, 1053–1059.

Krishna, A., Elder, R., & Caldara, C. (2010). Feminine to smell but masculine to touch? Multisensory congruence and its effect on the aesthetic experience. *Journal of Consumer Psychology, 20*, 410–418.

Lindström, M. (2005). *BRAND sense: Building powerful brands through touch, taste, smell*. Free Press.

Marks, L. E. (1987). On cross-modal similarity: Auditory–visual interactions in speeded discrimination. *Journal of Experimental Psychology: Human Perception and Performance, 13*(3), 384–394.

Mattila, A. S., & Wirtz, J. (2001). Congruency of scent and music as a driver of in-store evaluations and behavior. *Journal of Retailing, 77*, 273–289.

McGurk, H., & MacDonald, J. (1976). Hearing lips and seeing voices. *Nature, 264*, 746–748.

Odgaard, E. C., Arieh, Y., & Marks, L. E. (2004). Brighter noise: Sensory enhancement of perceived loudness by concurrent visual stimulation. *Cognitive, Affective, & Behavioral Neuroscience, 4*, 127–132.

Oh, H., & Petrie, J. (2012). How do storefront window displays influence entering decisions of clothing stores? *Journal of Retailing and Consumer Services, 19*, 27–35.

Pittari, E., Moio, L., Arapitsas, P., Curioni, A., Gerbi, V., Parpinello, G. P., Ugliano, M., & Piombino, P. (2020). Exploring olfactory-oral cross-modal interactions through sensory and chemical characteristics of Italian red wines. *Foods, 9*, 1530.

Reber, R. (2011). Processing fluency, aesthetic pleasure, and culturally shared taste. In A. P. Shimamura & S. E. Palmer (Eds.), *Aesthetic science: Connecting minds, brains, and experience* (online ed.; 19 January 2012). Oxford Academic.

Roggeveen, A. L., Grewal, D., & Schweiger, E. B. (2020). The DAST framework for retail atmospherics: The impact of in- and out-of-store retail journey touchpoints on the customer experience. *Journal of Retailing, 96*, 128–137.

Senkowski, D., Saint-Amour, D., Höfle, M., & Foxe, J. J. (2011). Multisensory interactions in early evoked brain activity follow the principle of inverse effectiveness. *NeuroImage, 56*, 2200–2208.

Shams, L., & Seitz, A. R. (2008). Benefits of multisensory learning. *Trends in Cognitive Sciences, 12*, 411–417.

Spangenberg, E. R., Sprott, D. E., Grohmann, B., & Tracy, D. L. (2006). Gender-congruent ambient scent influences on approach and avoidance behaviours in a retail store. *Journal of Business Research, 59*, 1281–1287.

Spence, C. (2020). Senses of place: Architectural design for the multisensory mind. *Cognitive Research: Principles and Implications, 5*, 46.

Spence, C. (2022). Multisensory contributions to affective touch. *Current Opinion in Behavioral Sciences, 43*, 40–45.

Spence, C., & Velasco, C. (2018). On the multiple effects of packaging colour on consumer behaviour and product experience in the 'food and beverage' and 'home and personal care' categories. *Food Quality and Preference, 68*, 226–237.

Spence, C., Puccinelli, N. M., Grewal, D., & Roggeveen, A. L. (2014). Store atmospherics: A multisensory perspective. *Psychology & Marketing, 31*, 472–488.

Stanford, T. R., & Stein, B. E. (2007). Superadditivity in multisensory integration: Putting the computation in context. *NeuroReport, 18*, 787–792.

Stanford, T. R., Quessy, S., & Stein, B. E. (2005). Evaluating the operations underlying multisensory integration in the cat superior colliculus. *The Journal of Neuroscience, 25*, 6499–6508.

Stein, B. E., & Stanford, T. R. (2008). Multisensory integration: Current issues from the perspective of the single neuron. *Nature Reviews. Neuroscience, 9,* 255–266.

Stein, B. E., Stanford, T. R., & Rowland, B. A. (2020). Multisensory integration and the society for neuroscience: Then and now. *The Journal of Neuroscience, 40,* 11–13.

Stein, B. E., Stanford, T. R., Ramachandran, R. Perrault, T., &. Rowland, B. (2009). Challenges in quantifying multisensory integration: Alternative criteria, models, and inverse effectiveness. *Experimental Brain Research, 198,* 113–126.

Tang, X., Wu, J., & Shen, Y. (2016). The interactions of multisensory integration with endogenous and exogenous attention. *Neuroscience and Biobehavioral Reviews, 61,* 208–224.

Velazquez A., Vidal, L., Varela, P., & Ares, G. (2020). Cross-modal interactions as a strategy for sugar reduction in products targeted at children: Case study with vanilla milk desserts. *Food Research International, 130.*

Werner, S., & Noppeney, U. (2010). Superadditive responses in superior temporal sulcus predict audiovisual benefits in object categorization. *Cerebral Cortex, 20,* 1829–1842.

Yau, J. M., DeAngelis, G. C., & Angelaki, D. E. (2015). Dissecting neural circuits for multisensory integration and crossmodal processing. *Philosophical Transactions of the Royal Society of London. Series B, Biological Sciences, 370,* 20140203.

Zellner, D. A., & Kautz, M. A. (1990). Color affects perceived odor intensity. *Journal of Experimental Psychology: Human Perception and Performance, 16,* 391–397.

6

Factors That Accelerate or Inhibit the Effects of Cues in a Retail Store

6.1 Shopping Motives

> **DID YOU KNOW?**
> - Shopping motives represent the reasons why people shop.
> - Shopping motives may vary from fulfilling a specific task to recreation and personal pleasure.
> - An individual's response to a retail environment often depends on their purpose for visiting the store.

We briefly discussed shopping motives and the ways they can help explain our behaviour in different situations in Chapter 2. Motives are our goals or purposes, the reasons behind our behaviour—in a word, the factors that precede our actions and set us in motion. Typically, motives can answer the question of why we behave the way we do.[1]

Motives arise from the needs we want to fulfil. These needs may have to do with feelings of belonging, social prestige or self-development, for example.[2] We may simultaneously have several motives which prompt us to action, and we may not even be aware of all of them. "Motivation" is often used in parallel to "motive". Motivation refers to our efforts to fulfil whatever needs we may have at a given moment. Motivation describes how vigorously

---

[1] Collins and Montgomery (1969).
[2] Maslow (1943).

we work towards our goals, while motives are the reasons or goals that set us in motion. Many studies have focused on motives and motivation, from various different perspectives. This in itself speaks volumes about how central a concept the motive is for explaining our behaviour.[3]

There has also been extensive research into motives as it comes to shopping, and several such motives have been identified. Traditionally, the motives or reasons for visiting a store can be categorised into three fundamental classes:

- Product-oriented motives
- Experiential motives
- Combinations of the above.[4]

A consumer with a product-oriented motive will visit the store to purchase a specific product or acquire information about a product for a specific purpose. In such cases, the reason for visiting the store is the genuine need to buy something. Experiential motives relate to shopping as entertainment, or spending time without a specific need to buy. Such consumers may go to a store primarily to boost their mood, or just because they have nothing better to do and they want to alleviate boredom. Product-oriented and experiential motives may also be present simultaneously. Motives may be further categorised and specified in many other ways. For example, a consumer's motive may be bargain-hunting or just a desire to see what is available and what the latest trends are. The motive may even be that the consumer needs help or advice with something. Or the consumer may just want to be physically active or seek social interaction with others. Motives may also have to do with self-expression or the demonstration of social status.[5]

Suffice to say that there is a broad spectrum of motives for shopping, and it would be unreasonably time-consuming to go through every single one in the scope of this book. The main thing to understand is that the consumer's presence at a specific store at a specific time may be the result of many different types of motives. Whatever the current motive or purpose of the store visit may be, it will inevitably influence how the consumer shops, what they pay attention to, what they ignore, and what seems generally significant during the visit.[6]

---

[3] Hattie et al. (2020).
[4] Dawson et al. (1990).
[5] Noble et al. (2006), Morschett et al. (2005) and Arnold and Reynolds (2003).
[6] Bitner (1992).

We can assume that from the retailer standpoint, motives relating to experience-seeking offer fertile ground for employing multisensory cues and their influence. Consumers with such motives are likely to be shopping with all of their senses open to receive and interpret various cues, and they are also more prone to impulse purchases[7] However, if the only motive to visit a store is to buy a specific product to satisfy a specific need, the impact of cues may be more limited. But even in such a case, we should not rule out or even downplay the impact of cues—they just have to be tuned to serve that motive and the resulting shopping style. This means that it is important that the retailer can support the customer in attaining the goals they have set for their shopping.

> Today's large supermarkets tend to offer two alternative shopping routes for their customers. There is a long route for "weekend shoppers", who have more time and are interested in browsing the product assortment, and a short one for "weekday shoppers", who want to do their shopping as quickly as possible and with minimum effort. Thus, the layout of these stores is designed to serve two different shopping motives.

6.2 Mood

> **DID YOU KNOW?**
> – Mood is a semi-persistent mental state or general feeling. Examples of mood states could be excitement, worry and cheerfulness.
> – Moods tend to be less intense than emotional states and are not necessarily triggered by a specific stimulus.
> – Each customer steps into a retail environment in a particular mood—for example, they may be feeling curious, happy or energised. Such mood states are likely to affect as well as be affected by the physical and social environment of the store.

This book has already extensively discussed consumer emotions and how significant they can be in terms of choice behaviour. Specifically, several sections have referred to emotional states that can be triggered rapidly by clues. Studies indicate that our emotional states may make us approach something or leave an area, for example. Mood is often discussed alongside

---

[7] See e.g., Williams et al. (1985), Bellenger and Korgaonkar (1980) and Kaltcheva and Weitz (2006).

emotions, and sometimes, they are used interchangeably. However, mood is its own concept with a distinct meaning.

Fundamentally, a mood is a more permanent state than an emotion. Where an emotional state is of short duration and passes quickly, a mood lasts longer. Furthermore, our emotions vary in intensity from one extreme to another, whereas moods are less intense experiences that are less powerfully felt. Another defining feature is that emotional states are triggered by a stimulus, while it is more challenging to identify the origin of a prevailing mood.[8] There may not even be a particular reason for our mood, and we may not be able to explain why we are in a specific mood.

Moods can be described and categorised in many different ways. We may say we are in a good mood, happy or calm, or we may be melancholy, irritated or restless. The spectrum of moods is extensive, but they are typically discussed in general terms as positive or negative. Studies have established that our moods influence us in many ways. For example, positive moods have been found to increase willingness to help, kindness and generosity. A person in a positive mood may give money to charity or leave an unusually large tip for a waiter. Meanwhile, someone in a negative mood may want to retreat to watch their favourite TV show or immerse themselves in a book. It has also been found that people may seek to alleviate a negative mood by shopping or spending time with friends. All in all, our moods may lead to a wide variety of different reactions.[9] Another important observation is that moods may influence what we pay attention to and what kind of information we seek from our environment. For example, if we are in a negative mood, we may be more likely to seek negative information and positive information when we are in a positive mood. A positive mood may make us see the world through rose-tinted glasses, while a negative mood may drive us to the other extreme, to only pay attention to problems and see everything in a negative light.[10]

It should be obvious that the mood of the consumer will inevitably influence their shopping experience as well as the way they react to the stimuli they encounter while at a store. As Puccinelli et al. concluded in their article: "When people feel good, they process and prefer different information and products than when they feel bad. Their mood also affects how consumers interact with personnel in a retail environment.[11]" Some studies indicate that consumers in a positive mood spend more money on their shopping

---

[8] Köster and Mojet (2015).
[9] Luomala and Laaksonen (2000).
[10] Swinyard (1993) and Köster and Mojet (2015).
[11] Puccinelli et al. (2009, p. 23).

and make more impulse purchases than consumers in a negative mood[12] On the other hand, it also seems that a consumer in a positive mood is able to resist temptation and delay gratification, while a negative mood makes us more susceptible to temptation and likely to seek instant gratification.[13] For example, being in a bad mood may spur us to make unhealthy choices at the grocery store. One study showed that the negative impacts of a bad mood on the shopping experience were significantly stronger than the positive impacts of a good mood.[14] In other words, a bad mood seems to have a bigger impact on the shopping experience than a good one. It is also important to note that the shopping environment can influence the mood of customers. For example, a pleasant shopping environment and good customer service may improve a customer's mood, while an unpleasant environment and poor service can turn a customer's good mood into irritation.[15]

> Snacks like chips, crackers and nuts are products that we typically purchase on impulse without prior planning. Some studies have found that over 80% of shoppers buy snacks on impulse. This is not surprising, as impulse products are generally low-cost convenience goods that are purchased frequently and demand minimum cognitive effort from the consumer. Neither is it unexpected that studies have indicated a link between our prevailing mood and the tendency to make impulsive snack purchases. A negative mood is a particularly powerful driver of impulse buying snacks. Buying snacks on impulse is often a way of alleviating a bad mood.[16]

All in all, retailers should understand how the moods of consumers influence their shopping behaviour, and how they can best react to different moods. A consumer may come to a store specifically because they are inspired by a good mood, or conversely, to seek relief from a melancholy one. Whatever the mood we are in when we enter a store has an impact on how we observe our environment and how reckless we are with our spending. Mood has a great impact on our shopping experience, but these impacts may go in either direction, and they are highly individual.[17]

---

[12] Ozer and Gültekin (2015) and Pornpitakpan et al. (2017).
[13] Swinyard (1993).
[14] Babin and Darden (1996).
[15] Gardner (1985).
[16] Tran (2022).
[17] Bitner (1992).

6.3 Self-Control

> **DID YOU KNOW?**
> - Self-control (or self-regulation) represents the capacity to regulate our behaviour and resist temptation.
> - Spontaneous impulse purchasing is often seen as a failure in self-control.

This book does not explore the personalities of consumers in any particular depth, or how these personalities are reflected in choice behaviour. However, it is clear that our personality is reflected in everything we do, directly or indirectly.[18] For example, our personality is the reason we often behave in the same way in different situations. A personality is a very stable thing and therefore brings consistency to the things we do.

Even though this book does not cover personalities as such, one feature of the personality should be discussed, as it has been found to have a significant impact on our shopping behaviour and particularly why one person is more prone to make impulse purchases than another. This factor is self-control.[19] Self-control means self-discipline or willpower. In practical terms, our self-control manifests in our ability to resist temptation or to delay gratification.[20] We need self-control both in daily tasks and to reach long-term goals, such as studying or maintaining a healthy lifestyle. Self-control is a very important characteristic. Without self-control, reaching goals would be virtually impossible.

We obviously also use self-control to regulate our behaviour during shopping. Studies have shown that individuals with weaker self-control are more likely to make impulse purchases,[21] while strong self-control guards against such impulses. A consumer with strong self-control is likely to walk through a store without succumbing to impulse purchases, no matter how many temptations they encounter during their visit. Correspondingly, a consumer with poor self-control is likely to make an impulse purchase at the very beginning of their shopping experience with minimal encouragement from cues.

From a managerial viewpoint, giving consumers more options to choose from and encouraging them to spend more time in the store, thus depleting their

---

[18] Kassarjian (1971) and Fraj and Martinez (2006).
[19] Gillebaart (2018) and Roberts and Manolis (2012).
[20] Ainslie (1975).
[21] Roberts and Manolis (2012).

> self-control resources, can be an effective way to boost sales.[22] Retailers can also try to appeal to consumers with limited self-control by launching grab-and-go stations, power aisles, countertop display units or similar shelving solutions.

While the impact of self-control on behaviour is easy to understand, it is more difficult to recognise inner self-control from the outside, at least beforehand. Consequently, it is a difficult factor to account for when setting cues. However, an understanding of consumer self-control and its impacts on choice behaviour can help us realise why some methods will influence one consumer but not another.

6.4 Rules of Thumb

> **DID YOU KNOW?**
> – Rules of thumb are mental shortcuts (heuristics) which simplify our decision-making and help us make decisions quickly and with less cognitive effort.
> – We use rules of thumb especially when the choice is not important to us or if we are in a hurry.

It is impossible to discuss consumer choice without mentioning rules of thumb or heuristics. Rules of thumb are methods or general solutions which the consumer uses to simplify and ease their decision-making, for example at a specific moment of choice. For example, Willman-Iivarinen emphasises that heuristics are typically used in decision-making due to our restricted cognitive abilities and desire to lower decision-making costs.[23] Rules of thumb have also been called mental shortcuts.

In practice, rules of thumb may mean that when making a choice, the consumer will only pay attention to certain aspects or instinctively apply a very simple solution to make a choice. We are most likely to use rules of thumb when the choice is not particularly important or if we are in a hurry. Even though rules of thumb often make decision-making easier and minimise our cognitive effort, they may not always guarantee the best possible result and may even lead us astray. This means that the accuracy of our decision-making might suffer when heuristics are applied.

---

[22] Yim (2017).
[23] Willman-Iivarinen (2017).

One well-known rule of thumb is the satisfying heuristic.[24] A consumer employing the satisfying heuristic will go through options one by one, pick the first option that they deem satisfactory, and stop browsing the options. The selected option may not be the best one, but the consumer feels it is satisfactory enough to choose in that specific situation. Another example is the elimination-by-aspects heuristic. With this heuristic, the consumer first chooses the most important criterion and then eliminates all options that do not meet the minimum requirement. Elimination rounds are repeated until a single option remains.[25,26] There are many other heuristics,[27] and we may all have our very own rules of thumb to make various decisions. Willman-Iivarinen points out that some heuristics might be used intentionally and deliberately, but some heuristics can be used rather automatically, even on unconscious level.[28]

It is important for retailers to understand these mental shortcuts or at least to be aware that consumers have them. Understanding consumers' specific rules of thumb may help understand why they make the choices they do.

6.5 Routines and Habits

> **DID YOU KNOW?**
> - Routines and habits are formed through frequent repetitions.
> - Once formed, routines and habits do not require conscious effort and they can guide us automatically without our awareness.
> - Consumer repetition does not necessarily indicate the existence of a routine or habit. Repetition, such as purchasing the same product again and again, might be a sign of continued preference and attitudinal loyalty for the product.

It is impossible to understand choice behaviour without discussing routines and habits. Routines are automated actions or practices which guide and structure our daily lives from morning until night. They provide predictability and order to our lives.[29] Routines are characterised by temporal consistency and similarity of behaviour. Typically, we follow routines without

---

[24] Ibid.
[25] Tversky (1972).
[26] Willman-Iivarinen (2017).
[27] Kahneman and Tversky (1974).
[28] Willman-Iivarinen (2017).
[29] Heinonen (2012).

making conscious decisions.[30] While habits and routines have similar meanings, the concepts also have their differences.[31] According to studies, habits are associated with a cue tied to a specific time, place, social environment or event, which makes us behave according to our habits.[32] In other words, our habitual behaviour is activated by context cues. As Wood and Neal stated: "[…] when people perceive habit-related context cues, they often perform the habitual response with minimal guidance from goals and intentions.[33]" According to Martin and Morich, even unconscious recognition of a context and contextual cues is enough to trigger a habit.[34] Routines are usually not associated with a trigger. Although there are differences between a routine and a habit, they have more similarities than differences as forms of behaviour.

Every one of us has several routines and habits that guide our behaviour when we go shopping. We often do not even realise they exist if we do not consciously think about them. Often we only notice our routines and deeply ingrained habits when the surrounding context changes and we realise that our established ways of operating no longer work. For example, if our local grocery store closes, we will have to find a new store and learn to shop there, or if our local store changes the location of products or pathways inside the store, we have to stop using our autopilot at least for the moment and learn new ways of moving through the store. These types of situations may be highly stressful for consumers.

An interesting and difficult question regarding habits is whether a consumer's repeated choice of a specific product or store is force of habit or a sign of purchase loyalty. If we were to ask this of the company marketing the product, they would surely attribute the behaviour to loyalty. But if we were to turn to a sociologist, they would likely say that people repeatedly choose the same thing out of habit. Research shows that purchase loyalty and habits are easily confused. Seen from the outside, it is often very difficult to determine whether the repeated choice is caused by habit or loyalty. The difference is that purchase loyalty arises from a combination of conscious evaluation and positive attitudes, whereas habits are created through repeated behaviours without our conscious processing of why we are doing what we are

---

[30] Nuutinen (2012).
[31] Arlinghaus and Johnston (2019) and Neal et al. (2012).
[32] Martin and Morich (2011).
[33] Wood and Neal (2009, p. 581).
[34] Martin and Morich (2011).

doing.[35] A choice made based on purchase loyalty is by definition a conscious act, while a habitual choice is unconscious and automatic.[36]

It is important for retailers to be aware of the routines and habits of their customers. It is particularly crucial to recognise established, even unconscious behavioural models and to serve customers in a way that does not require them to frequently change these models. Customers with strong routines and habits often find the smallest changes to their shopping environment annoying. Additionally, deeply rooted routines and habits may make us rather immune to various stimuli during our shopping.

6.6 Involvement

> **DID YOU KNOW?**
> - From the viewpoint of consumer choice, involvement means the extent to which the consumer cares or is concerned about what they buy, and whether they are motivated to make the right choice.
> - A highly involved consumer tends to create a smaller evoked set and larger inept set than a consumer with low involvement.

One factor which has a significant impact on our choice behaviour is our level of involvement[37] The level of involvement measures how important a particular choice is for the consumer. The importance of the choice is determined by the individual needs, values and interests of the consumer.[38] A choice that may hold tremendous significance for one person may be entirely irrelevant to someone else. Similarly, the level of involvement may be permanent or highly situation specific.[39] In fact, it is typical for the choice of a particular product to feel of little importance on day-to-day basis, but in some specific situations the choice of that same product may become highly important. For example, when we are buying a present for an important person or arranging a party, even choices we make every day gain tremendous importance.

The basic assumption is that the more important the choice, the more careful the consumer's consideration, and correspondingly, the less important

---

[35] Liu-Thompkins and Tam (2013).
[36] Wood and Neal (2009) and Hoyer (1984).
[37] Michaelidou and Dibb (2008) and Laaksonen (1994).
[38] Zaichkowsky (1985).
[39] Michaelidou and Dibb (2008).

the choice, the less care expended to make it. According to research, involvement primarily influences the amount of information gathered and the extent of comparison between options. The terms commonly used are limited and extended choice process, which are largely defined by the level of involvement or the perceived importance of the choice. The stronger the involvement, the more extended the choice process, with more different stages included. In such a case, the choice itself is also more carefully considered. Correspondingly, the lower the level of involvement, the more limited the choice process, with fewer stages in the selection process. In such cases, consumers also employ less consideration. If the choice is of particularly low importance, the consumer may use various rules of thumb or simple choice tactics to make the selection easier. For example, the consumer may choose the option which most others have picked, or which is the cheapest.[40] It is said that in the case of low levels of involvement, various positive or negative cues tend to guide our choices because we do not want to engage in extensive information processing.[41]

Researchers have made an interesting observation about how the consumer's level of involvement influences the composition of the choice set. From the available options (i.e., the choice set), it is possible to separate the ones the consumer has a positive attitude towards and which they might purchase (i.e., the evoke set) from ones the consumer has a negative attitude towards and which they will exclude from the selection process (i.e., the inept set). When the level of involvement is high, the number of options that qualify and can be considered becomes smaller, whereas if the level is low, the number of potential options is larger. This is because a consumer with a high level of involvement is usually very demanding, using strict evaluation criteria to support the choice process, and considering only a small set of options to fulfil these criteria. This makes the number of potential options smaller. Meanwhile, consumers with a low level of involvement will not have many criteria, or the criteria are significantly laxer, meaning that the consumer may be willing to accept a broader range of different options.[42]

According to studies, the purchasing of affordable and frequently bought groceries, such as milk, coffee or toast, follows a limited or routine choice process, while the purchasing of more expensive and rarely bought specialist products, such as sports equipment or home electronics, consumers use an extended choice process. Naturally, there are exceptions, but this is a general

---

[40] Hoyer (1984).
[41] Petty and Briñol (2012).
[42] Belonax and Javalgi (1989).

overview of what level of consideration consumers typically use for which types of purchasing situations.

6.7 The Presence of Others

> **DID YOU KNOW?**
> - Consumers might feel pressured to behave in a certain way to avoid social sanctions.
> - The presence of friends is likely to increase the urge to purchase, while the presence of family members is likely to decrease it.

It is well established that consumers are susceptible to a range of social influences when making decisions or choices. The key is to know what kinds of expectations the consumer believes others are placing on their behaviour. These expectations have to do especially with what the consumer finds acceptable, and may be associated with friends, spouses, family or colleagues.

When we talk about the social impacts relating to our choice behaviour, we are usually dealing with subjective norms. Subjective norms and their impacts have been extensively studied, especially in conjunction with consumer attitudes with the goal of understanding our intentions to act a certain way. A subjective norm consists of the things individuals believe that are expected of them and ways they believe others think they should behave.[43] A subjective norm is usually based on the consumer's normative beliefs regarding how likely their important others are to consider a specific ongoing behaviour, such as buying second-hand clothes, to be acceptable or objectionable. In addition to such normative beliefs, the intensity of the individual's motivation to behave according to the expectations of others influences their subjective norm.[44]

If the consumer believes that their important others would approve of a specific behaviour, such as thrift shopping, they are more likely to engage in that behaviour. Correspondingly, a belief that others would object to the behaviour makes it likely that the individual will avoid it. The intensity of this effect correlates to how motivated the consumer is to act according to the expectations of others. The subjective norm is often called a perceived social pressure to behave in a specific way. The extent to which the subjective

---

[43] Uusitalo (1997).
[44] Ajzen (1991).

norm or social pressure influences us relates to which direction we perceive the expectations to be coming from.

Xuoming Luo has conducted a study comparing shopping with friends to shopping with family.[45] In the study, Luo examined the social impacts of these two accompanying groups on consumer behaviour (specifically impulsive purchasing) based on two experimental settings with imagined shopping scenarios. These scenarios differed in terms of who the research participant was to imagine they were shopping with (friends or family) and what the degree of cohesion of the group was thought to have. Different participants were given different scenarios to read. After reading the scenarios, the participants answered a survey on impulse purchasing and the extent to which they considered themselves to be susceptible to the influence of others. Luo found that in the study, the presence of friends increased the participants' impulse purchases, while the presence of family members decreased them. The effects were greater the more cohesive or closer the shopping group was thought to be. Shopping with very close friends or family members came with a different set of expectations than shopping with friends or family who were considered more distant. Luo's study is a good illustration of how much the company in which we shop can determine what we consider acceptable behaviour. Based on this study, it could be said that consumers find it acceptable to relax and be impulsive with close friends, while they want to present a more prudent persona to family members.

Social influence can be also non-interactive, meaning that the mere presence of others in social situations influences us. For example, Dahm et al. explored queuing in a retail setting and found that queues can cause a negative social pressure particularly for those customers who reach the head of a queue and start using a retail service.[46] Argo et al. also studied non-interactive social influence in a retail context and found that non-interactive social presence of others affects consumers when the social presence is large (vs. small) and is in close (vs. far) proximity.[47] The presence of others may also lead to spontaneous mimicry. This means that the mere perception of another's postures, mannerisms and other behaviours automatically increases the likelihood of engaging in the same behaviour. Spontaneous mimicry was discussed briefly in Chapter 4.

It is **important for retailers to understand how a consumer's behaviour may be dependent on the group with whom they are visiting the store. If a consumer enters the store together with others, they are susceptible to their

---

[45] Luo (2005).
[46] Dahm et al. (2018, p. 218).
[47] Argo et al.(2005).

expectations and to the behavioural norms of the group. Unspoken expectations and social norms may have a significant impact on how the consumer behaves in the store and what they choose for their shopping basket.

> To take advantage of the presence of others and peer influence, retailers could launch promotions to encourage consumers to shop with their friends. A "bring a friend and get a discount" type of promotion could be a nice way to gain new customers and increase foot traffic, while providing an opportunity to boost impulse purchases among customers.

6.8 Time Pressure

> **DID YOU KNOW?**
> - Consumers who make purchases under time pressure tend to simplify their decision-making.
> - When pressed for time, consumers place more weight on the features they consider most important and are more likely to focus on finding negative quality cues.
> - Consumers are more likely to act habitually when they are under time pressure.

Time pressure, or the sense of urgency experienced by the consumer, also affects decision-making and is a common feature of the retail environment. As Dhar and Nowlis have noted: "[...] we know that a number of decisions are made by consumers under time pressure and that consumers often spend a limited amount of time making decisions in many product categories.[48]"

Time pressure may influence the amount of time a consumer can use to gather and process information before coming to a decision. The less time there is available, the less opportunity the consumer has to search for information to support a decision. A consumer under time pressure must also process the information they collect very quickly. It is generally understood that consumers under time pressure will be very selective in searching and using information, and will seek to focus on a few critical cues or some unique features.[49] Consumers are more likely to act habitually when pressed

---

[48] Dhar and Nowlis (1999, p. 382).
[49] Dhar and Nowlis (1999), Nilsson et al. (2017) and Willman-Iivarinen (2017).

for time.[50] Studies have also found that individuals under time pressure will focus more on finding negative quality cues than consumers with a more relaxed schedule.[51] Thus, it seems that the information-seeking process becomes skewed when consumers have little time. Researchers believe that this is because when consumers are in a hurry, they want to protect themselves from mistakes. This is particularly true in decision-making situations which involve some form of risk.[52] Consumers under time pressure may be more likely to simplify their decision-making, e.g., by using heuristics.[53] A time pressure is considered particularly challenging if the time allocated for the decision is less than usual, or less than is required to make the decision. Such time pressures have been found to increase consumer stress.

> Our increasingly dynamic and stressful lifestyles have generated a demand for convenient food consumption. Therefore, it is not surprising that "on-the-go" consumption is a growing trend in the retail industry. On-the-go refers to immediate food consumption while in transit from one place to another. To alleviate consumers' time scarcity and make their lives a bit easier, many retailers are now offering on-the-go products such as ready-to-eat snacks, healthy smoothies and other portable drinks. On-the-go consumption has also created demand for new package design that takes into account that the food is eaten in transit.

Chaturvedi has established that time pressures are associated with impulse purchases. According to Chaturvedi, impulse purchases become more likely if the consumer experiences intense time pressure, or conversely, if they have ample time to make their purchases. Meanwhile, a reasonable time limit had no impact on impulsive buying. Based on the study, Chaturvedi has stated that the likelihood of impulse purchases is at its highest when consumers have less than 15 or more than 60 minutes to shop.[54]

It is important for retailers to understand the impact of time pressures and urgency on consumers' choice behaviour, and to develop and provide consumers with solutions, including cues, which enable a pleasant shopping experience even when the consumer is in a hurry.

---

[50] Wood and Neal (2009).
[51] Wright (1974).
[52] Wright and Weitz (1977).
[53] Dhar and Nowlis (1999).
[54] Chaturvedi (2015).

6.9 Familiarity of the Environment

> **DID YOU KNOW?**
> - In a familiar environment, consumers are likely to switch to autopilot, while in a less familiar environment they are likely to be more aware of their shopping behaviour.
> - Consumers with low category familiarity are more likely to engage in impulsive buying than consumers with high category familiarity.

The familiarity of the environment is known to act as a moderating variable between store-level factors or cues, and purchasing behaviour. Familiarity refers to the perceived level of prior knowledge that consumers have on a particular store. Consumers accumulate familiarity through direct or indirect experiences.[55]

Otterbring et al. have claimed that customers who are less familiar with the store and its layout are more likely to direct their attention towards in-store cues,[56] even though it has also been argued that customers who are familiar with the store have a greater ability to use the store environment to guide their shopping needs. In their study, Otterbring et al. found that customers' store familiarity had a positive impact on navigational fluency. Navigational fluency, in turn, could affect actual choice behaviour. The familiarity of the environment may also determine whether we switch to autopilot when we enter the store. As Martin and Morchi have pointed out: "If the mind perceives an environment as familiar, the perception enables the unconscious to automate behaviour. If the consumer perceives the environment as novel, the conscious mind actively engages to interpret its surroundings and figure out what to do.[57]" Doucé et al. in turn argue that it is likely that consumers in a familiar retail store environments have developed a schema which makes the consumer more comfortable in coping with and assimilating the information that the familiar store and its sensory cues provide.[58] In general, we tend to use our past experiences and the resulting schemas when evaluating store environments.

Familiarity can also be explored on the category level, or even on the brand level. It has been established that consumers with less category familiarity are

---

[55] Alba and Hutchinson (1987).
[56] Otterbring et al. (2016).
[57] Martin and Morich (2011, p. 14).
[58] Douce et al. (2022).

more likely to engage in impulsive buying than consumers with high category familiarity.[59] Conversely, it can be assumed that consumers with high category familiarity are likely to be less impulsive than consumers with lower familiarity. This also indicates that consumers with low category familiarity are more influenced by store-level promotions than consumers with high category familiarity. Retailers should take this into account when tailoring their in-store promotion strategies.

6.10 Summary

It has been noted that the strength and direction of the relation between cues and various responses are moderated by personal and situational factors.[60] These factors either accelerate or inhibit the effects that cues may have. Thus, understanding these factors is highly relevant from the retailers' viewpoint. They can help understand why some customers can easily be nudged by cues, while others are entirely resistant to them.

This chapter has introduced nine accelerating or inhibiting factors, from shopping motives to involvement and time pressure. However, other factors, such as demographic features like age or gender, may also be significant response moderators. For example, research has shown that women are more sensitive to scents and better able to identify them,[61] meaning that women are likely to respond differently to olfactory cues than men. Likewise, it is said that teenagers' sense of smell is 200% stronger than adults.[62] Further studies will hopefully shed more light on these different response moderators.

Self-Reflective Questions
- Describe yourself as a consumer.
- What are the things that are central to you when you make consumption choices?
- How thoughtful are you as a consumer, and are there some consumption choices that you consider more carefully than others?
- To what extent do you consider shopping a pleasant way to spend time? Is shopping something that makes you relax and puts you in a good mood, or does it irritate you?

---

[59] Shukla and Banerjee (2014).
[60] Bitner (1992).
[61] Spangenberg et al. (2006).
[62] Lindström (2005).

- Do you have any particular rules of thumb that you use when making your selection decisions?
- How do you make your decisions if you are in a hurry?
- When shopping in a store you are familiar with, do you routinely use the same route and pick the same products for your shopping basket, or do you try to find something new in the store?
- Do you find that your shopping behaviour varies whether you are shopping alone or with your close friends or family?

Decision-Based Questions

- As a store manager, how would you consider the different shopping motives that customers may have when they come to the store? How should the different shopping motives be taken into account when planning the store environment?
- As a store manager, how would you consider the different routines and habits that customers may have? How should the routines and habits be taken into account when planning the store environment?
- As a store manager, how would you consider the time pressure that customers might have when they come to the store? How should the potential time pressure be taken into account when planning the store environment?
- As a store manager, how would you take advantage of the peer influence?
- As a store manager, how would you take into account the fact that customers' familiarity with the store is likely to vary?

References

Ainslie, G. (1975). Specious reward: A behavioral theory of impulsiveness and impulse control. *Psychological Bulletin, 82*, 463–496.

Ajzen, I. (1991). The theory of planned behavior. *Organizational Behavior and Human Decision Processes, 50*, 179–211.

Alba, J. W., & Hutchinson, J. W. (1987). Dimensions of consumer expertise. *Journal of Consumer Research, 13*, 411–454.

Argo, J. J., Dahl, D. W., & Manchanda, R. V. (2005). The influence of a mere social presence in a retail context. *Journal of Consumer Research, 32*, 207–212.

Arlinghaus, K. R., & Johnston, C. A. (2019). The importance of creating habits and routine. *American Journal of Lifestyle Medicine, 13*, 142–144.

Arnold, M., & Reynolds, K. (2003). Hedonic shopping motivations. *Journal of Retailing, 79*, 77–95.

Babin, B. J., & Darden, W. R. (1996). Good and bad shopping vibes: Spending and patronage satisfaction. *Journal of Business Research, 35*, 201–206.

Bellenger, D. N., & Korgaonkar, P. K. (1980). Profile the recreational shopper. *Journal of Retailing, 56*, 77–92.

Belonax, J., & Javalgi, R. (1989). The influence of involvement and product class quality on consumer choice sets. *Journal of the Academy of Marketing Science, 17*.

Bitner, M. J. (1992). Servicescapes: The impact of physical surroundings on customers and employees. *Journal of Marketing, 56*, 57–71.

Chaturvedi, R. K. (2015). The influence of availability of shopping time on impulse purchase tendency. *The IUP Journal of Marketing Management, XIV*, 47–62.

Collins, L., & Montgomery, C. (1969). The origins of motivational research. *European Journal of Marketing, 3*, 103–113.

Dahm, M., Wentzel, D., Herzog, W., & Wiecek, A. (2018). Breathing down your neck!: The impact of queues on customers using a retail service. *Journal of Retailing, 94*, 217–230.

Dawson, S., Bloch, P., & Ridgway, N. (1990). Shopping motives, emotional states, and retail outcomes. *Journal of Retailing, 58*, 34–57.

Dhar, R., & Nowlis, S. (1999). The effect of time pressure on consumer choice deferral. *Journal of Consumer Research, 25*, 369–384.

Douce, L., Willems, K., & Chaudhuri, A. (2022). Bargain effectiveness in differentiated store environments: The role of store affect, processing fluency, and store familiarity. *Journal of Retailing and Consumer Services, 69*, 1–12.

Fraj, E., & Martinez, E. (2006). Influence of personality on ecological consumer behaviour. *Journal of Consumer Behaviour, 5*, 167–181.

Gardner, M. P. (1985). Mood states and consumer behavior: A critical review. *Journal of Consumer Research, 12*, 281–300.

Gillebaart, M. (2018). The 'operational' definition of self-control. *Frontiers in Psychology, 9*.

Hattie, J., Hodis, F., & Kang, S. (2020). Theories of motivation: Integration and ways forward. *Contemporary Educational Psychology, 61*.

Heinonen, V. (2012). Arkielämän tutkimusperinteet, kulutus ja rutiinit, Kulutustutkimus. *Nyt, 1*.

Hoyer, W. D. (1984). An examination of consumer decision making for a common repeat purchase product. *Journal of Consumer Research, 11*, 822–829.

Kahneman, D., & Tversky, A. (1974). Judgment under uncertainty: Heuristics and biases. *Science, 185*.

Kaltcheva, V. D., & Weitz, B. A. (2006). When should a retailer create an exciting store environment? *Journal of Marketing, 70*, 107–118.

Kassarjian, H. (1971). Personality and consumer behavior: A review. *Journal of Marketing Research, VIII*, 409–418.

Köster, E. P., & Mojet, J. (2015). From mood to food and from food to mood: A psychological perspective on the measurement of food-related emotions in consumer research. *Food Research International, 76*, 180–191.

Laaksonen, P. (1994). *Consumer involvement: Concepts and research*. Routledge.
Lindström, M. (2005). *BRAND sense: Building powerful brands through touch, taste, smell*. Free Press.
Liu-Thompkins, Y., & Tam, L. (2013). Not all repeat customers are the same: Designing effective cross-selling promotion based on attitudinal loyalty and habit. *Journal of Marketing, 77*, 21–36.
Luo, X. (2005). How does shopping with others influence impulsive purchasing? *Journal of Consumer Psychology, 15*, 288–294.
Luomala, H. T., & Laaksonen, M. (2000). Contributions from mood research. *Psychology & Marketing, 17*, 195–233.
Martin, N., & Morich, K. (2011). Unconscious mental processes in consumer choice: Toward a new model of consumer behavior. *Journal of Brand Management, 18*, 483–505.
Maslow, A. H. (1943). A theory of human motivation. *Psychological Review, 50*, 370–396.
Michaelidou, N., & Dibb, S. (2008). Consumer involvement: A new perspective. *Marketing Review, 8*, 83–99.
Morschett, D., Swoboda, B., & Foscht, T. (2005). Perception of store attributes and overall attitude towards grocery retailers: The role of shopping motives. *The International Review of Retail, Distribution and Consumer Research, 15*, 423–447.
Neal, D. T., Wood, W., Labrecque, J. S., & Lally, P. (2012). How do habits guide behavior? Perceived and actual triggers of habits in daily life. *Journal of Experimental Social Psychology., 48*, 492–498.
Nilsson, E., Gärling, T. & Marell, A. (2017). Effects of time pressure, type of shopping, and store attributes on consumers' satisfaction with grocery shopping. *The International Review of Retail, Distribution and Consumer Research, 27*.
Noble, S., Griffith, D., & Adjei, M. (2006). Drivers of local merchant loyalty: Understanding the influence of gender and shopping motives. *Journal of Retailing, 82*, 177–188.
Nuutinen, O. (2012). Puheenvuoro: Valinta, vastuu ja rutiini. *Hybris, 1*.
Otterbring, T., Wästlund, E., & Gustfasson, A. (2016). Eye-tracking customers' visual attention in the wild: Dynamic gaze behavior moderates the effect of store familiarity on navigational fluency. *Journal of Retailing and Consumer Services, 28*, 165–170.
Ozer, L., & Gültekin, B. (2015). Pre- and post-purchase stage in impulse buying: The role of mood and satisfaction. *Journal of Retailing and Consumer Services, 22*, 71–76.
Petty, R. E., & Briñol, P. (2012). The elaboration likelihood model. In P. A. M. Van Lange, A. W. Kruglanski, & E. T. Higgins (Eds.), *Handbook of theories of social psychology* (pp. 224–245). Sage Publications Ltd.
Pornpitakpan, C., Yuan, Y., & Han, J. H. (2017). The effect of salespersons' retail service quality and consumers' mood on impulse buying. *Australasian Marketing Journal, 25*, 2–11.

Puccinelli, N. M., Goodstein, R. C., Grewal, D., Price, R., Raghubir, P., & Stewart, D. W. (2009). Customer experience management in retailing: Understanding the buying process. *Journal of Retailing, 85*, 15–30.

Roberts, J. A., & Manolis, C. (2012). Cooking up a recipe for self-control: The three ingredients of self-control and its impact on impulse buying. *Journal of Marketing Theory & Practice, 20*, 173–188.

Shukla, P., & Banerjee, M. (2014). The direct and interactive effects of store-level promotions on impulse purchase: Moderating impact of category familiarity and normative influences. *Journal of Consumer Behaviour, 13*, 242–250.

Spangenberg, E. R., Sprott, D. E., Grohmann, B., & Tracy, D. L. (2006). Gender-congruent ambient scent influences on approach and avoidance behaviours in a retail store. *Journal of Business Research, 59*, 1281–1287.

Swinyard, W. R. (1993). The effects of mood, involvement, and quality of store experience on shopping intentions. *Journal of Consumer Research, 20*(2), 271–280.

Tran V. D. (2022). Consumer impulse buying behavior: the role of confidence as moderating effect. *Heliyon, 8*.

Tversky, A. (1972). Elimination by aspects: A theory of choice. *Psychological Review, 79*, 281–299.

Uusitalo, L. (1997). Kuluttajien ympäristöä koskevat valinnat. *Liiketaloudellinen aikakauskirja, 1*, 15–31.

Williams, T., Slama, M., & Rogers, J. (1985). Behavioral characteristics of the recreational shopper and implications for retail management. *Journal of the Academy of Marketing Science, 13*, 307–316.

Willman-Iivarinen, H. (2017). The future of consumer decision making. *European Journal of Futures Research, 5*, 14.

Wood, W., & Neal, D. (2009). The habitual consumer. *Journal of Consumer Psychology, 19*, 579–592.

Wright, P. (1974). The harassed decision maker: Time pressures, distractions, and the use of evidence. *Journal of Applied Psychology, 59*, 555–561.

Wright, P., & Weitz, B. (1977). Time horizon effects on product evaluation strategies. *Journal of Marketing Research, 14*, 429–443.

Yim, M.Y.-C. (2017). When shoppers don't have enough self-control resources: Applying the strength model of self-control. *Journal of Consumer Marketing, 34*, 328–337.

Zaichkowsky, J. (1985). Measuring the involvement construct. *Journal of Consumer Research, 12*, 341–352.

7

Key Points of This Book

7.1 Cue Diversity

One of the main messages of this book is that as consumers we are exposed to a large number of different cues whenever we go shopping. Cues are sensory stimuli which we may sense and experience in different ways, and which may influence us on a conscious or unconscious level.[1] For example, we see, hear and smell many different cues as we move around a store. Cues are meaningful in many ways. For example, empirical evidence supports the idea that cues provide us with information that influences our perceptions of the store and helps us to make judgements. Furthermore, it is important to understand that when we step in a retail store, we are enveloped with multisensory experiences. Even if we are not aware of it, our visit in a store is always multisensory in nature.

From this holistic perspective, it can be said that any physical or non-physical element of a store the consumer encounters or senses while shopping could be seen as a potential cue which may influence the consumer and their behaviour. Cues are something that surround us from the moment we enter into the store until the moment we leave. One could say that basically anything that we can perceive in a store using our senses can be called cue. Shapes, curves, colours, temperature, surfaces, weight, perfumes and so on are all cues. It is also important to note that these different cues, even tiniest ones, can convey specific meanings to us. Numerous studies have demonstrated that certain cues can be linked to certain features or benefits of the

---

[1] Biswas (2019).

store. For instance, high ceilings communicate freedom or handwritten typeface is associated with a human touch. Neat and sparse displays, in turn, are associated with more expensive brands. Odd-ending pricing is a sign of great deal whereas even pricing indicates quality. Chapter 4 has introduced these meanings rather extensively.

In practice, cues associated with shopping in a store environment can be classified in many ways. This book references a well-established method of classifying cues in physical retail environments into ambient, design and social cues[2]:

- Ambient cues are non-visual, background conditions in the store environment. Such cues include lighting, temperature, background music and scents.
- Design cues are the aesthetic and functional cues in the store environment which help the consumer understand the retail context as a space and set of functions. Design cues include, for example, store architecture, layout and colour palette.
- Social cues relate to other people, such as the number of retail staff, their clothing and body language. It is said that social cues can affect us significantly because we have a natural tendency to perceive and interpret other people.

Although the above classification is multifaceted and includes all key environmental elements, it does not take into account cues that can have an impact at the moment a choice is being made. Thus, in addition to the cues that are related to the general atmosphere of our shopping journey, this book also has dedicated sections for the following cues that are more directly related to the moment of choice:

- Haptic cues; primarily information we receive when we hold the product in our hands, i.e., information that comes via the sense of touch. Haptic cues can be, for example, weight or softness.
- Merchandise-related cues; cues that we face when assessing the product offering and making the product choice in the front of shelf. The way products are organised on the shelf is an example of merchandise-related cues.

---

[2] See, e.g., Baker et al. (2002), Kumar and Kim (2014) and Roggeveen et al. (2020).

- Pricing-related cues; cues that signals about the prices or offers. Pricing-related cues like 0.99 pricing often try to persuade us that the offer is unbeatable.

By taking into account all these various cues, this book has provided a comprehensive overview of the cues that exist in a retail environment and thus has expanded the current knowledge of sensory marketing and its multifaceted nature.

Explicit and Implicit Cues

The types of cues discussed above may be grouped into explicit and implicit cues. This classification helps to understand the nature of cues and how they affect us. The division of cues into explicit and implicit has mainly been discussed in terms of product or packaging design,[3] and less studied on the store level. However, this classification also works on the store level and helps to categorise a wide spectrum of cues into two basic groups.

Explicit cues are cues that can be clearly observed while shopping, and their goal is to influence consumer choice, such as impulse buys, in a very direct and targeted manner. Explicit cues may be clearly formulated verbal statements (e.g., "Today only" or "Maximum three packs per customer") that the consumer is expected to recognise and engage with right on the spot.[4] Price is also an example of an explicit cue. It is said that consumers tend to use explicit cues as easy-to-process sources of information when assessing the quality and making judgements.[5] Implicit cues, in turn, are more subtle, almost hidden and the consumers may not be consciously aware of them or how their behaviour is affected by these cues during their visit. Furthermore, even if implicit cues are observed, the information that they provide might not be that obvious or easy to comprehend. One could say that implicit cues connote abstract and highly associative meanings whereas explicit cues convey more concrete information and literal meanings. Table 7.1 describes the features of explicit and implicit cues.

Cues in a retail environment can be categorised either as explicit or implicit cues, even though in some cases it may be difficult to differentiate between the two. For example, ambient cues (e.g., scents or background music) and design cues (e.g., the colour palette in the store) are primarily implicit cues

---

[3] See, e.g., Ooijen et al. (2017) and Karjalainen (2007).
[4] Karjalainen (2007).
[5] Ooijen et al. (2017).

Table 7.1 Explicit and implicit cues

Explicit cues	Implicit cues
Observable	Hidden and subtle
Concrete information	Abstract meanings
Easy-to-process	Difficult to comprehend
Likely to affect on a conscious level	Likely to affect unconsciously
Influence the moment of choice	Influence in the background
Primarily help to make judgements	Primarily engender emotional responses

which influence and guide consumer choice indirectly from the background. These are rather abstract or hidden sensory inputs that we might not pay that much, or any, attention to when we walk around the store and make our choices. Meanwhile, some cues like product displays, odd-ending pricing or info related to scarcity or popularity of products are more observable and affect at the moment of choice. In other words, these cues are explicit in nature and can persuade or otherwise impact consumer choice and opinion in a very straightforward. For example, explicit cues can create a sense of urgency around a product offering that then motivates consumers to act fast and make a purchase before it is too late. However, even in the case of the most explicit cues, the consumer may not be fully aware of how they are being influenced.

As a side note, whether one is interested in studying explicit or implicit cues, semiotics[6] could offer significant help in understanding the meanings that cues convey. Implicit cues like background colours or shapes in particular may communicate meanings that can only be fully understood after thorough semiotic analysis. For retailers, the ability to grasp these semantic meanings would be very valuable. By understanding what cues actually communicate, retailers could ensure that their stores truly resonate with their customers and generate the intended responses among them. Understanding the meanings that cues convey would also help ensure that there is a semantic match (congruence) between the cues. In addition, retailers who have an idea what the cues really communicate can invest their money more wisely.

Tactical and Strategic Cues

Another way of categorising cues in the retail environment is to classify them into tactical and strategic cues. This classification rests on the role and purpose each cue has for the business operations of the store. It is important

---

[6] See, e.g., Mick (1986).

to note that cues that are under the retailer's control may be used for very different purposes.

Tactical cues are intended to generate immediate effects in the customer and may be used, for example, to draw attention or to increase the number of impulse buys. Typically, tactical cues can be rapidly deployed and do not necessarily require extensive investments from the store. Tactical cues are part of the daily business and marketing efforts of the store and may have to do with the ways products are displayed or prices marked. For example, cues with simple and persuasive messages like "Limited edition" or "Today only" can be seen as tactical cues. Meanwhile, strategic cues have to do with the overall image of the store and its brand building. The main goal of strategic cues is to help the store gain and maintain the targeted position in the minds of consumers. One could say that strategic cues are part of a retailer's storytelling. Thus, strategic cues are not about immediate effects; they produce outcomes in the long run and help the store differentiate itself from competitors. For this reason, strategic cues often require more planning and investments from the store. Strategic cues may be also more difficult to change after they have been set, i.e., they are relatively stable. It is clear that strategic cues and their use should be included in the store's strategic planning. Compared to tactical cues, strategic cues convey more profound meanings, like key benefits (e.g., quality, fun, convenience or safety) or even values of the store, and may include cues in the store's retail design, or cues relating to the soundscape and scents in the store. Table 7.2 describes the central differences between tactical and strategic cues.

The diversity of the cues and, above all, their ability to engage all our senses, is undeniably the aspect that makes the physical retail environment such a unique consumer context, setting it apart from online retail environments. However, whether explicit or implicit, tactical or strategic, all cues must be managed correctly for the multisensory nature of the retail environment to be translated into a tangible competitive advantage and superiority

Table 7.2 Tactical and strategic cues

Tactical cues	Strategic cues
Seek immediate effects	Seek long-term effects
Focus on behavioural reactions	Related to overall impressions
Quick to implement	Require preparation
Part of the daily work of the store	Part of the strategic planning of the store
Convey simple meanings	Convey profound meanings
Related to product displays and pricing promotions, etc.	Related to store design, audio branding and signature scents, etc.

factor. In particular, cues should be seen as an opportunity to communicate with consumers and convey intended meanings or messages to them. If poorly managed and haphazardly used, cues can result in confusion or sensory overload of the clientele. We will discuss such practical measures more at a later point.

7.2 Cue Impact

Several studies, many of which have been extensively referenced in this book, have established that cues do indeed have an impact on us, and emerging research keeps supporting this finding. It is widely stated that cues offer information that can shape how we feel, think or act while we are visiting a store. For example, Baker et al. argue that empirical evidence supports the idea that information from cues influences consumers' assessments of a store.[7] We are also becoming increasingly aware of the joint effects of cues, even though there is still very little research into specific cue combinations.[8] What we know is that consumers tend to respond differently to cue combinations than to individual stimuli.[9] Assessing the joint effects (i.e., the impact of multiple cues) is very demanding and requires skills such as in-depth understanding of cue (in)congruence (see Chapter 5). Overall, it can be said that existing research supports the view that cues separately or together do, or at least have the potential to, impact us.

Even though the impact or potential impact of cues is undeniable, a cue is not a magic bullet that will automatically lead to a specific effect every time. We observe cues selectively,[10] and the processing and interpretation of sensory observations is also always influenced by our previous experiences and the given setting. It is said that explaining cue impact requires profound understanding of how we perceive things and how our mind works.[11] While it is highly challenging to fully explain the impact of cues, this book endeavours to shed some light on the mechanisms through which cues influence us.

---

[7] Baker et al. (2002).
[8] Spence (2020).
[9] Helmefalk and Berndt (2018).
[10] When it comes to the filtering the incoming stimuli (cue), individuals can be classified either as screeners or non-screeners. Screeners are relatively selective individuals whereas non-screeners are less selective, and therefore, they are more sensitive to stimulus changes (Donovan & Rossiter, 1982; Mehrabian & Russell, 1974). One could assume that the level familiarity with the environment determines at least partly to what extent individual engage in selective observation (Martin & Morich, 2011).
[11] Kumar and Kim (2014) and Krishna (2012).

In short, cue impacts can be seen as emotional responses, cognitive evaluations or impulse purchases. Cue impacts can be also divided into conscious and unconscious impacts. In addition, various response moderators which can have a significant effect on how cues influence us are likely also in play.

Emotional Response

According to research, it seems that cues in a retail store either alone or in combination often trigger specific types of transient emotional states, which, if sufficiently intense, may lead to a behavioural reaction.[12] In other words, cues are likely to engender emotional responses in us. This means that cues that we sense in a store can make us feel, for example, relaxed or excited. Emotional states occurring in the moment are typically something that we are consciously experiencing. Numerous studies have demonstrated that pleasure and arousal are core emotional states that are influenced by external cues, such as music, colours or odours, and that they also have a potential to influence our behaviour, for example, whether we approach a store or avoid it.[13,14] In other words, pleasure and arousal as emotional states mediate the effects of in-store cues on our behaviour. Pleasure refers to the degree to which the person feels happy, relaxed or satisfied in the situation, whereas arousal refers to the degree to which a person feels stimulated, excited or active.[15] Both pleasure and arousal can be seen as continuums that have low and high ends. For example, a person can feel less aroused or even non-aroused in the situation, or they can experience high levels of arousal. Adjectives such as sleep and boredom are used to describe low levels of arousal whereas high levels of arousal are described as alertness and excitement.

According to studies, our arousal may increase in a complex environment, fast-tempo music, bright lighting or the scent of grapefruit, while pleasure may be increased by blue or green colours in the store's colour palette, slow-tempo music or a unified design appearance in the store setting.[16] Many

---

[12] Mehrabian and Russell (1974), Donovan and Rossiter (1982) and Roggeveen et al. (2020).

[13] The literature typically talks about two different behavioural reactions evoked by emotional states: approach and avoidance. This means that our emotional states can make us approach a target (such as a store) or avoid it. This "approach-avoidance" classification, introduced by Mehrabian and Russell (1974), has been extensively used to describe the behavioural reactions of consumers to environmental stimuli and the emotional states they evoke.

[14] Mehrabian and Russell (1974) and Kaltcheva and Weitz (2006).

[15] Donovan and Rossiter (1982).

[16] According to Mehrabian and Russell (1974), the information rate or "information load" of an environment is directly related to arousal. A high-load environment, i.e., environment that is novel and complex makes us feel excited and alert (see Donovan & Rossiter, 1982). However, one should

similar examples are described in Chapter 4. There has been considerable research regarding the kinds of behavioural reactions pleasure and arousal can provoke among consumers. The general understanding is that moderate or high levels of pleasure and arousal enhance approach behaviours, although the effects of arousal have been considered less clear.[17] Nevertheless, in an ideal situation, the retailer will discover a combination of cues which enables them to simultaneously control both arousal and pleasure in exactly the right way. For example, studies have shown that if an environment features cues that increase our arousal while we are experiencing the setting as pleasurable, we will want to approach the environment and spend time there.[18] The above means that although pleasure and arousal are more or less independent dimensions they affect us together. As Ridgway et al. stated "[…] consumers who find an environment pleasant and arousing will want to explore the environment, communicate and interact with others in the environment, and report greater satisfaction with the environment.[19]" However, creating such positive joint effects is by no means simple and may yield unexpected results, including sensory overload.[20] Some cues also seem to easily trigger negative emotions, like irritation. Such cues include congestion in the store, long lines to the cashier as well as general disarray.

Cognitive Evaluations

When we walk into a retail store and face various cues, we are not only emotionally touched, but we also evaluate the store and its cues cognitively. This means that we engage in at least some sort of thinking and reasoning while we are exploring the store. Through our cognitive processes we are able to convert cues into meaningful information and come to a conclusion about the store.[21] Cognitive evaluations might affect psychological factors like our mental images or attitudes towards the store.[22] For example, cues like warm-coloured backgrounds or low ceilings can create an immediate perceptual

---

keep in mind that an extremely high information load that leads to high levels of arousal may evoke unpleasant feelings.
[17] Kaltcheva and Weitz (2006) and Ridgway et al. (1990).
[18] Donovan and Rossiter (1982).
[19] Ridgway et al. (1990, p. 140).
[20] Doucé and Adams (2020).
[21] Kumar and Kim (2014) and Roggeveen et al. (2020).
[22] Bardzil and Rosenberger (1996) have argued that the elaboration likelihood of a cue information can vary from high to low, depending on the personal relevance and consequences of the information. Bardzil and Rosenberger state that when the personal relevance and consequences of a cue are high, and it is more likely that a consumer will use the information cognitively and give the information

image in our minds. In fact, academic literature on cues often discusses how cues like store design or the number of employees on the floor can influence or enhance our quality, service and price impressions of the store. For instance, Baker et al. found that the store environment affects consumers' perceptions of the price and quality of merchandise as well as the quality of employee service.[23] All in all, there is strong evidence that cues have significant effects on consumers' cognitive evaluations of retailer image in quality, service and price.

Visual cues may trigger specific mental pictures or impressions in consumers[24] and may have a particularly powerful impact in shaping the first impression. This means that cues that we perceive immediately after entering a store can influence our subjective opinions or expectations on the store. For example, just the width of passageways or the shape of physical objects in the store can generate specific impressions regarding the quality of the store or the retailer's competence. Lighting and its brightness can also impact the impressions we develop of a store and its price level, and the way the staff are dressed may influence our impression of their professionalism and the quality of the store in general. Such impressions or mental images may then reflect, for example, on our purchasing intentions. One central cue that influences how we think about a store has to do with the selection of goods and especially the number of available options. Ailawadi and Keller expressed this nicely by stating "you are what you sell".[25] Similarly, the floor plan of the store and the ease of shopping influence our opinion of the store. In terms of individual products, cues that shape our impressions and expectations may be haptic, such as the weight of the product or the surface texture of the packaging. Just the choice to mark a reduction in price as a percentage or absolute value may impact consumers' impressions of the price of the product.

An interesting question regarding cue impact is whether consumers first think or feel when they step in a retail store and become surrounded by cues. This is a difficult question to answer,[26] and many researchers disagree on the matter. Some researchers argue that cognitive evaluations precede emotional states, while others argue that emotional states come first. Although there is no clear answer to this question, it has been argued that a person cannot have an emotional response in the absence of some sort of a cognitive appraisal

---

thorough consideration. Low personal relevance and consequences, in turn, lead to processing information cues peripherally or heuristically without engaging in extensive cognitive evaluation. For more about the Elaboration Likelihood Model (ELM), see, e.g., Petty and Briñol (2012).

[23] Baker et al. (2002).
[24] Spence et al. (2014).
[25] Ailawadi and Keller (2004).
[26] Lin (2004) and Bettman (1986).

of the stimulus,[27] which would seem logical. However, it should be noted that our behaviour is often unconsciously guided by the environment, which makes the above discussion even more complex.

Spontaneous Impulse Purchases

A spontaneous impulse purchase that is made in the store is a good example of an impact created by cues.[28] Impulse buying is generally understood as something we do without conscious thinking or pre-planning. It is said that we engage very often in impulse buying while shopping and this sort of unintentional and unplanned behaviour is motivated by external cues to a large extent. As Dijksterhuis et al. state, "[…] some of our choices are likely made without any information processing at all, neither just before we pick a product, nor earlier. […] Here […] we truly buy things on impulse. In other words, attitudes are bypassed completely. These impulse choices are usually strongly affected by subtle cues in the environment".[29] Such an impulse buy that is done on the spot may be, for example, the result of cues that communicate limited availability or restrictions on purchase amounts. Indicating that a product is a "best seller" may also result in impulse purchases. These sorts of cues or selling slogans often make consumers feel an urgent or irresistible need to buy the promoted product immediately without any real reasoning or an evaluation of need. Sometimes we may choose a product simply because it happens to be conveniently within reach, or we see others choosing it. For some, the aroma of freshly-baked bread may lead to an impulsive decision to add a warm baguette into their shopping cart. Thus, sudden impulse purchases that do not involve conscious reasoning may be explained by the store setting and its myriad cues, and the urgent need to buy or sensory experiences that cues stimulate right on the spot. However, it should be remembered that the antecedents of impulse purchases may also arise from much deeper in our minds. This is to say that various psychological factors or internal triggers, such as desires, wishes or cravings, may cause impulse buys or at least make the consumer more susceptible to them.[30] Impulse purchases are not motivated by external cues or promotional stimuli alone.

---

[27] Kumar and Kim (2014).
[28] Piron (1991) has defined impulse purchase "as a purchase that is (1) unplanned, (2) the result of an exposure to a stimulus, (3) decided on-the-spot".
[29] Dijksterhuis et al. (2005, p. 194).
[30] Beatty and Ferrell (1998).

It should be also noted that there are many different kinds of impulse purchases, including pure impulse buying and reminder impulse buying.[31] Pure impulse buying is truly buying on impulse and is something that breaks a normal buying pattern, whereas reminder impulse buying refers to purchases that are triggered by some sort of reminders that the consumer perceives in the store (e.g., seeing the product in another customer's shopping cart or on the shelf) and then recalls the need of the product (e.g., the stock at home is low). It is said that pure impulse purchases do not have such a reminder component.

Conscious and Unconscious Impacts

The described impacts of cues can be either conscious or unconscious. When cues influence us consciously, we observe the cue with our senses, interpret the information that is provided according to our conscious mind, and then we may (or may not) react to it, for example, by selecting a specific product. In the literature, this kind of chain is known as the conscious information processing model. Key phases of this model are our conscious sensory observations and the conscious processing of such observations. Conscious processing can involve either high or a relatively low levels of elaboration and reasoning. The processing of sensory information also involves our previous experiences, information and knowledge structures that are stored in our memory, among other things. The outcome of this conscious processing could be, for example, a mental image or change in our attitudes that may affect our behaviour. Emotional states are also primarily conscious experiences, although some of our emotional reactions can be unconscious. Through our conscious process we also decode semantic meanings that cues convey to us, although this can also happen without our full awareness.[32] A simple example of conscious information processing can be found Baker et al.'s article: "[…] consumers attend to design, social, and ambient environment cues when evaluating stores, because they believe that these cues offer reliable information about product-related attributes such as quality, price, and the overall shopping experience […] For example, a customer entering a store with tile floors, the smell of popcorn, fluorescent lighting, and Top-40 music may access from memory a 'discount store' schema and infer that the store's merchandise is low priced and of average

---

[31] See more about various types of impulse buying Stern (1962).
[32] Velmans (1991).

quality and that the store has minimal service.[33]" Without going further into the conscious effects of cues, we may assume that conscious effects are the ones we are aware of and which we elaborate at least to some extent, and which we can also verbally explain to other people with some accuracy.[34]

Meanwhile, unconscious effects bypass our conscious information processing and affect our behaviour sort of directly. It has been said that a large part of the effects of cues take place beyond our full awareness and conscious control. For example, Dijksterhuis et al. state that our behaviour often unfolds unconsciously as a result of the mere perception of cues in the environment. This means that just being exposed to a cue—even without consciously processing it—can trigger a response among us. Spontaneous impulse purchases that are made very quickly on the spot without any reasoning or prior thought can be seen as an example of unconscious effects, but also the way or speed we move in the store or where we stop as well as what we approach or avoid are very often choices that are made unconsciously and affected by subtle cues.[35] When describing unconscious effects, it might seem like we react to cues like mindless robots. Obviously this is not the case. Although effects bypass our conscious processing, it does not mean that nothing happens in our mind.[36] While this book does not delve deeper into our mind or the mechanisms of how cues affect us on an unconscious level, the literature in this field does discuss, for example, attitudes that are automatically activated. Automatically activated attitudes refer to well-learned and highly accessible attitudes that can be easily triggered by specific stimuli (such as cues) without any conscious effort.[37] Something we see or otherwise sense activates some sort of an evaluation spontaneously and makes us react before we engage in conscious reasoning. Nonconscious mimicry, in turn, is an example of the unconscious effects of social cues[38] In general, it is said that our behaviour is highly contagious and we tend to mimic unconsciously other people's behaviour (the effect is known as automatic perception–behaviour link).[39] Taken together, we can assume that the multisensory retail environment is full of cues that have the ability to trigger unconscious responses in us. However, it may be very difficult for us to verbally describe such unconscious effects in ourselves, even though we may be fully aware of the existence

---

[33] Baker et al. (2002, p. 122).
[34] Bargh (2002).
[35] Dijksterhuis et al. (2005).
[36] Bargh and Morsella (2008).
[37] Goodall and Slater (2010).
[38] Martin and Morich (2011).
[39] Dijksterhuis et al. (2005).

of the cues (e.g., we can see that the retail store has a green background colour but we are not aware of how this colour affects us).

Lastly, an unconscious effect may also occur when we are unaware of even being exposed to a cue, let alone its influence.[40] In other words, there is a lack of awareness of both the cue being observed and the influences or effects the cue may have.[41] This is often labelled as subliminal influencing. It has been claimed that the most subtle or implicit cues, such as faint scents, influence us in exactly this manner.[42] Music or lighting may also operate similarly in some situations. For example, just the tempo of the background music in a store may impact the speed at which customers move inside it. Similarly, small changes in the temperature or the direction of the airflow in the store may trigger effects in consumers without their awareness. These cues are, in a way, hidden, and we might not be aware of them while we are at the store. However, such cues can affect us despite their invisibility.[43] For example, based on studies on consumer priming, we know that even very brief exposure to a hidden cue may lead to changes in consumer behaviour without the consumer being in any way aware of the cue and its effect.[44] Hidden or invisible cues are probably the most subtle way to influence consumers. However, generating such unconscious effects is very challenging in the store environment and requires in-depth understanding of how the mind of the consumer works. In this, we also come to an ethical question: to what extent is it morally permissible to influence consumers in such subliminal ways?

Response Moderators

This book has emphasised that the effects of cues are dependent on a range of factors that can either enhance or inhibit their effects. These factors are called response moderators[45] and may include shopping motives, self-control, routines and habits, rules of thumb and degree of involvement. Simply the reason we are visiting the store probably has a very strong impact on how we observe and interpret cues. Routines and habits also often mean we make choices as if on autopilot, which may thwart the effects of cues. Similarly, time pressures or the person we are shopping with may have a significant impact on how we function at the store, how we observe the cues and what

---

[40] Bargh (2002), Martin and Morich (2011) and Samson and Voyer (2012).
[41] Bargh and Morsella (2008).
[42] De Luca and Botelho (2019).
[43] Ansorge et al. (2014) and Minton et al. (2017).
[44] Karremans et al. (2006), Laran et al. (2011) and Tsalikis (2015).
[45] Bitner (1992).

Linking Cues to the Quality of the Shopping Experience

Cues in the store environment play a key role in shaping the quality of our shopping experience. First of all, cues convey various meanings and thus can evoke expectations regarding shopping at the store. For example, how the store looks externally affects the initial impressions we have about the store. The way the staff is dressed also creates expectations in us regarding the competence of the staff and the quality level of the entire store. The perceived price level of the store is another strong cue that feeds expectations. There are many similar examples. By setting various cues, the retailer can either raise, or consciously try to curb, the expectations of their customers.

In addition to expectations, cues also affect the actual shopping experience, i.e., what we experience when shopping in a store. For example, cues such as scents and sounds can trigger strong emotional states during our visit in the store. The cues can also guide our movement in the store, or they can help us find the products we are looking for. On the other hand, we can encounter cues that make us irritable during our shopping. Such cues include, for example, untidiness, overcrowding or long checkout lines. Of course, these or other cues alone do not determine our shopping experience, but they can make our in-store experience better or worse.

Based on the above, it is important to understand that cues are not only means of influencing how the customer acts during the visit in the store or what they choose for their shopping cart, but they are also relevant in terms of the quality of the entire shopping experience. At best, cues help raise the quality of the shopping experience in a significant way. On the other hand, cues may also ruin the quality of the shopping experience, for example, by creating expectations that cannot be met. Figure 7.1 describes the effect of cues on the quality of the shopping experience.[46]

In sum, it is important to understand that cues generate expectations for the store, which it must then be able to meet. If the expectations generated by the cues do not correspond to actual shopping experiences, the customers will be disappointed, and the quality of shopping experience is likely to be poor.

---

[46] Parasuraman et al. (1985).

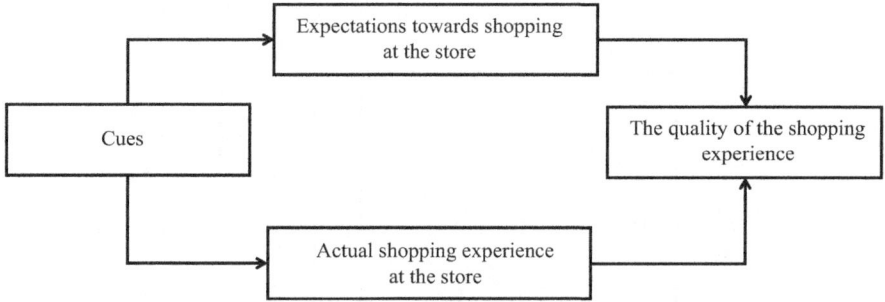

Fig. 7.1 Linking cues to the quality of the shopping experience

7.3 Summary: The Overall View of the Impacts of Cues on Our Choices

The impacts cues may have on our behaviour have been summarised in Fig. 7.2. The figure is based on the Stimulus-Organism-Response (S-O-R) model[47] in which cues can be defined as stimuli (S) that affect the internal states (O) of the customer, which then may have an effect on behaviour (R). In line with this idea and as the figure illustrates, the effects of cues alone or in combination may proceed through our consciousness as conscious sensory observations and their interpretations, potentially evoking some emotional states (i.e., emotional response) or shaping, for example, our mental images or attitudes (i.e., cognitive evaluations) that may or may not influence our actual behaviour. In this view, the cues are information that our senses register, and our mind consciously process (with high or low levels of elaboration), and based on this processing psychological factors are formed with potential behavioural responses. This could be considered a rather conventional way of seeing and explaining the impact of cues. There is no doubt that the so-called conscious information processing explanation works to some degree, but quite often cues impact us on an unconscious level, meaning that our conscious processing is bypassed. In such cases, the cue has an effect without the sensory observation being consciously processed or even registered. Our behaviour is just initiated automatically and unconsciously when we are exposed to the cue. For example, Dijksterhuis et al. argue that most of our choices are actually caused by unconscious effects of various subtle cues in the environment.[48]

---

[47] For more on this, see, e.g., Mehrabian and Russell (1974) and Donovan and Rossiter (1982).
[48] Dijksterhuis et al. (2005).

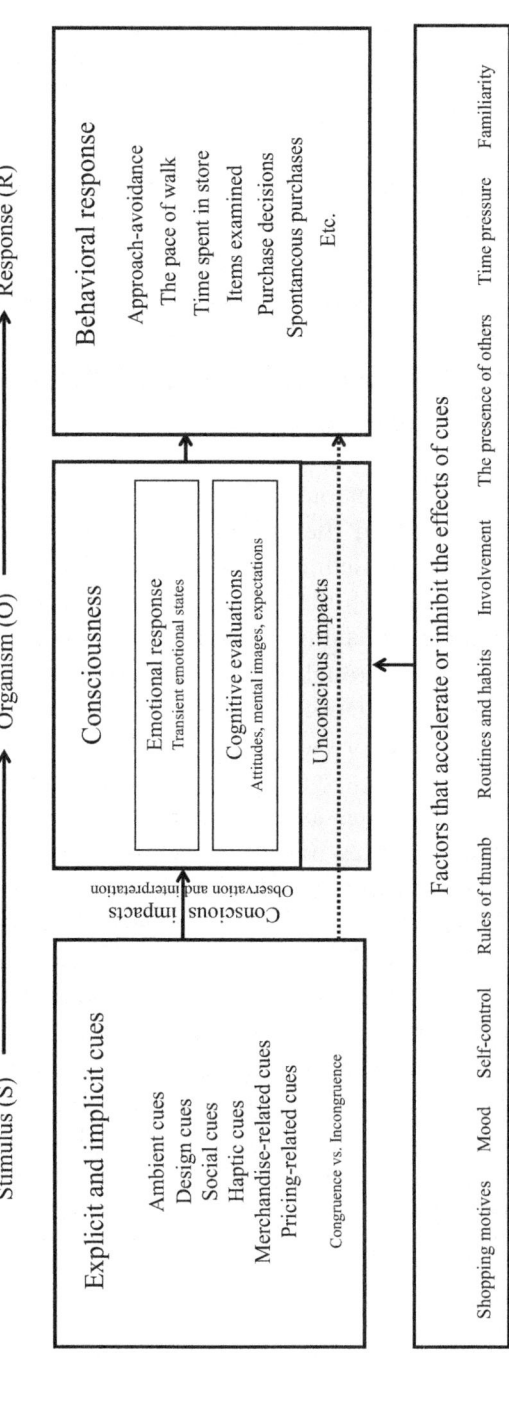

Fig. 7.2 Overall view of the impacts of cues on our behaviour

It should be noted that the behavioural responses during our visit in a store might take many forms. Behavioural reactions may manifest, for example, as the consumer approaching or avoiding some sections or aisles, changes to the pace at which they walk in the store or spontaneous impulse purchases. It is also important to understand that there may be no behavioural response even if the consumer's consciousness has been influenced. This means that the impacts of cues should not be evaluated solely based on behavioural reactions.

It should also be reiterated that in a multisensory retail environment, and different cues entwine in our mind and generate joint effects. In other words, our brain constantly combines different kinds of information from different sources.[49] This also means that customers perceive a store environment holistically, and thus, multiple cues influence customers at the same time.[50] For this reason, it may be difficult to differentiate conscious and unconscious effects of cues in practice. In fact, it has been shown that conscious and unconscious information processing are likely to occur at the same time.[51] It may be possible to regulate the number and effects of cues under strictly controlled laboratory conditions or in an experimental setting, but in a real-world retail environment it is much more challenging. Related to this, researchers should focus on developing better methodologies and research design when evaluating the conscious and unconscious effects of multiple cues on consumer behaviour. Particularly, perceived cue (in)congruence is an important factor to take into account in further studies.

In addition, it should be borne in mind that each store visit and the cues we encounter during such visits will also form experiences and potentially long-lasting memories, which will in turn influence our next visit and the ways in which we interpret cues in that situation. Naturally our psychological characteristics and other individual and social factors will always have an impact on how we function during moments of choice, how we observe cues and, ultimately, how they influence us. For example, consumers may experience the retail store in different ways depending on their motivation or degree of involvement. This all highlights the fact that explaining cue impact is a very complex matter and requires that several factors be taken into account simultaneously. Perhaps one of the main things to remember is that the impact of cues arises from the person, the store environment and the ongoing interaction between the two.[52]

---

[49] Seilheimer et al. (2014).
[50] Spence et al. (2014).
[51] Ren et al. (2021).
[52] Lin (2004).

References

Ailawadi, K., & Keller, K. (2004). Understanding retail branding: Conceptual insights and research priorities. *Journal of Retailing, 80*, 331–342.

Ansorge, U., Kunde, W., & Kiefer, M. (2014). Unconscious vision and executive control: How unconscious processing and conscious action control interact. *Consciousness and Cognition, 27*, 268–287.

Baker, J., Parasuraman, A., Grewal, D., & Voss, G. (2002). The influence of multiple store environmental cues on perceived merchandise value and patronage intentions. *Journal of Marketing, 66*, 120–141.

Bardzil, J., & Rosenberger, P. (1996). Atmosphere: Does it provide central or peripheral cues? In R. Belk & R. Groves (Eds.), *AP—Asia Pacific advances in consumer research* (Vol. 2, pp. 73–79). Association for Consumer Research.

Bargh, J. (2002). Losing consciousness: Automatic influences on consumer judgment, behavior, and motivation. *Journal of Consumer Research, 29*, 280–285.

Bargh, J., & Morsella, E. (2008). The unconscious mind. *Perspectives on Psychological Science, 3*, 73–79.

Beatty, S., & Ferrell, E. (1998). Impulse buying: Modeling its precursors. *Journal of Retailing, 74*, 169–191.

Bettman, J. R. (1986). Consumer psychology. *Annual Review of Psychology, 37*, 257–289.

Biswas, D. (2019). Sensory aspects of retailing: Theoretical and practical implications. *Journal of Retailing, 95*, 111–115.

Bitner, M. J. (1992). Servicescapes: The impact of physical surroundings on customers and employees. *Journal of Marketing, 56*, 57–71.

De Luca, R., & Botelho, D. (2019). The unconscious perception of smells as a driver of consumer responses: A framework integrating the emotion-cognition approach to scent marketing. *AMS Review, 11*, 145–161.

Dijksterhuis, A., Smith, P., van Baaren, R., & Wigboldus, D. (2005). The unconscious consumer: Effects of environment on consumer behavior. *Journal of Consumer Psychology, 15*, 193–202.

Donovan, R., & Rossiter, J. (1982). Store atmosphere: An environmental psychology approach. *Journal of Retailing, 58*, 34–57.

Doucé, L., & Adams, C. (2020). Sensory overload in a shopping environment: Not every sensory modality leads to too much stimulation. *Journal of Retailing and Consumer Services*, Elsevier, 57.

Goodall, C. E., & Slater, M. D. (2010). Automatically-activated attitudes as mechanisms for message effects: The case of alcohol advertisements. *Communication Research, 37*, 620–643.

Helmefalk, M., & Berndt, A. (2018). Shedding light on the use of single and multi-sensory cues and their effect on consumer behaviours. *International Journal of Retail & Distribution Management., 46*, 1077–1091.

Kaltcheva, V. D., & Weitz, B. A. (2006). When should a retailer create an exciting store environment? *Journal of Marketing, 70*, 107–118.

Karjalainen, T. (2007). It looks like a Toyota: Educational approaches to designing for visual brand recognition. *International Journal of Design, 1*, 67–81.

Karremans, J. C., Stroebe, W., & Claus, J. (2006). Beyond Vicary's fantasies: The impact of subliminal priming and brand choice. *Journal of Experimental Social Psychology, 42*, 792–798.

Krishna, A. (2012). An integrative review of sensory marketing: Engaging the senses to affect perception, judgment and behaviour. *Journal of Consumer Psychology., 22*, 332–351.

Kumar, A., & Kim, Y.-K. (2014). The store-as-a-brand strategy: The effect of store environment on customer responses. *Journal of Retailing and Consumer Services, 21*, 685–695.

Laran, J., Dalton, A., & Andrade, E. (2011). The curious case of behavioral backlash: Why brands produce priming effects and slogans produce reverse priming effects. *Journal of Consumer Research, 37*, 99–1014.

Lin, I. Y. (2004). Evaluating a servicescape: The effect of cognition and emotion. *International Journal of Hospitality Management, 23*, 163–178.

Martin, N., & Morich, K. (2011). Unconscious mental processes in consumer choice: Toward a new model of consumer behavior. *Journal of Brand Management, 18*, 483–505.

Mehrabian, A., & Russell, J. (1974). *An approach to environmental psychology*. The Massachusetts Institute of Technology.

Mick, D. (1986). Consumer research and semiotics: Exploring the morphology of signs, symbols, and significance. *Journal of Consumer Research, 13*, 196–213.

Minton, E. A., Cornwell, T. B., & Kahle, L. R. (2017). A theoretical review of consumer priming: Prospective theory, retrospective theory, and the affective–behavioral–cognitive model. *Journal of Consumer Behaviour, 16*, 309–321.

Ooijen, I., Fransen, M. L., Verlegh, P. W., & Smit, E. G. (2017). Packaging design as an implicit communicator: Effects on product quality inferences in the presence of explicit quality cues. *Food Quality and Preference, 62*, 71–79.

Parasuraman, A., Zeithaml, V. A., & Berry, L. (1985). A conceptual model of service quality and its implications for future research. *Journal of Marketing, 49*, 41–50.

Petty, R. E., & Briñol, P. (2012). The elaboration likelihood model. In P. A. M. Van Lange, A. W. Kruglanski, & E. T. Higgins (Eds.), *Handbook of theories of social psychology* (pp. 224–245). Sage Publications Ltd.

Piron, F. (1991). Defining impulse purchasing. In R. H. Holman & M. R. Solomon (Eds.), *NA—Advances in consumer research* (Vol. 18, pp. 509–514). Association for Consumer Research.

Ren, S., Shao, H., & He, S. (2021). Interaction between conscious and unconscious information-processing of faces and words. *Neuroscience Bulletin, 37*, 1583–1594.

Ridgway, N. M., Dawson, S. A., & Bloch, P. H. (1990). Pleasure and arousal in the marketplace: Interpersonal differences in approach-avoidance responses. *Marketing Letters, 1*, 139–147.

Roggeveen, A. L., Grewal, D., & Schweiger, E. B. (2020). The DAST framework for retail atmospherics: The impact of in- and out-of-store retail journey touchpoints on the customer experience. *Journal of Retailing, 96*, 128–137.

Samson, A., & Voyer, B. (2012). Two minds, three ways: Dual system and dual process models in consumer psychology. *AMS Review, 2*, 48–71.

Seilheimer, R. L., Rosenberg, A., & Angelaki, D. E. (2014). Models and processes of multisensory cue combination. *Current Opinion in Neurobiology, 25*, 38–46.

Spence, C. (2020). Senses of place: Architectural design for the multisensory mind. *Cognitive Research: Principles and Implications, 5*, 46.

Spence, C., Puccinelli, N. M., Grewal, D., & Roggeveen, A. L. (2014). Store atmospherics: A multisensory perspective. *Psychology & Marketing, 31*, 472–488.

Stern, H. (1962). The significance of impulse buying today. *Journal of Marketing, 26*, 59–62.

Tsalikis, J. (2015). The effects of priming on business ethical perceptions: A comparison between two cultures. *Journal of Business Ethics, 131*, 567–575.

Velmans, M. (1991). Is human information processing conscious? *Behavioral and Brain Sciences, 14*, 651–726.

8

Engaging in Sensory Marketing in Practice

8.1 Integrating Sensory Marketing into Retail Marketing

Based on everything discussed thus far, we see that sensory marketing holds tremendous potential. As sensory marketing has the ability to stimulate our senses such as sight, touch and hearing, it can affect us in a way that other modes of marketing cannot. Thus, sensory marketing or, more precisely, the use of sensory cues, should be as systematic and controlled as the use of other marketing mix tools. For example, the retailer can use cues as sensory inputs to influence what a customer selects while shopping, how the customers move through the store or how much time they spend there. Cues can also be the factors that, if well implemented, generate positive images and feelings in consumers, leaving them with pleasant memories and making them return to the store or to recommend it to friends.[1] More broadly speaking, managing physical stores is not just about selling or placing products on the shelf, it is more about storytelling and creating multisensory experiences.[2] Physical stores with their cues are a critical part of brand building. As Ailawadi and Keller stated in their highly influential article: "From a branding perspective, an appealing in-store atmosphere offers much potential in terms of crafting a unique store image and establishing differentiation".[3] Particularly in competition with digital platforms and algorithms, the multisensory experiences and

---

[1] Biswas (2019).
[2] Alexander and Cano (2020).
[3] Ailawadi and Keller (2004, p. 333).

cues associated with visiting a physical store can provide a retail company a unique means of setting itself apart and specialising on the market. Sensory cues can provide something that customers cannot get online.

It is also important to understand that consumers entering the store will always see and experience various sensory stimuli. The question is whether the retailer seeks to somehow control these stimuli for the clientele, or whether they are yet to emerge and influence the customers freely with no planning or efforts to attain a particular effect. While it is obvious that completely controlling every potential sensory stimulus is impossible, the most critical cues should be in the hands of the retailer.

Using cues is primarily about the desire and will to use these stimuli as part of the retailer's other influencing efforts and the ability to link the cues to the operation of the retailer. Engaging in sensory marketing does not necessarily require huge capital or major behind-the-scenes resources. Employing cues typically comes down to very small things which are more a question of innovation and creativity than deep pockets. Just changing the background music can generate changes in consumer behaviour, as can changing even prices to 0.99-style odd pricing (or vice-versa). Certainly there are also cues that require more planning and potentially greater investments. It is naturally crucial for the retailer to be aware of the kinds of effects various cues are likely to have. For example, the impact of colours on customers may be surprising and should be studied beforehand.

The retailer should also be aware of the joint effects of cues and must possess the skill and vision to manage and coordinate cues from this standpoint as well. For example, the retailer should understand how the congruity of cues is reflected on how pleasant the store is to visit, or how the management of cues and tensions between them can be used to influence the arousal level of consumers. This means that big-picture thinking is vital when the retailer engages in sensory marketing. At the same time it should be borne in mind that using cues may lead to sensory overload,[4] and visual and auditory stimuli should be employed with particular caution. Sensory marketing is not same as running a disco; it is something that must be conducted with cautious and "less is more" type of thinking. This is to say that it is possible to be too excessive or even annoying in the use of cues. Just like with any method of influencing consumer behaviour, the use of cues requires that they are evaluated and managed from the perspective of the company according to its strategic objectives.

---

[4] Homburg et al. (2012) and Doucé and Adams (2020).

Furthermore, cues can have very different functions or missions at the store level.[5] For instance, by skilfully using colours or lighting, the retailer can draw customers' attention and steer their movements, while making them feel comfortable during their visit at the store. Visual complexity can be used in a way that it encourages customers to explore and browse, while visual coherence tends to make the store more pleasant. Scents and music are subtle cues that can be used to evoke pleasure (or, alternatively, arousal) during shopping. Formal employee clothing can be an efficient way to generate an impression of professionalism. Pricing-related cues, in turn, can direct customers to make more impulse purchases. Thus, cues can be used for different purposes and the retailer should have a solid understanding of which cues suit which purposes. The ability to select the right cues and set them in the right manner at the right place and at the right time is very crucial for the retailer. This is not an easy task, as there is an endless amount of cues to select from and most cues can be implemented in various ways.

This book has provided information that can help retailers select and use sensory cues both in their daily operations and also on the strategic level. Figures 8.1 and 8.2 illustrate a few simple cues and their effects (Fig. 8.2) based on existing literature (discussed in more detail in Chapter 4). However, it should be noted that the impacts described should be regarded with some reservation while bearing in mind that something that works in one retail environment may not work in another. Similarly, it should be understood that the joint effects of several cues may lead to very different consumer reactions than the use of a single cue as the only means of influence. All in all, the intended effects might differ from the perceived effects.

8.2 The Connection of Cues to the Customer Promise

Sensory marketing must match the retailer's brand positioning. More specifically, cues must be in harmony and in line with the retailer's customer promise[6] (or, alternatively, value proposition) and targeted strategic positioning of the store in the minds of consumers. It is also important that

---

[5] Kotler (1973) has proposed that the sensory qualities of the store can have three functions: (i) to create attention, (ii) to communicate certain messages to potential and actual customers or (iii) to create or heighten an appetite (affect) for certain goods, services or experiences. Ballantine et al. (2010), in turn, classified retail atmospheric cues into (i) attractive cues that draw consumers' attention and elicit approach behaviours and (ii) facilitating cues that facilitate product engagement.

[6] Customer promise defines the value or experience that the retailer offers to its customers.

Fig. 8.1 Retail store as a bundle of cues

the cues suit each other and communicate similar things or meanings to customers. If the intention is to generate tension between cues, this should be done in a controlled manner which suits the overall retail environment.

The connection of cues to the customer promise means that whether the retailer seeks to provide fast service or to differentiate itself more through price, quality or the overall shopping experience determines how and what kinds of cues should be used. For example, if the retailer is seeking to brand itself as providing low prices, it should use cues like bright lights, Top 40 hits in the background and odd pricing. These cues convey meanings that are linked to affordable prices. However, if the retailer aims to build a high-quality brand image, cues should include soft lighting, classical music and even pricing. If cues and the meanings or messages that they communicate are not in line with the customer promise and other marketing activities, consumers may become confused. For example, a store striving for price-oriented image may confuse its customer if one cue suggests the store has low prices, while another creates an image of expensive offering. Such blunders are easy to make if the store is not aware of how consumers interpret the retail environment and its cues. Thus, it is critical to understand the target customer segment when using cues. The retailer must be aware of the meanings people in its target segment associate with various cues, and which things they find important. Incorrect interpretations and

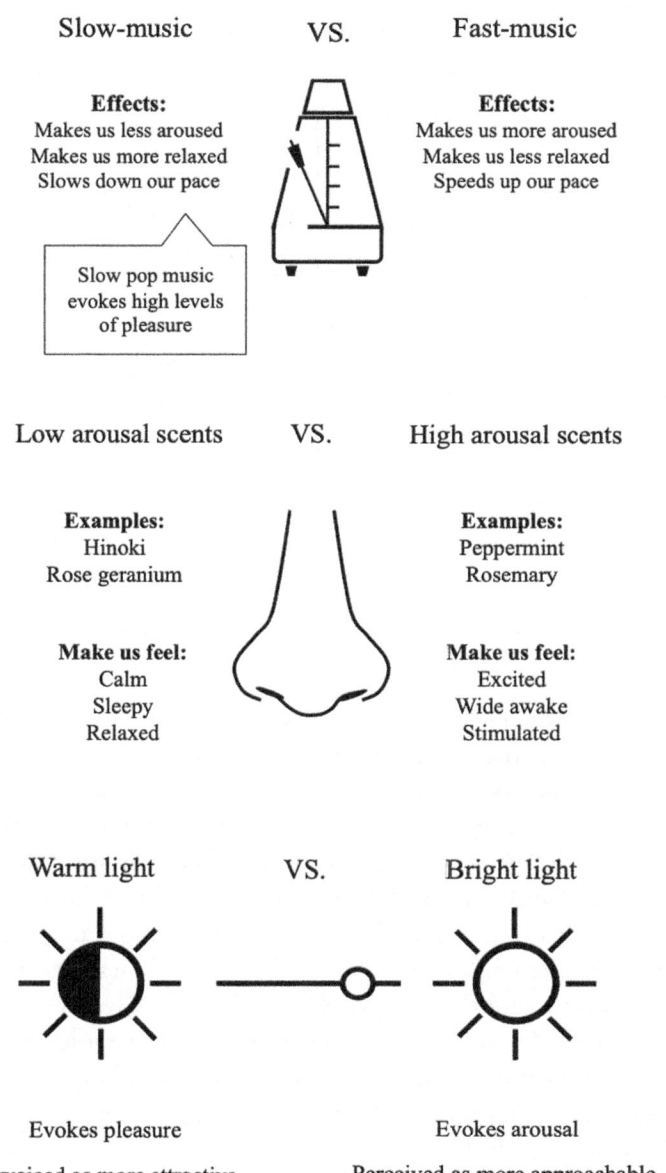

Fig. 8.2 Examples of the effects of cues in a retailing setting

conclusions about the preferences of the customers may be disastrous for the store (Fig. 8.3).

The above emphasises the fact that individual cues should not be seen as separate magic bullets, but rather as a key part of the retailer's storytelling and long-term brand building. Cues that help the retailer in its branding

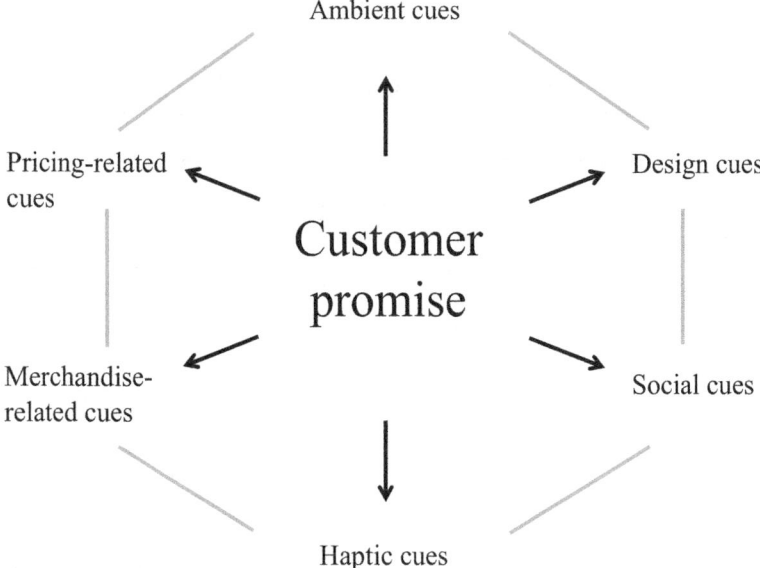

Fig. 8.3 A customer promise directs the use of cues in practice

efforts are called strategic cues. Strategic cues are tied to the overall image of the store and the entire shopping experience, and as such are cues which also require more consideration from the retailer. Strategic cues have the potential to convey more profound or larger meanings to customers and may include cues relating to the soundscape, scents or store design. Besides strategic cues, retailers can use more simple tactical cues to generate immediate reactions in the customers. In the optimal situation, tactical cues enable quick wins for the store, for example, in the form of increased impulse buys. Tactical cues may include, for example, product displays or various ways of marking prices or discounts. However, tactical cues should always be used in a way that does not threaten the brand building efforts or fulfilling the customer promise. This means that there must be some sort of congruence between tactical cues and strategic cues. On the other hand, when tactical cues are moderately incongruent with more stable strategic cues, it generates arousal among consumers and increases their interest to explore the store.[7]

---

[7] Roggeveen et al. (2020).

8.3 Managing Cue Congruence

We have already repeatedly discussed the fact that there is a broad range of cues that may influence consumers. Consumers are targeted by cues from every direction and at every stage of the purchasing experience, particularly in a retail environment. However, this diversity of cues must not lead to a situation where the joint effect of the cues is uncontrollable chaos or sensory overload, or confusion among the customers arising from conflicting cues. The goal of the store must be for the shopping environment and its many cues to be a pleasant overall experience that enhances the arousal level of the consumers to an appropriate degree. To reach this goal, it is essential that the cues like store design, music and scents fit together and generate a coherent, balanced whole in the minds of the consumers. Cues that might be very different in nature should still communicate or convey similar things to consumers. Cue congruence is the situation where there is a match between different cues. The match can be semantic (e.g., the cues convey meanings of affordable prices) or may have to do with the emotions that cues generate (e.g., relaxing background music combined with relaxing lavender scent). The match does not have to be perfect, but cues should seem to naturally fit together from the viewpoint of consumers.

When the cues match, consumers will get the impression that things are rolling along smoothly and that there is nothing suspicious about the purchasing process or environment, or anything that might trigger uncertainty, negative emotions or an avoidance reaction.[8] Everything makes sense. Thus, congruent multisensory store environments form a base for an enjoyable shopping experience.[9] However, in some situations, it may be possible or even recommendable to deliberately generate a degree of tension or conflict between the cues to arouse the interest of the customers and satisfy their curiosity. For example, a luxurious department store can be decked in bright yellow during a campaign, or a discount store can play classical background music. Sometimes just peculiar staff uniforms or products placed in unusual locations can act as a stimulating surprise factor. However, any incongruent stimulation must be done in a controlled manner and be appropriate for the overall setting. It is known that excessively gimmicky or incongruent environments ultimately become unpleasant, although they might generate arousal and interest to explore. This is all to emphasise that cues should not be considered or managed as individual, separate methods of influence. Instead, they should be thought of as parts of a whole and managed as such. If cues

---

[8] Imschloss and Kuehnl (2017).
[9] Spence et al. (2014) and Helmefalk (2017).

are managed as individual influence tactics without any mutual match or connection to the customer promise, it will become difficult to discern what the store actually represents or what its goal is.

8.4 Measuring Cue Effectiveness

Sensory marketing is a mode of influence that requires proper management and coordination. This also means that the effectiveness of cues on consumer behaviour must be evaluated and tracked systematically. For example, the retailer should be aware of the extent to which the cues increase impulse buys and change the structure of the customer's shopping basket, or how cues influence the paths customers take in the store. Necessary and efficient corrective measures can only be made if the impacts of cues are tracked. The use of some tactical cues may be discontinued very quickly if the impacts are not as desired. Similarly, the retailer should be aware of the impact of cues on the shopping experience and the price and quality impression of the store, or the positioning of the store in customer impressions more extensively. This is particularly important for strategic cues. Even though it may be difficult to ascertain the impacts of cues and separate them from the impacts of other efforts, the retailer should have one or more methods of evaluating how the cues are working and whether they are yielding the intended results. This is the only way to make significant improvements to the retailer's sensory marketing efforts.

Naturally, when assessing cue effectiveness at a physical store, any retailer should monitor what customers are actually buying and at what quantities. For example, basket size is a good metric to track when cues are set or some changes are made to the store. Real purchase data is likely to tell an experienced retailer a great deal about whether cues are having their intended effects. If there is no impact on actual purchases, it is likely that cues are not working as they should. However, in some cases cues are not used for boosting sales but rather for building the brand and overall image of the store. Thus, evaluating cue effectiveness is more than just measuring sales or basket sizes.

Foot traffic (number of shoppers) is widely used measure to assess marketing and advertising efforts in retailing. Foot traffic also provides a general idea of whether cues help pull customers in. The number of shoppers can be easily followed by traffic counting systems (e.g., sensors at store entrances). Getting people to step inside the store is great, but it is not enough. Ideally those who come to the store are converted into buying customers. Thus, retailers should track the conversion rate, or the percentage of visitors to a retail store who make a purchase. The higher the percentage, the more "persuasive" the store is. Furthermore, a high conversion rate indicates that in-store cues are likely to produce the intended effects, although it can be also a sign of something else, such as skilful sales staff. If the conversion rate stays very low, it should be seen as a red flag.

For many retailers, it could be very useful to develop measures to also assess the cross-channel conversion rate. The cross-channel conversion rate tells to what extent visits at the physical store drive or guide customers to the retailer's online store. In other words, while customers visit the store and browse there, they might end up doing their actual purchases online, ideally at the retailer's own online shop. This kind of behaviour where customers first visit the store but then purchase online is known as "showrooming."[10,11] Reasons behind showrooming might be, for example, out-of-stock situations or long queues at the store. Those customers who only switch channels but not the retailer are called "loyal showroomers."[12,13] Thus, one could say that non-buying behaviour at the store is not always a sign of a problem with the store or its cues; the store itself with all its cues may work well, but actual purchases just take place outside of the store. At its best, when loyal showroomers make purchases online, they might purchase more products and have a larger basket size than they otherwise would at the physical store. Thus, measuring the cross-channel conversion rate could reveal the value of the physical store from a new viewpoint. By tracking the cross-channel conversion rate, retailers can also gain a better understanding of how customers move across different channels and touchpoints in their shopping journey. All in all, there is a need for new kinds of "omnichannel metrics" as retailing becomes more digitalised and borders between digital and physical channels disappear (Fig. 8.4).

Customers' navigation patterns, common shopping paths and the time spent in the store are also relevant issues to follow when cues are used. These can be tracked by using various indoor location detection systems, which have become quite sophisticated in recent years. With these technologies, it may be possible to monitor the paths of customers or shopping carts quite precisely, even down to a few inches, to see at which points customers stop

---

[10] Verhoef et al. (2015), Flavián et al. (2020) and Viejo-Fernández et al. (2020).

[11] An opposite to showrooming is "webrooming" which refers to the behaviour where information is first searched online but actual purchases are done offline (Flavián et al., 2020).

[12] Arora et al. (2020).

[13] Showroomers can also engage in free-riding behaviour, i.e., "competitive showrooming", where consumers first use one retailer's (Retailer A) physical store in their planning and information gathering but then switch to a competing retailer's (Retailer B) channel (online shop) to make their actual purchases (Flavián et al., 2020; Viejo-Fernández et al., 2020). This kind of free-riding behaviour is problematic for the retailers and can weaken their profitability.

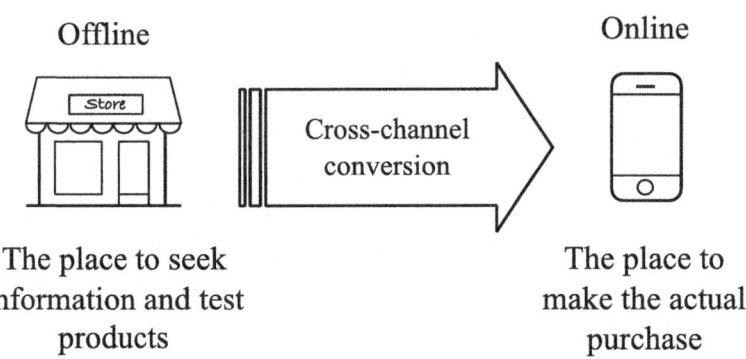

Fig. 8.4 Cross-channel conversion in the case of showrooming

while shopping, or which path they choose. Such location information, which can be packaged in the form of heat maps, may quickly reveal how certain cues influence the shopping behaviour of consumers and where the hot zones and cold zones of the store are located. This kind of location information can be very valuable when assessing how well cues work in a physical retail setting.

Cue effectiveness can also be assessed by observing customer behaviour either in-house or with the help of a third-party expert. Such observation can yield fairly comprehensive information on how specific cues are noticed and what kinds of reactions they evoke in customers, such as changes to browsing behaviour. At its best, observation can produce very detailed information, for example, on items examined or time spent in front of displays. Observation can also reveal some specific shopping habits. However, observation is a challenging method at a larger scale. It must also be done very deliberately to avoid generating misleading insights. For example, observation should be done in a way that customers are not aware that they are being observed.

Meanwhile, eye-tracking technologies may be used to study how consumers make observations in a retail environment, including which cues they look at and for how long.[14] Traditionally this method has required extensive preparation and considerable work and has consequently been unsuitable for long-term use. However, as technology and its applications have developed, the use of this method has become significantly easier, and more and more retail companies are using eye-tracking to collect increasingly precise information on how customers make observations during their shopping visit. We can only assume that eye-tracking methods and equipment will

---

[14] The parameters that are measured in eye-tracking are fixation, pupil dilation, smooth pursuit movement, saccade, microsaccade and blinking (Adhikari, 2023). Fixation is the most important measure because it reveals the focus of the subject's gaze.

continue to develop in the coming years, bringing progressively accessible and affordable applications to the market for collecting this type of data.

One interesting option for measuring the effect of cues is to take advantage of wearable technologies, such as smart watches. Wearable technology often measures movement, body temperature and heart rate. When such physical metrics are combined with, for example, precise location or eye-tracking data, a store can gain unique information on the physical reactions of its customers at various stages of their shopping experience and for different sensory stimuli. However, few stores currently have the opportunity to collect, let alone aggregate, such data.

Customers entering the store can also be interviewed, ideally before and after the shopping visit (e.g., to ask them what they intend to buy and what they actually bought) to determine the impact of cues on shopping behaviour. Customer interviews could reveal, for example, to what extent customers engage in spontaneous impulse buying, or the reason for non-buying behaviour. Such interviews also provide an opportunity to explore the consumer's shopping motives, mood states, self-control and other similar issues. Interviews can help retailers explore customers' expectations or overall shopping experience in more detail. Besides customer interviews, retailers can conduct customer surveys to find out what customers think about the store more broadly and what kinds of images they attach to the retailer.

Finally, the practical implementation of cues and their quality can also be evaluated using mystery shoppers. Mystery shopping is a simple way of assessing the quality of a store from the customer standpoint. In practice, mystery shoppers are specially trained test customers, who visit the store as normal customers, but observe the store and its features, such as lighting or product presentation, according to predetermined criteria.

8.5 Responsibilities and Limitations Related to Sensory Marketing

It is obvious that engaging in sensory marketing and the management of cues is easier if a person or team with the necessary know-how is explicitly appointed to be in charge of the efforts. Otherwise the planning, testing and use of cues becomes nobody's responsibility, and ultimately their practical use and evaluation comes to nothing. This is especially important for larger retail units.

In practice, the use of cues may be dependent on the store's business models. Business models in the retail industry may be roughly divided into two main types: ones based on a store-specific business idea and independent, self-directing work; and ones based on a shared, unified business idea and centralised decision-making.[15] It can be assumed that in business models which allow more freedom and self-management for individual stores, and it may be easier to use and test cues than in business models which have more centralised management. Centrally-led business models typically have a highly standardised plan for each individual store and provide next to no opportunity to deviate from concept handbooks or general rules. Such a business model may also make it difficult to use or experiment with cues. On the other hand, in a centrally-led business model, best practices can be rapidly spread from one store to the next, which may be more difficult in a business model based on independent store-specific operations. No matter what the business model, it should not be allowed to excessively dictate or restrict how the retail environment is managed and how the use and testing of cues is carried out at the store level. One potential solution supporting the testing of cues for major retail chains could be to establish dedicated test stores. Such test locations could have more freedom to experiment with various cues and to track their impact on consumers.

A retailer may also take advantage of the competence of its suppliers or manufacturers of branded goods in the use of cues. Often these companies have important skills in their specific product groups. Suppliers and manufacturers may also have a great deal of up-to-date data on consumers and markets which may be necessary when deciding on practical solutions. In the best-case scenario, sensory marketing is a cooperation between different parties. However, it is important for the retail company to remain in the lead of this cooperation, and for the cues to be managed according to the strategic customer promises and chosen target groups. Otherwise there is the risk of the cues serving a single manufacturer but not the store at large.

8.6 Cultural Specificity of Cues

A retail store or chain and its locations always operate in a specific context and culture, with largely shared values, norms and practices. Culture also entails various symbols or signs, such as specific words, colours, images or even gestures, which may all have a special meaning in a given culture. Such symbols and their meaning may not be legible to people outside the culture, or they may evoke unintended meanings and impressions. This is what we

---

[15] Kautto and Lindblom (2004).

mean by the cultural specificity of cues—cues and the related communication must be compatible with the cultural context in which the retailer operates. That way environmental cues will address the local clientele of the retail location in a way that they understand and communicate the kinds of things and meanings that have positive implications. Meanwhile cues that work against the local culture are more likely to cause nothing but confusion or even disapproval among consumers.

Visual cues may invite particularly different interpretations from one culture to the next. The significance ascribed to colours is a good illustration of this.[16] For example, purple has been found to communicate to Japanese and Chinese people that a product is expensive, while US consumers associate purple with affordable products. They consider the colour for expensive goods to be grey, which the Japanese and Chinese interpret as indicating cheap prices.[17] Clothing conventions also vary across cultures. What may be appropriate dress in one culture may seem offensive in another. Very small gestures, such as bowing, may also carry great meaning in some cultures. While in Japan it is common for retail employees to bow deeply when a customer exits the store, the same gesture could be extremely confusing in another culture. What works in one market area or one country may not work in another.

The cultural specificity of cues is of course particularly relevant to retail companies which operate simultaneously in several different cultural contexts. Major international retail chains are a good example of this. However, the cultural specificity of cues should also be considered on the local level for the immediate surroundings of the store. The cultural context of the store may be very different in the centre of the capital city, in a smaller town or in a rural area. This means that cultural specificity should also be considered within individual countries, with understanding of the cultural features of each region. Retail companies often come across additional cultural barriers when they expand their operations and market area by opening an online store. In the course of such digital expansion, the company may encounter various cultural tensions which may be unexpected. For example, what is attractive to Nordic online shoppers may leave their Asian counterparts nonplussed. Cultural specificity should be considered in all channels, and especially in the ways cues are used.

Managing cues according to the cultural context demands specialised cultural competence from the store. Such cultural competence includes the capacity of a retail company to read the prevailing values, appreciations,

---

[16] Madden et al. (2000).
[17] Jacobs et al. (1991).

symbols and signs in its market environment, as well as its ability to use this literacy in its operations and in the use of cues. Robust cultural competence may constitute a significant resource for the store.[18]

8.7 Summary

For many retailers, even for the largest online retailers like Amazon and Zalando, physical presence is an essential part of their business strategy and a way to differentiate themselves from competitors and communicate with consumers about their benefits and values.[19] It is largely acknowledged that physical presence is one of the most powerful ways to communicate and create intimate and long-lasting experiences in the field of retailing. The multisensory nature of physical stores is often a source of shopping enjoyment and pleasure.[20] Many shoppers also search for immediate satisfaction and convenience from physical locations. Also, physical stores might drive more traffic to online stores and thus help improve the retailers' overall performance. And for many consumers, the physical store is still the place to make purchases, although they may prefer the Internet as an information source. All in all, stores can have a larger role in retailers' business models than one could think. Furthermore, retail stores enable human interaction and can act as community centres driving socialisation.[21] Thus, even in the era of digitalisation, the retail store holds enormous power and value in our lives.

> In 2021, **Google** opened its first-ever physical retail store in New York. The Google Store is located in Chelsea and is a space where customers can experience and have hands-on interaction Google's hardware and services. Google describes the store in the following words: "As you approach our new store, the first thing we hope you'll notice are beautiful physical and digital product displays lining the store's windows, which offer a peek into our products and their features. And as you enter the store, you will find a light-filled space that's centered around experiencing the helpfulness of our products".[22]

Running a physical retail store in a way that addresses our senses and creates satisfying in-store experiences is challenging task. Retailers must have a solid understanding of sensory marketing and how our senses can be engaged

---

[18] Uusitalo and Joutsenvirta (eds.) (2009).
[19] Gilad (2022).
[20] Cox et al. (2005).
[21] Alexander and Cano (2020).
[22] Ross and Allen (2021).

or stimulated during our visit. Particularly, there is a need to be aware of the joint effects of cues, and retailers must possess the skill and vision to manage and coordinate cues from this standpoint as well. For example, the retailer should understand how the congruity of cues is reflected on how pleasant the store is to visit, or how the management of cues and tensions or even conflicts between them can be used to influence the arousal level of consumers. Retailers should also possess sensitivity for cultural issues and have skills to manage cues according to the local cultural context. One key issue is also to understand how cues are in line with the retailer's customer promise and how cues can be used as a part of storytelling and creating the company image. In other words, sensory marketing is not just about achieving immediate effects, and it is more about long-term brand building. Measuring whether cues work as they should is a complex issue and requires various metrics and holistic observation of behavioural responses and customers' internal evaluations.

It should be noted that this chapter has intentionally avoided giving strict normative guidelines and left it up to the reader to evaluate how sensory marketing might best be implemented in practice. When using sensory cues and other means of influencing behaviour, it is crucial for them to always be evaluated and managed from the company's own perspective and matching with its customers' preferences.

Decision-Based Questions
- As a store manager, how would you use cues to draw consumers' attention?
- As a store manager, how would you use cues to help your customers navigate the store?
- As a store manager, how would you use cues to encourage your customers to explore and browse?
- As a store manager, how would you use cues to make your customers visit at the store as pleasant as possible?
- As a store manager, how would you use cues to make your customers visit at the store as exciting as possible?
- If you would be in the position of the store manager in a store that intends to stand out with its high quality, what kind of cues would you use to create this particular image?
- If you would be in the position of the store manager in a store that intends to stand out with its affordable prices, what kind of cues would you use to create this particular image?
- If you would be in the position of the store manager in a store that is targeted for young people, what kinds of cues would you use to appeal this segment?
- If you would be in the position of the store manager in a store that is targeted for seniors, what kind of cues would you use to appeal this segment?

- What kinds of cues in a store environment tend to convey similar meanings, i.e., have a semantic match?
- What are the most essential things in creating seamless customer experiences in an omnichannel environment?
- How would you assess or measure whether cues had their intended impact?
- What kinds of cues need to be localised or adapted for local preferences and what kinds of cues can be standardised across various markets?

References

Adhikari, K. (2023). Application of selected neuroscientific methods in consumer sensory analysis: A review. *Journal of Food Science, 88*, A53–A64.

Ailawadi, K., & Keller, K. (2004). Understanding retail branding: Conceptual insights and research priorities. *Journal of Retailing, 80*, 331–342.

Alexander, B., & Cano, M. B. (2020). Store of the future: Towards a (re)invention and (re)imagination of physical store space in an omnichannel context. *Journal of Retailing and Consumer Services, 55*, 101913.

Arora, S., Parida, R. R., & Sahney, S. (2020). Understanding consumers' showrooming behaviour: A stimulus–organism–response (S-O-R) perspective. *International Journal of Retail & Distribution Management, 48*, 1157–1176.

Ballantine, P. W., Jack, R., & Parsons, A. G. (2010). Atmospheric cues and their effect on the hedonic retail experience. *International Journal of Retail & Distribution Management, 38*, 641–653.

Biswas, D. (2019). Sensory aspects of retailing: Theoretical and practical implications. *Journal of Retailing, 95*, 111–115.

Cox, A., Cox, D., & Anderson, R. (2005). Reassessing the pleasures of store shopping. *Journal of Business Research*, Elsevier, *58*, 250–259.

Doucé, L., & Adams, C. (2020). Sensory overload in a shopping environment: Not every sensory modality leads to too much stimulation. *Journal of Retailing and Consumer Services*, Elsevier, *57*.

Flavián, C., Gurrea, R., & Orús, C. (2020). Combining channels to make smart purchases: The role of webrooming and showrooming. *Journal of Retailing and Consumer Services, 52*, 1–11.

Gilad, Z. (2022, July 7). *Should E-commerce merchants have a physical presence?* Forbes.

Helmefalk, M. (2017). *Multi-sensory cues in interplay and congruency in a retail store context: Consumer emotions and purchase behaviors* (Linnaeus University Dissertations No 297/2017).

Homburg, C., Imschloss, M., & Kühnl, C. (2012). *Of dollars and senses—Does multisensory marketing pay off? IMU research insights*. University of Mannheim.

Imschloss, M., & Kuehnl, C. (2017). Don't ignore the floor: Exploring multisensory atmospheric congruence between music and flooring in a retail environment. *Psychology & Marketing, 34*, 931–945.

Jacobs, L., Keown, C., Worthley, R., & Ghymn, K. (1991). Cross-cultural colour comparisons: Global marketers beware! *International Marketing Review, 8*, 21–30.

Kautto, M., & Lindblom, A. (2004). Ketju - Kaupan ketjuliiketoiminta. Otava.

Kotler, P. (1973). Atmospherics as a marketing tool. *Journal of Retailing, 49*, 48–64.

Madden, T. J., Hewett, K., & Roth, M. S. (2000). Managing images in different cultures: A cross-national study of color meanings and preferences. *Journal of International Marketing, 8*, 90–107.

Roggeveen, A. L., Grewal, D., & Schweiger, E. B. (2020). The DAST framework for retail atmospherics: The impact of in- and out-of-store retail journey touchpoints on the customer experience. *Journal of Retailing, 96*, 128–137.

Ross, I., & Allen, N. (2021, June 16). *Open for business: A look inside our Google Store in NYC.* Blog Google.

Spence, C., Puccinelli, N. M., Grewal, D., & Roggeveen, A. L. (2014). Store atmospherics: A multisensory perspective. *Psychology & Marketing, 31*, 472–488.

Uusitalo, L., & Joutsenvirta, M. (eds.). (2009). Kulttuuriosaaminen - tietotalouden taitolaji. Gaudeamus.

Verhoef, P., Kannan, P., & Inman, J. (2015). From multi-channel retailing to omnichannel retailing: Introduction to the special issue on multi-channel retailing. *Journal of Retailing, 91*, 174–181.

Viejo-Fernández, N., Sanzo-Pérez, M. J., & Vázquez-Casielles, R. (2020). Is showrooming really so terrible? start understanding showroomers. *Journal of Retailing and Consumer Services, 54*, 102048.

9

What to Explore Next?

9.1 Joint Effects and Sensory Overload

Even though an increasing amount of information is available on cues and their impacts, there is a great need for further research. In terms of using cues, it would be especially important to generate knowledge on the joint effects of cues, or what kinds of reactions various combinations of cues generate. The study of such multisensory cues is particularly important in multisensory environments, like retail stores. At the time of writing, very little research on such joint effects exists. For example, Helmefalk has pointed out that the number of studies that have explored cues that engage three or more senses is significantly limited.[1] This is largely because studying joint effects is very challenging and requires an in-depth understanding of themes such as cross-modal interaction and multisensory integration. Further, before embarking on research into joint effects, the researchers must carefully consider which combinations of cues are relevant and can even be studied. Otherwise the number of potential cue combinations is nearly infinite. In an ideal situation, researchers would be able to find combinations which would be important in terms of consumers' experiences of pleasure and arousal, for example, and which could then be used to control these emotional states in a useful way. The challenges of managing joint effects were discussed in more detail in Chapter 5, where the seesaw effect was introduced. We would need more

---

[1] Helmefalk (2017).

in-depth study into the seesaw effect in various shopping environments and among various customer groups.

Sensory overload should also be studied in conjunction with joint effects, meaning the point at which the stimulation of the senses of customers with cues or cue combinations goes too far.[2,3] Unfortunately, very little data on this currently exists.

9.2 Studying How Cues Are Related to Perceived Safety

The most recent global pandemic has brought consumers' experiences of health security into the forefront. Previously, there had been little consideration of this factor or of how it can be influenced with cues in retail environments. Perceived health security should be considered more in research on the impacts of atmospheric cues in retail environments, but also in practical measures. For example, it would be interesting to know which cues lead the consumer to believe that it is safe to visit a store. Do face masks among staff promote a sense of security, or do they suggest that the consumer should be worried? How does having products freely available for everyone to touch influence the consumer's sense of health security, and consequently, the willingness to buy?

Retailers may find that the ability to communicate health security may become an increasingly important method for attracting consumers to physical shopping settings. This view is supported by the recent survey conducted by Wang et al., which showed that consumers now have higher expectations for in-store safety.[4]

9.3 The Ethics of Influence in Consumer Marketing

A major theme which can be expected to grow in significance is the ethics of influencing consumers. Particularly methods which can be used to influence consumers subliminally are in dire need of more extensive public discussion and clearer ethical guidelines. However, as influencing already takes so many

---

[2] Homburg et al. (2012).
[3] Doucé and Adams (2020).
[4] Wang et al. (2020).

forms and is so ubiquitous, this is a challenging task. It is very difficult for us as consumers to articulate or even identify what kinds of influencing can be considered responsible, and what constitutes manipulation or otherwise questionable methods. As our culture becomes ever more digital and new kinds of shopping environments, social media channels and applications become more common, and the ethical questions surrounding influencing will become ever more difficult to answer. Already many social media platforms have been built mainly for commercial purposes, with never-ending entertainment available for users who are unlikely to comprehend how extensive, and how targeted, influencing they are exposed to when they spend time in these digital environments. Influencing with distorted or even entirely fabricated information is also becoming more common. We have seen many unfortunate examples of this in recent years. It is more important than ever to have a conversation about the ethics of influencing.

9.4 Sensory Marketing in an Omnichannel Environment

In these days, it is very common for retailers to have many different channels through which they operate and seek to reach their customers and meet their needs. Furthermore, channels are becoming highly integrated from the customer perspective, meaning that the distinctions between physical and online locations are vanishing to a large extent. Business models where digital (online) and physical (offline) channels are merged into a single, seamless customer experience is called omnichannel retailing.[5] Verhoef et al. have stated that in omnichannel retailing "channels are interchangeably and seamlessly used during the search and purchase process."[6] In practice, this could mean, for example, testing a product first at a physical location, then ordering the item by smartphone and finally picking it up at a nearby parcel locker, perhaps later to return it to the store. It is clear that in omnichannel retailing the role of the physical store changes and stores become part of a larger and more connected shopping experience.[7]

Thus, as omnichannel retailing is becoming more common and the natural borders between channels are beginning to disappear, customers can experience retailers more holistically than ever. This compels retailers to consider

---

[5] Lemon and Verhoef (2016).
[6] Verhoef et al. (2015, p. 175).
[7] Alexander and Cano (2020).

their presence in different channels simultaneously and assess how these channels can work and communicate seamlessly for their customers. The key is to realise that making technological solutions or interfaces compatible is not enough for omnichannel retailing, and it requires unifying communication and marketing across all channels. Omnichannel retailing drives retailers to deliver smooth and borderless shopping experiences regardless of the channel. This poses a difficult question for sensory marketing: how does multisensory stimulation manifest in an omnichannel customer experience[8]? It is clear that stimulating customers' senses across numerous touchpoints in an omnichannel environment is a highly complex task. For example, to what extent can retailers facilitate unified multisensory customer experiences in omnichannel environments? The reality is that even in an omnichannel environment, digital and physical locations and touchpoints have their own special features and limitations which should always be considered when engaging in sensory marketing. Omnichannel retailing also requires its own measurement metrics (e.g., to capture the cross-channel conversion rate) to assess how sensory marketing affects customers' borderless shopping behaviour.

Although omnichannel retailing has raised a great deal of interest among researchers, multisensory omnichannel experiences are not fully understood yet and the coming years will hopefully bring more research on sensory marketing in an omnichannel environment. In fact, it is said that understanding and designing multisensory omnichannel experiences is one of the top priorities in service research in the future.[9]

9.5 Digital Sensory Marketing

An interesting potential development has to do with digital environments and the choice behaviours that manifest there. It is particularly fascinating to follow the directions that virtual reality will take in the future, and whether it can be fully adopted to online and digital retailing. Meta, previously known as Facebook, is currently driving this development, as they have already launched their own Metaverse environment. The Metaverse is largely based on virtual reality. Virtual reality may have unexpected impacts on consumer choice behaviour, and it would be interesting and important in many ways to study them. At the moment, there is little data available on the topic.[10]

---

[8] Stead et al. (2022).
[9] Ibid.
[10] Biswas (2019).

The impacts may be particularly great if haptic feedback can be integrated as a natural part of virtual reality. With such haptic feedback, a consumer visiting an online store or digital marketplace might even be able to feel a material or get a sense for how much an object weighs. For example, Petit et al. have forecasted that "[…] haptic stimulations might one day, perhaps, help to communicate different material properties concerning the products via the Internet […]. These new haptic-enabling technologies can also help the consumer to understand how the product works, by interacting physically with it at a distance.[11]" With haptic feedback, virtual reality and online stores or digital marketplaces that use it could be a step closer to physical shopping environments and the multisensory experiences they provide. The effects could radiate throughout consumers' shopping behaviours.

All in all, it is crucial to generate research information on how our senses can be stimulated in digital environments and what kinds of impacts different influencing methods can evoke. Some novel sensory-enabling technologies that stimulate consumers' senses in online environments already exist.[12] For example, there are wearable systems that produce olfactory, thermal and airflow stimuli to simulate real-world environmental conditions. There are even some experiments where sensory-enabling technology has been used to stimulate the sense of taste. However, as Petit et al. point out, there are many biological and technical challenges that need to be solved before such systems become commercially viable. Digital sensory marketing is a fascinating, but currently little-studied, phenomenon.

9.6 Neuroscience and Neuromarketing

In consumer studies, a key question has to do with methodology—which tools are used to generate empirical data on consumers and their choice behaviour. The range of available methods is extensive, and there is no single right way of creating information. The studies discussed in this book are primarily based on experimental research. Experiments are a widely used method to study the impact of individual cues or other external stimuli on consumers. The benefit of such studies is that it is possible to control what kind of cue, such as music, the research subject is exposed to, and to observe their reactions very closely. On the other hand, experimental studies are often based on very artificial, even laboratory-like settings and entirely imaginary

---

[11] Petit et al. (2019, p. 50).
[12] Petit et al. (2019).

shopping situations. The problem is that experimental studies rarely correspond to real-life shopping situations and environments, and consequently, their results can easily be called into question.

One alternative way of addressing the minds of consumers is neuromarketing or consumer neuroscience.[13] Koushik Adhikari defines neuromarketing as a relatively new and fast-growing subdiscipline in marketing research that combines psychological knowledge with medical sciences primarily to understand the needs, values, decisions and emotions of the consumer in a decision-making context.[14] Bazzani et al., in turn, emphasise that while traditional marketing methods aim to primarily explain customers' conscious actions and choices, and consumer neuroscience tries to offer objective and replicable measures of neural processes arising during decision-making.[15]

A central feature of neuromarketing is that it applies neuroscientific tools to understand how the consumer's mind works. For example, brain imaging can be used to understand what is really happening in the brain of the consumer when they are consciously or unconsciously exposed to a stimulus. Adhikari summarises the core idea of neuromarketing studies thus: "[…] the focus is to understand the subliminal and subconscious processes happening in the brain of the consumer in response to stimuli."[16] Neurophysiological data can reveal, for example, the perceived pleasantness of a commercial, or how easily it can be memorised.[17] Neuroscientific methods have also been used to investigate adequate price levels for products. Neuroscientific methods include the EEG (electroencephalography) and fMRI (functional magnetic resonance imaging). Both methods monitor activity in the brain either by measuring magnetisation (fMRI) or measuring changes in electrical activity across the scalp (EEG).[18] The neuroscience toolbox also includes some simpler methods such as measuring skin temperature and heart rate.

Neuroscientific methods may be able to generate information which is unavailable through other means, and they could be particularly helpful in studying multisensory cues. However, it is clear that neuroscientific methods require a distinct set of specialist skills, instruments and often considerable financial resources. On the other hand, new, lighter, more intelligent or

---

[13] Harrell (2019).
[14] Adhikari (2023).
[15] Bazzani et al. (2020).
[16] Adhikari (2023, p. A55).
[17] Ibid.
[18] Niedziela and Ambrose (2021).

more affordable technological solutions are being released on the market—including smart devices based on wearable technology as well as applications which enable the study of bodily reactions in a completely new way. Such technological innovations may offer researchers a completely new category of possibilities for studying cues and stimuli, also in a retail environment. However, researchers should not think that neuroscience is the golden key to unlock the mysteries of our mind. As Niedziela and Ambroze state: "[…] it is important to recognise that any non-conscious activity is not easy to measure. The human brain is far too complicated to reduce to a simple algorithm read by one device to deliver a straightforward answer.[19]" Neuroscience methods would best be used in combination with other methods, not as stand-alone methods.[20] There are also some ethical issues that need be addressed when neuroscience methods are used for commercial purposes.[21] There are already some concerns whether neuroscience is able to reveal our brain's "buy button" that marketers could manipulate without our awareness.

Consumer choice behaviour cannot be studied with experimental studies and neuroscientific methods alone. To understand in more depth why consumers behave in the way they do, we could use methods of participant observation or ethnography. An ethnographic researcher lives as part of the consumer's daily life, observing their behaviour in their natural living and working environments. Such observation often produces unique data on consumers and helps us see the social and cultural underpinnings of consumer behaviour which would otherwise remain obscured. Neither should we ignore traditional interview or survey studies. If well executed, such studies can provide rich information on consumers and their behaviour as well as the background factors behind the behaviour, such as motives, attitudes and values. The value of interview or survey studies is usually greatest when they can be repeated at regular intervals.

References

Adhikari, K. (2023). Application of selected neuroscientific methods in consumer sensory analysis: A review. *Journal of Food Science, 88*, A53–A64.

Alexander, B., & Cano, M. B. (2020). Store of the future: Towards a (re)invention and (re)imagination of physical store space in an omnichannel context. *Journal of Retailing and Consumer Services, 55*, 101913.

---

[19] Niedziela and Ambrose (2021).
[20] Adhikari (2023).
[21] Spence (2020).

Bazzani, A., Ravaioli, S., Trieste, L., Faraguna, U., & Turchetti, G. (2020). Is EEG suitable for marketing research? A systematic review. *Frontiers in Neuroscience, 14*, 594566.

Biswas, D. (2019). Sensory aspects of retailing: Theoretical and practical implications. *Journal of Retailing, 95*, 111–115.

Doucé, L., & Adams, C. (2020). Sensory overload in a shopping environment: Not every sensory modality leads to too much stimulation. *Journal of Retailing and Consumer Services*, Elsevier, *57*.

Harrell, E. (2019). Neuromarketing: What you need to know. *Harvard Business Review, 97*, 64–70.

Helmefalk, M. (2017). *Multi-sensory cues in interplay and congruency in a retail store context: Consumer emotions and purchase behaviors* (Linnaeus University Dissertations No 297/2017).

Homburg, C., Imschloss, M., & Kühnl, C. (2012). *Of dollars and senses—Does multisensory marketing pay off? IMU research insights*. University of Mannheim.

Lemon, K., & Verhoef, P. (2016). Understanding customer experience throughout the customer journey. *Journal of Marketing, 80*, 69–96.

Niedziela, M. M., & Ambrose, K. (2021). The future of consumer neuroscience in food research. *Food Quality and Preference, 92*, 104124.

Petit, O., Velasco, C., & Spence, C. (2019). Digital sensory marketing: Integrating new technologies into multisensory online experience. *Journal of Interactive Marketing, 45*, 42–61.

Spence, C. (2020). On the ethics of neuromarketing and sensory marketing. In J. Martineau & E. Racine (Eds.), *Organizational neuroethics. Advances in neuroethics*. Springer.

Stead, S., Wetzels, R., Wetzels, M., Odekerken-Schröder, G., & Mahr, D. (2022). Toward multisensory customer experiences: A cross-disciplinary bibliometric review and future research directions. *Journal of Service Research*.

Verhoef, P., Kannan, P., & Inman, J. (2015). From multi-channel retailing to omnichannel retailing: Introduction to the special issue on multi-channel retailing. *Journal of Retailing, 91*, 174–181.

Wang, Y., Xu, R., Schwartz, M., Ghosh, D., & Chen, X. (2020). COVID-19 and retail grocery management: Insights from a broad-based consumer survey. *IEEE Engineering Management Review, 48*, 202–211.

10

Concluding Remarks

One of the main messages of this book is that physical retail stores with their multisensory features play an important role in our daily lives. In many cases, our local brick-and-mortar store is the place where we can try products and get personal help or advice if needed. Visually and otherwise engaging physical store environments can also provide us with inspiration and new ideas, or they can just make us feel good or excited. At their best, retail stores can create unforgettable experiences.

However, the digital world is developing at a dizzying pace, and the natural borders between physical and digital channels are eroding. Showrooming and webrooming are already examples of new modes of shopping behaviour and signals how physical and digital channels are moving towards integrated omnichannel environments.[1] Alexander and Cano state that a key facilitator of this channel convergence is the increasing dominance of mobile devices, which have already changed consumer purchasing behaviours in many ways.[2] However, fast-moving digitalisation will not render the physical store obsolete. Even in the highly digitalised future, we as consumers have a need to experience things with all our senses, and to gather genuine all-encompassing experiences. It is hard to even imagine a future where we do not want to have tactile sensations, engage in lively social interaction or enjoy the audio-visual stimuli with our own eyes and ears.

---

[1] Flavián et al. (2020).
[2] Alexander and Cano (2020).

This book has shown that physical stores can respond to our need to gain sensory-based experiences. Physical stores can appeal to all our five senses in a way that any other channel or shopping type can. One could say that physical stores have a natural and even overwhelming advantage over online stores, digital platforms and other similar non-physical formats. This advantage just needs to be seized. This is where sensory marketing steps in. Sensory marketing is a marketing activity that helps retailers to engage the consumers' senses and influence their perceptions, judgement and behaviour.[3] This book has emphasised that sensory marketing is above all about communicating with customers in a very holistic way. By utilising sensory marketing, retailers can convey specific semantic meanings and create a strong emotional connection with their customers. Sensory marketing also offers a way to help customers navigate in the store and make their shopping experience as smooth and convenient as possible. And of course, sensory marketing helps to boost sales if it is conducted in the right manner. Even very small things may have a significant impact on consumers and their purchasing behaviour.

Sensory marketing should not be considered a simple marketing trick—it is a highly demanding practice that requires specific capabilities and skills from retailers. When engaging in sensory marketing, the retailer must have a solid understanding of several issues, including consumer psychology, semiotics, service design and even neuromarketing. It is essential that retailers have a good understanding of the multisensory nature of retail stores and particularly how to manage multisensory cues in a way that the store evokes pleasant and stimulating shopping experiences. It is also crucial to understand how sensory marketing can be linked to long-term strategic brand building. In addition, retailers must possess strong cultural expertise to successfully manage sensory cues in various markets. It is equally obvious that retailers must be able to address issues relating to ethical and responsible influencing. All these factors together provide a solid foundation for sensory marketing.

One can assume that sensory marketing will become even more challenging in coming years, since consumer preferences and consumption trends are constantly changing, and consumers' wants and needs becoming more difficult to anticipate. Anyone who works in the retail industry knows that what is today considered a pleasant or trendy shopping environment might be hopelessly outdated tomorrow. Also, growing concern for the environment and increasingly critical attitudes towards consumerism are likely to bring new challenges in the field of retailing, and the ways stores should communicate with their customers. Furthermore, the boundaries of physical

---

[3] Krishna (2012) and see also Krishna (2010).

retail stores have become blurred, as retailers are expanding their businesses to different directions with an aim to create more holistic service offerings for their customers. There are already various hybrid concepts such as grocerants where grocery stores and restaurants have merged to offer new kinds of solutions for customers. These developments among others are likely to bring new challenges also for sensory marketing.

Furthermore, in the future, physical store environments will increasingly incorporate new technologies, such as augmented reality (AR), smart touchscreen mirrors or customer service robots, which can change the shopping experience in many ways. For example, retail service robots can help consumers navigate in the store, or robots can offer personalised customer service and product advice. In the most dramatic visions of the future, service robots would be humanoids, designed to resemble humans and to replicate facial features and body language.[4] It will be interesting to see how the new and emerging technologies will change the way how physical stores are built in the future and what kinds of responses new technology-driven innovations evoke among consumers.

No matter which direction the market environment evolves in the coming years, sensory marketing will be one of the most important marketing activities for retailers to evoke favourable responses among their customers and generate memorable shopping experiences.

References

Alexander, B., & Cano, M. B. (2020). Store of the future: Towards a (re)invention and (re)imagination of physical store space in an omnichannel context. *Journal of Retailing and Consumer Services, 55*, 101913.

Flavián, C., Gurrea, R., & Orús, C. (2020). Combining channels to make smart purchases: The role of webrooming and showrooming. *Journal of Retailing and Consumer Services, 52*, 1–11.

Krishna, A. (2010). *Sensory marketing. Research on the sensuality of products.* Routledge.

Krishna, A. (2012). An integrative review of sensory marketing: Engaging the senses to affect perception, judgment and behaviour. *Journal of Consumer Psychology, 22*, 332–351.

Song, C., & Youn-Kyung, K. (2022). The role of the human-robot interaction in consumers' acceptance of humanoid retail service robots. *Journal of Business Research, 146*, 489–503.

---

[4] Song and Youn-Kyung (2022).

Glossary

Ambient cues: Primarily nonvisual cues that often affect the consumer on a unconscious level. In a retail environment, typical ambient cues are background music, scents and lighting.

Approach behaviour: A desire to stay in the store environment and willingness to explore it.

Arousal: An emotional state. Describes how active or alert we feel, or to what extent we experience, for example, excitement during our visit at the store. Although arousal effects are less consistent, arousal is likely to have a positive impact on impulse purchases and time spent in the store, for example. However, high arousal environments might cause sensory overload.

Attitude: Attitude expresses our evaluation or opinion of something or someone. Attitudes reflect either favourable or unfavourable assessments. Often based on some sort of elaboration and conscious information processing. Our attitudes can affect how we behave or intend to behave.

Automatically activated attitudes: Highly accessible attitudes that come to our mind spontaneously (automatically) when we perceive or are exposed to something.

Avoidance behaviour: A desire to leave the environment or a tendency to minimise interaction with the environment.

Behavioural response: An actual act or change in our behaviour. Can be observed and measured. For example, browsing and selecting products, the pace of walking in the store and communicating with the staff are behavioural responses.

Choice: A behavioural response. Refers to actual purchase decisions (incl. impulse purchases) but also conscious and unconscious decisions to approach or avoid the retail environment.

Cognitive evaluations: Refers to conscious information processing that requires some sort of cognitive reasoning and elaboration. Through our cognitive evaluations we are able to convert cues into a meaningful information and make judgements, for example, about the store.

Conscious choice: A choice that has a conscious intent and is under our control. Something that we can verbally explain.

Conscious impact: A chain of effects triggered by a cue, which progresses through conscious information processing to a possible behavioural response.

Conscious information processing: Information processing of which we are aware. The starting point of information processing is receiving sensory information. Processing the information can involve either high or a relatively low levels of elaboration and reasoning. Information processing is a part of perception.

Conscious mind: Being aware and knowing what is going on. Refers to our ability to observe, judge and make deliberate decisions such as specific choices. Our conscious thoughts are verbally reportable.

Consciousness: Covers all factors and processes internal to the consumer's mind, such as motives, attitudes and emotions, as well as perception and interpretation. In the broadest sense, it also includes the unconscious parts of our mind.

Consumer psychology: A field of study that explores how our motives, beliefs, emotions and other psychological factors affect how we behave. Combines many disciplines.

Cross-channel conversion: Describes to what extent customers move across different channels during their shopping journey. For example, customers might first test products at the physical store but then make the actual purhcases online.

Cross-modal interaction: Information received from one sense affects how we perceive information from another. For example, our visual perception affects how we process nonvisual information.

Cues: Stimuli that can we can sense during our shopping journey. In a store environment cues can appeal to any of our five senses. From an information processing perspective, cues are information that can carry various meanings. Cues can guide our choices either on a conscious or unconscious level.

Cue congruence: A situation where the cues communicate in a similar fashion and evoke similar emotions or convey similar meanings to customers. There is a match between cues from the viewpoint of customers. Increases the pleasantness of the store environment but can make customers less excited.

Cue incongruence: A situation where the cues are somehow in conflict and evoke or convey contradictory emotions or meanings to customers. There is a mismatch between cues from the viewpoint of customers. Increases the arousal and interest to explore the store but might also lead to feelings of unpleasantness.

Design cues: Aesthetic and functional cues of the retail environment. Design cues are primarily visual in nature. Store design, colours and layout are examples of design cues.

Emotional response: An emotional reaction to perceived stimuli such as cues.

Emotional state: An emotion that is transient and can be experienced intensively. Emotional states occur in response to specific cues. Pleasure and arousal are our core emotional states.

Explicit cue: A cue that is clearly observable during our visit at the store and whose aim is to influence our choices in a very straightforward way. For example, verbal statements such as "Today only" or "Max 3 per person" can be seen as explicit cues.

Fluency theory: Fluency theory explains our internal evaluations and preferences by focusing on the ease of processing a stimulus such as a cue. The core idea of the fluency theory is rather simple: if consumers process sensory information easily, positive feelings such as pleasure and self-confidence are evoked. Ease of processing signals most of all safety and absence of threat.

Gestalt theory: Explains our perceptions and perceptual experiences. Based on the idea that we try to simplify and organize complex images or visual elements in our mind. The theory emphasizes that stimuli like separate cues can be grouped in meaningful way and seen as a whole.

Habit: Something that we do often and regularly. Tends to occur unconsciously.

Haptic cues: Cues that stimulate our sense of touch, i.e., cues that we can feel, for example, on our hands or fingertips. For example, the weight of an object or the softness of the surface material are haptic cues.

High-arousal cues: Cues that evoke high levels of arousal in us. For example, fast and loud music or red color can be seen high-arousal cues.

Image: Subjective perception or impression regarding an object, such as a retail store. For example, we may have an image of the store as a high-quality or inexpensive place to make purchases.

Implicit cue: A subtle or hidden cue which the consumer may not consciously notice while shopping in the store. For example, delicate scents and low volume music are primarily implicit cues.

Impulse purchase: A spontaneous choice that has not been consciously considered or planned in advance.

Information processing model: Explains and describes how we receive, organise, interpret, store and use information. Information can be processed either through the central route (i.e., by thorough cognitive thinking) or peripheral route (i.e., by simple inference). Information processing is typically seen as a conscious process but it can also take place on an unconscious level, and often unconscious information-processing occurs at the same time with conscious processing.

Involvement: Describes how important or relevant a choice is to the consumer.

Interpretation: Part of the perception process. Through interpretation we give meaning to the sensory information we receive.

Internal evaluations: Something that takes place in our mind. In this book refers to emotional responses or cognitive evaluations.

Inverse effectiveness: Multisensory integration is enhanced in a situation where sensory inputs (in at least one modality) are relatively weak (low in intensity).

Joint effects: Describes the effects that take place when two or more cues (e.g., music and scents) affect in combination.

Merchandise related cues: Cues conveying information about the store's product offering and its features, and more broadly also about the entire store and its positioning efforts. For example, the manner of presentation or merchandise arrangement can be seen merchandise related cues.

Moderator: A factor that affects the strength of relationship between two variables.

Mood: Refers how we feel at a particular time. Has a low intensity and can be long-lasting. Mood is not caused by a particular stimulus.

Motives: The reasons, goals or purposes of our behaviours. Based on our needs and can be either conscious or unconscious.

Multisensory: Something that involves or appeals to more than one of our senses.

Multisensory enhancement: Refers to synergistic effects of multisensory integration. At its best, multisensory integration leads to enhanced response that is greater than the sum of its unisensory parts. This is called superadditive multisensory response.

Multisensory integration: Various types of information from multiple sources are integrated in our brains into a coherent and meaningful percept.

Pleasure: An emotional state. Describes the extent to which we feel pleasure, satisfaction, or joy during our visit at the store. Pleasure as emotional state is strongly linked to approach behaviour whereas displeasure is linked to avoidance.

Perception: Refers to both receiving and processing (such as organising and interpreting) sensory information. Perception is a process that helps us to understand the world around us.

Pricing related cues: Psychological cues related to pricing.

Priming: Refers to a situation where we are exposed to a certain cue (prime) without our awareness and this exposure can affect how we behave later. Priming is based on increased knowledge activation in our mind.

Processing fluency: Refers to the ease with which information flows through our mind. Processing is fluent if the flow of information is fast and easy.

Retail store: In this book, the physical context where we primarily engage in browsing and purchasing. Also, a place where we are exposed to various cues. Can also be called the brick-and-mortar or offline channel.

Seesaw effect: Describes a situation where increasing pleasantness of the store by cue congruence decreases the arousal levels of consumers, while increasing consumers' arousal levels by cue incongruence lead to decrease in pleasantness of the store.

Semantic match: A situation where cues convey similar meanings to us. Refers to cue congruence.

Semantic meanings: Often abstract features, qualities or benefits that cues communicate to us. For example, odd-ending pricing communicates savings or affordable prices whereas even pricing indicates quality.

Senses: Our five basic senses are sight, hearing, smell, taste and touch. Senses allow us to interact with the outer world. Our senses gather information all the time, even if we don't think about it consciously.

Sensory dominance: The relative importance of different senses in detecting or identifying sensory signals. Very often sight is seen as a sense that dominates our sensing.

Sensory information: Information that our senses provide us from the outer world. Sensory information can take different forms. Cues are sensory information.

Sensory marketing: A marketing activity that aims to appeal to one or more of our five senses to trigger some specific responses in our mind or actual behaviour. In this book, coordinated use of sensory cues for influencing purposes is called sensory marketing.

Sensory overload: A situation where the information that we receive exceeds our ability to process this information. Sensory overload may lead, for example, to leaving the store.

Shopping experience quality: Based on the comparison of our expectations and actual experiences that we gain at the store. Cues have potential to either to elevate shopping experience quality or degrade it.

Showrooming: A mode of behaviour where a consumer first visits at the store to gather information but then makes the purchase online. Customers who only change the channel but not the retailer are called loyal showroomers.

Situational variables: All the factors that are specific to a time and place and which can affect our current behaviour on the spot. Situational variables can be distinguished from stable personal features such as personality and certain stimulus (object) attributes such as features of the brand.

Social cues: Cues related to sales staff and other customers in the store.

Social norms: Shared and typically unwritten rules of acceptable behaviour.

S-O-R: Describes the chain of influence triggered by cues. "S" stands for external cue (Stimulus), "O" is the component (human mind) that mediates the effects of cue (Organism), and "R" is the actual behavioural reaction (Response), such as choosing a product. The original S-O-R model emphasises our internal emotional states (pleasure and arousal) as mediating variables between cues and actual behavioural responses.

Strategic cues: Cues that support a retailer's overall image and brand building efforts. Primarily stable cues that convey profound meanings. Part of the retailer's strategic planning.

Superadditive multisensory response: Occurs when exposure to two or more sensory inputs (cues) simultaneously leads to a response that is significantly greater than the impact of the individual sensory signals.

Tactical cues: Cues aimed at an immediate behavioural response. Cues that primarily convey simple meanings. Part of the retailer's daily operations.

Unconscious choice: A choice that arises in the absence of conscious intent and guidance or control. Something that is difficult or even impossible to explain verbally.

Unconscious impact: A chain of effects triggered by a cue that bypasses the conscious information processing and causes a behavioural response without our awareness and conscious control.

Unconscious mind: Part of our mind that is beyond our conscious awareness and control. Something that we cannot verbally explain or report.

Visual coherence: Store design that is easy to understand. Everything makes sense. Generates pleasure but can make the store too predictable and boring.

Visual complexity: Store design that is difficult to understand. There is something peculiar in the design. Generates arousal but might also just confuse us.

Index

A

Ambient cues 34, 43, 44, 61, 180, 181
Approach behaviour 33, 53, 150, 186, 201
Arousal 17, 18, 44, 45, 47, 48, 51, 54, 56, 57, 63, 65, 89, 142, 146–150, 152, 185, 186, 200, 201, 204, 205, 213, 217
Attitude 2, 6, 12–14, 16, 19, 28, 36, 110, 122, 147, 165, 167, 168, 186, 188–190, 193, 223, 226
Automatically activated attitudes 190
Avoidance behaviour 18, 53, 89, 149

B

Behavioural response 13, 28, 195, 213

C

Choice 1–6, 11–14, 18–22, 27–31, 33–35, 38, 47, 49, 58, 68, 78, 79, 95, 101–103, 106, 110, 111, 115, 118, 119, 122, 161–168, 171–173, 180–182, 187, 188, 190, 191, 193, 195, 220–223
Cognitive evaluations 122, 185–187, 193
Conscious choice 21
Conscious impact 29
Conscious information processing 11, 18, 21, 189, 190, 193
Conscious mind 16, 19, 172, 189
Consciousness 9, 28, 193, 195
Consumer psychology 6, 21, 22, 39, 226
Cross-channel conversion 207, 208, 220

Index

Cross-modal interaction 143–145, 151, 217
Cue congruence 139, 146–150, 152, 205
Cue incongruence 148–150, 152

D

Design cues 34, 60–62, 70, 79, 111, 123, 180, 181

E

Emotional response 17, 45, 49, 50, 67, 122, 146, 182, 185, 187, 193
Emotional state 16–18, 28, 48, 54, 55, 60, 84, 85, 88, 159, 160, 185, 187, 192, 193, 217
Explicit cue 181, 182

F

Fluency theory 39, 77, 148

H

Habit 1–3, 20, 164–166, 174, 191, 208
Haptic cues 35, 94–97, 111, 147, 180
High-arousal cues 142

I

Image 1, 2, 14–16, 20, 21, 28, 44, 49, 52, 56, 67–69, 73, 76, 98, 119, 141, 146, 148, 183, 186, 187, 193, 199, 202, 204, 206, 209, 210, 213
Implicit cue 181, 182, 191
Impulse purchase 2, 19, 20, 27, 32, 35, 70, 71, 94, 122–124, 159, 161, 162, 169, 171, 185, 188–190, 195, 201

Information processing model 39
Internal evaluations 28, 122, 213
Interpretation 11, 16, 21, 184, 193, 202, 211
Inverse effectiveness 139
Involvement 11, 20, 79, 117–119, 166, 167, 173, 191, 195

J

Joint effects 28, 35, 137, 141, 146, 147, 150–152, 184, 186, 195, 200, 201, 205, 213, 217, 218

M

Merchandise-related cues 35, 97, 98, 180
Moderator 152, 173, 185, 191
Mood 29, 57, 158–161, 173, 209
Motives 2, 12, 21, 157–159, 173, 174, 191, 209, 223
Multisensory 28, 31, 32, 38, 123, 137–141, 143, 145, 147, 149–152, 159, 179, 183, 190, 195, 199, 205, 212, 217, 220–222, 225, 226
Multisensory enhancement 139, 140, 153
Multisensory integration 138–141, 151, 217

P

Perception 9, 11, 14, 21, 48, 72, 73, 100, 102, 103, 110, 111, 114, 117, 137, 138, 141, 143–145, 148, 169, 172, 179, 187, 190, 226
Pleasure 3, 17, 31, 32, 44, 45, 50, 56, 62, 63, 71, 108, 149, 150, 185, 186, 201, 212, 217
Pricing-related cues 35, 111, 122, 181, 201

Priming 20, 191
Processing fluency 148

R

Retail store 28, 32, 33, 38, 39, 53, 56, 74, 89, 91, 122, 123, 138, 145, 151, 152, 172, 179, 185–187, 191, 195, 202, 207, 210, 212, 217, 225–227

S

Seesaw effect 150, 151, 217, 218
Semantic match 145, 146, 182, 214
Semantic meanings 72, 74, 77, 79, 123, 146, 182, 189, 226
Senses 3, 9–12, 14, 18, 20, 21, 27, 28, 33–35, 38, 50, 51, 53, 56, 62, 66, 68, 80, 81, 94, 96, 97, 117, 122, 137–139, 141–145, 149–152, 159, 170, 173, 179, 180, 183, 185, 189, 190, 199, 205, 212, 217, 218, 220, 221, 225, 226
Sensory dominance 225
Sensory information 9–11, 16, 21, 33, 38, 62, 139, 189
Sensory marketing 21, 22, 27, 29, 30, 32, 33, 35, 36, 38, 53, 141, 146, 150, 181, 199–201, 206, 209, 210, 212, 213, 220, 221, 226, 227
Sensory overload 36, 142, 143, 152, 153, 184, 186, 200, 205, 218
Shopping experience quality 100, 192
Showrooming 207, 208, 225
Situational variables 34
Social cues 34, 83, 84, 89, 92, 93, 180, 190
Social norms 29, 170
Stimulus-Organism-Response (S-O-R) 28, 39, 193
Strategic cues 182, 183, 204, 206
Superadditive multisensory response 139

T

Tactical cues 183, 204, 206

U

Unconscious choice 19, 20
Unconscious impact 185
Unconscious mind 35

V

Visual coherence 63, 64, 201
Visual complexity 63, 64, 142, 201

SPRINGER NATURE

GPSR Compliance

The European Union's (EU) General Product Safety Regulation (GPSR) is a set of rules that requires consumer products to be safe and our obligations to ensure this.

If you have any concerns about our products, you can contact us on ProductSafety@springernature.com

In case Publisher is established outside the EU, the EU authorized representative is:

Springer Nature Customer Service Center GmbH
Europaplatz 3
69115 Heidelberg, Germany

The manufacturer's authorised representative in the EU is Springer Nature Customer Service Centre GmbH, Europaplatz 3, 69115 Heidelberg, Germany. If you have any concerns regarding our products, please contact ProductSafety@springernature.com

Printed and bound by CPI Group (UK) Ltd, Croydon, CR0 4YY

25/03/2026

02078170-0002